Street by Street

COVEN . . .
RUGBY
BEDWORTH, BIRMINGHAM NEC, KENILWORTH

Baginton, Balsall Common, Brownsover, Bulkington, Dunchurch, Hampton in Arden, Hillmorton, Long Lawford, Meriden, Tile Hill, Wolston

2nd edition November 2003
© Automobile Association Developments Limited 2003

Original edition printed May 2001

Ordnance Survey® This product includes map data licensed from Ordnance Survey ® with the permission of the Controller of Her Majesty's Stationery Office. © Crown copyright 2003. All rights reserved. Licence number 399221.

Published by AA Publishing (a trading name of Automobile Association Developments Limited, whose registered office is Millstream, Maidenhead Road, Windsor, Berkshire SL4 5GD. Registered number 1878835).

Mapping produced by the Cartography Department of The Automobile Association. (A01723)

A CIP Catalogue record for this book is available from the British Library.

Printed by GRAFIASA S.A., Porto, Portugal

The contents of this atlas are believed to be correct at the time of the latest revision. However, the publishers cannot be held responsible for loss occasioned to any person acting or refraining from action as a result of any material in this atlas, nor for any errors, omissions or changes in such material. This does not affect your statutory rights. The publishers would welcome information to correct any errors or omissions and to keep this atlas up to date. Please write to Publishing, The Automobile Association, Fanum House (FH17), Basing View, Basingstoke, Hampshire, RG21 4EA.

ML034z

Key to map pages .... ii–iii

Key to map symbols iv–1

Enlarged map pages 2-3

Main map pages 4-71

Index – towns & villages 72

Index – streets 73-85

Index – featured places 86-88

Acknowledgements 88

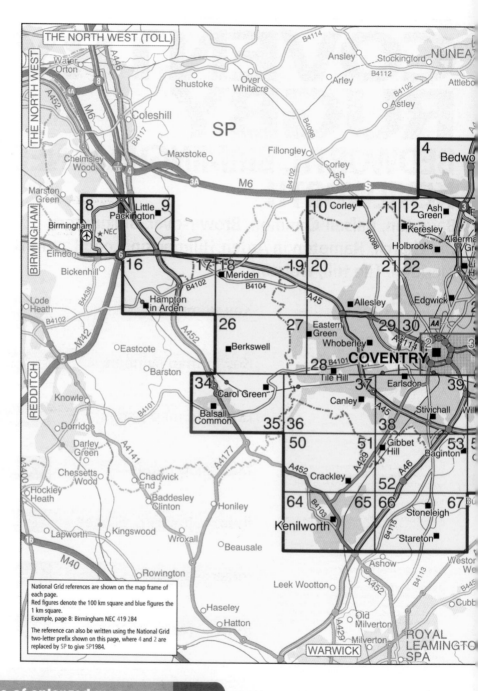

Scale of enlarged map pages 1:10,000 6.3 inches to 1 mile

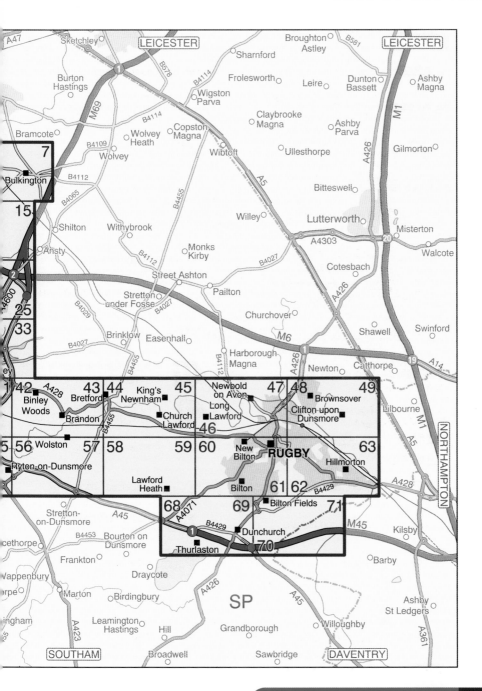

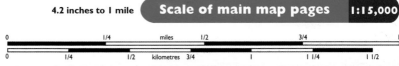

Junction 9	Motorway & junction	⊖	Underground station
Services	Motorway service area	—⊖—	Light railway & station
	Primary road single/dual carriageway	+++++++++++	Preserved private railway
Services	Primary road service area	LC	Level crossing
	A road single/dual carriageway	•—•—•—•	Tramway
	B road single/dual carriageway	------------	Ferry route
	Other road single/dual carriageway	····················	Airport runway
	Minor/private road, access may be restricted	—··—··—··	County, administrative boundary
← ←	One-way street	ⱱⱱⱱⱱⱱⱱⱱⱱⱱ	Mounds
	Pedestrian area	**17**	Page continuation 1:15,000
============	Track or footpath	**3**	Page continuation to enlarged scale 1:10,000
▮▮▮▮▮▮▮▮	Road under construction		River/canal, lake
[==={	Road tunnel		Aqueduct, lock, weir
AA	AA Service Centre	465 ▲ Winter Hill	Peak (with height in metres)
P	Parking		Beach
P+▭	Park & Ride		Woodland
▭	Bus/coach station		Park
	Railway & main railway station		Cemetery
	Railway & minor railway station		Built-up area

	Featured building		Abbey, cathedral or priory
	City wall		Castle
A&E	Hospital with 24-hour A&E department		Historic house or building
PO	Post Office	Wakehurst Place NT	National Trust property
	Public library	M	Museum or art gallery
i	Tourist Information Centre		Roman antiquity
i	Seasonal Tourist Information Centre		Ancient site, battlefield or monument
	Petrol station, 24-hour Major suppliers only		Industrial interest
†	Church/chapel		Garden
	Public toilets		Garden Centre Garden Centre Association Member
	Toilet with disabled facilities		Garden Centre Wyevale Garden Centre
PH	Public house AA recommended		Farm or animal centre
	Restaurant AA inspected		Zoological or wildlife collection
Madeira Hotel	Hotel AA inspected		Bird collection
	Theatre or performing arts centre		Nature reserve
	Cinema		Aquarium
	Golf course	V	Visitor or heritage centre
	Camping AA inspected		Country park
	Caravan site AA inspected		Cave
	Camping & caravan site AA inspected		Windmill
	Theme park		Distillery, brewery or vineyard

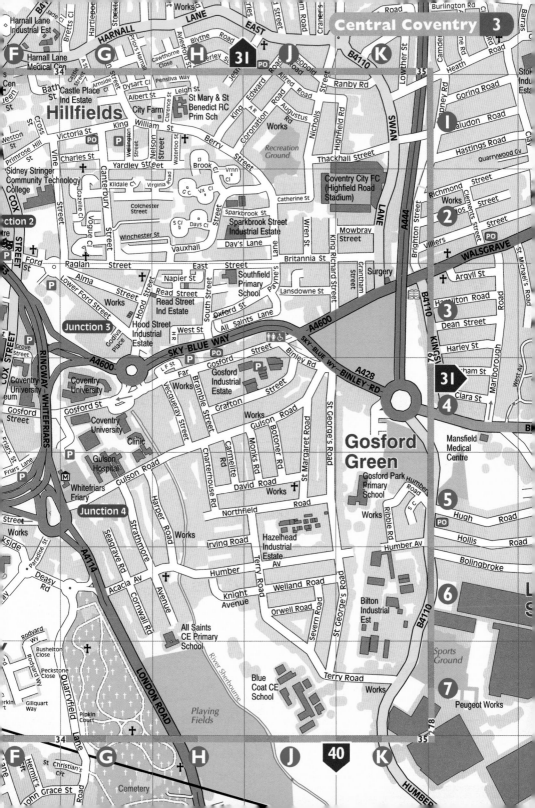

4

Cowley Wood

A   B   C   D

433   34

88

1

Sole End Farm

Astley Lane

Bedworth Lane

Cow Lees

Woodlands Lane

Dove Cl

Way

2

87

Bedworth Woodlands

affs Farm

3

Astley Hall Farm

Bedworth Heath

Astley Lane

Wildey Rd

Marriott Rd

Lindl Rd

H Rd

Coventry Way

Juniper Cl

The Pines

The Syms

Lyndale

The Laurels

Laburnum Wy

The Alders

Celandine

The Willows

Fern Gv

The Limes

Bluebell Drive

The Beec

Smorrall Lane

Highfield House Farm

Ashington Road

Blyth Cl

Whitburn Rd

Cardigan Road

Tenby

Newdigate Primary School

Anderton Road

Blair Dr

Market End

Smercote Cl

PO

Smorrall

†

Lane

Primrose Dr

Colu

Foxglove

LCl

Brt

ne Wy

4

286

Mayor

Newcomen

Keenan Dr

Keenan Dr

Dark

Bellairs AV

Glet

Kathleen AV

PO

Rd

Raynor

Dowty Ct

Howells AV

Newey AV

Robinson Rd

Lane

Potters Rd

Topp's Drive

Cashmore Rd

Henson Rd

Hammersle

Goodyers End

Hospital Lane

Drive

Humphrey Dav

Melrose AV

McMahon Rd

Goodyer End Prir School

Maynard AV

Jeffrey Close

Moat Dr

Acorn

Farm

Goodyers

End

Lane

5

M6

A   **12**   B   C   D

433   34

Newland Hall Farm

Breach Brook

Royal Oak Lane

Newland

1 grid square represents 500 metres

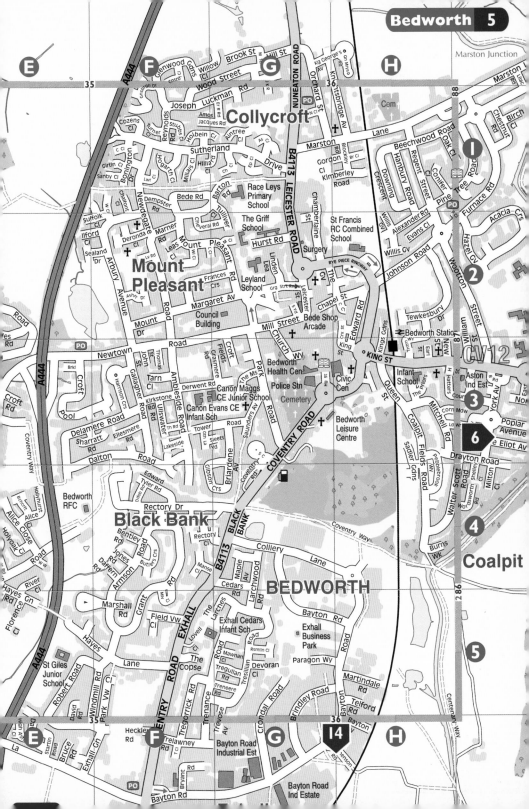

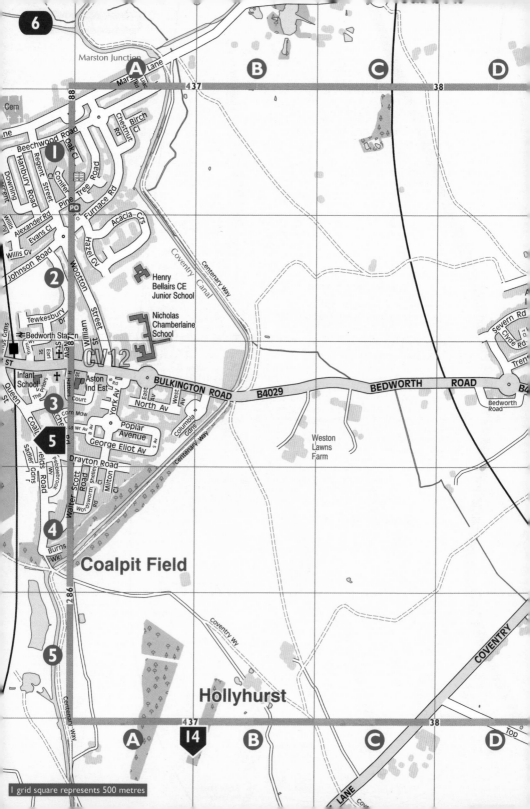

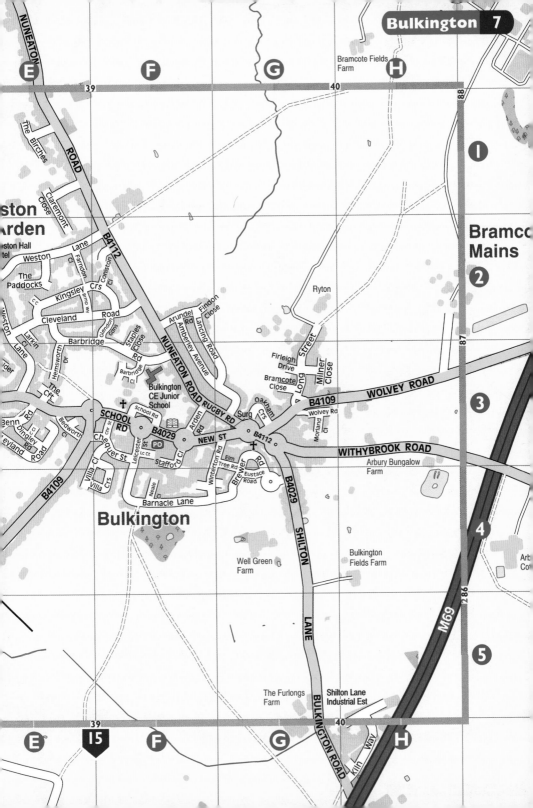

E F G H

NUNEATON

ROAD

39 40 88

I

Bramcote Fields
Farm

Bramco
Mains

2

Ryton

87

The Birches

ston
arden

Claremont
Close

eston Hall
tel

Weston
Cl

Lane

Farndon
Cl

The
Paddocks

Kingsley Crs

Benad Wy

B4112

Conlston Cl

Cleveland Road

Barbridge Rd

Glendon
Gdns

Staples
Close

Arundel
Rd

Findon
Close

Lancing Road

Amberley Avenue

Firleigh
Drive

Long Street

Milner
Close

Wolvey Rd

Bramcote
Close

WOLVEY ROAD

B4109

3

Larkin
Cl

Hemsworth
Dr

Barbridge
Cl

Bulkington
CE Junior
School

NUNEATON ROAD

RUGBY RD

Surg

Oakham
Crs

Morland Rd

WITHYBROOK ROAD

Arbury Bungalow
Farm

Weston Lane

The
Cft

SCHOOL
RD

School Rd

Chr St

Arden Rd

B4112

B4029

B4109

Benn
Rd

Bedworth
Rd

Chequer St

Leicester St

PO
Lc Ct

Stafford Cl

NEW ST

Winterton Rd

Elm
Tree Rd

Brewer Rd

Eustace
Road

SHILTON

LANE

4

2286

Bulkington
Fields Farm

Arb
Co

Villa Cl

Villa Crs

Neale

Barnacle Lane

eveland
Road

Dingley
Rd

Bulkington

Well Green
Farm

M69

5

The Furlongs
Farm

Shilton Lane
Industrial Est

BULKINGTON ROAD

Kiln Way

39 40

E 15 F G H

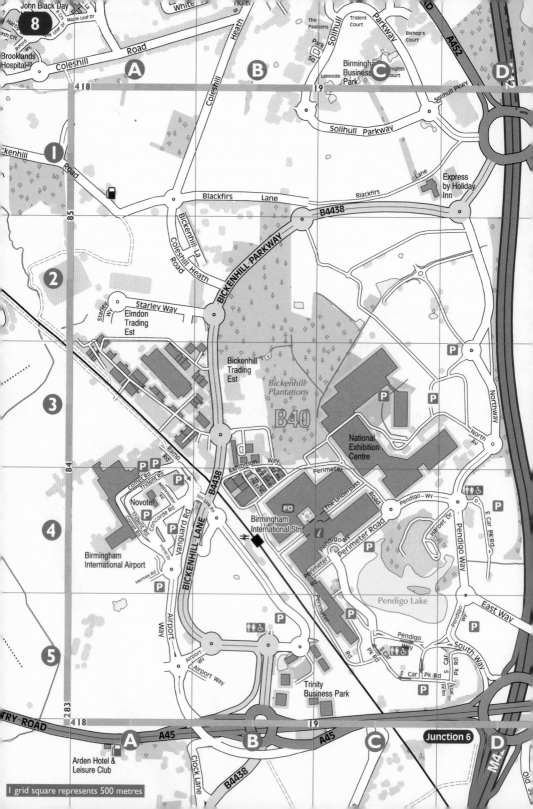

E F G H

21 22

1

85

2

Little
Packington

River Blythe

3

84

ROAD

A446

arden
entre

Fishpool Lane

Packington Lane

Park Farm

Warwickshire County

Solihull

Middle Bickenhill Lane

CHESTER ROAD

Packington
Hall

Hall Pool

4

Middle
Bickenhill

The Mill
Farm

5

East Way

Coventry Road

COVENTRY ROAD

BIRMINGHAM ROAD

283

Ston**F**bridg **16**

E F G H

21 22

KENILWOR

Pasture Farm

Geary's
Heath

cle
m
al

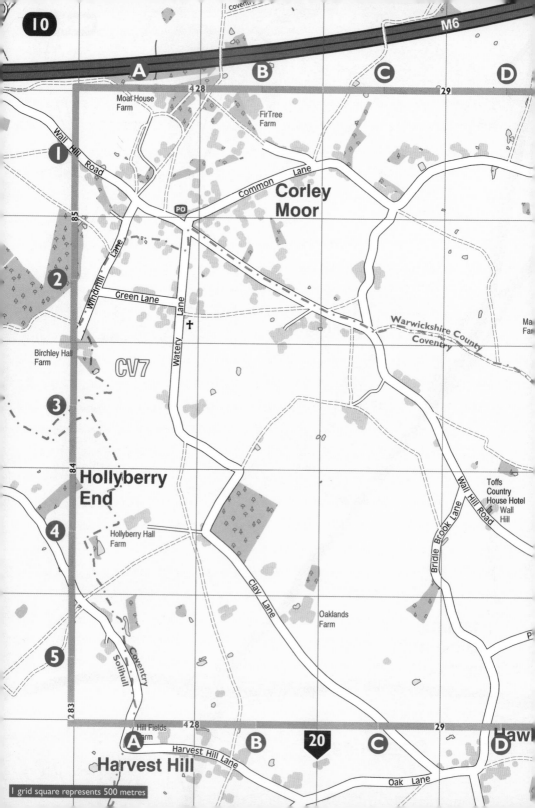

10

M6

A

428

B

29

C

D

Wall Hill Road

Moat House Farm

FirTree Farm

1

85

Common Lane

PO

Corley Moor

Windmill Lane

2

Green Lane

Watery Lane

✝

Warwickshire County

Coventry

Ma Fa

Birchley Hall Farm

CV7

3

84

Hollyberry End

Toffs Country House Hotel

Wall Hill

4

Hollyberry Hall Farm

Bridle Brook Lane

Wall Hill Road

5

Coventry Solihull

Clay Lane

Oaklands Farm

P

2 83

428

29

Hill Fields Farm

A

B

20

C

D Haw

Harvest Hill

Harvest Hill Lane

Oak Lane

1 grid square represents 500 metres

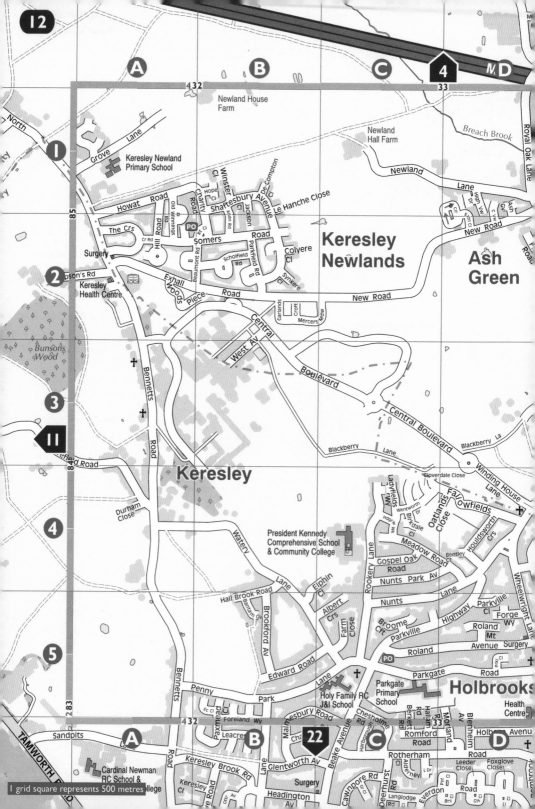

12

A · · B · · C · **4** M D

Newland House Farm

North

Grove Lane

I

Keresley Newland Primary School

Newland Hall Farm

Breach Brook

Royal Oak Lane

Newland Lane

Howat Road

Old Winnings Rd

Charity

Winster Cl

Hope Cl

Shaftesbury Avenue

De Compton Cl

Jackson

Le Hanche Close

New Road

The Crs

Hill Road

PO

Somers

Road

Acfen Rd

Parkfield Rd

Scholfield Rd

Colyere Cl

Colvere Cl

Keresley Newlands

Ash Green

2

Surgery

pson's Rd

Keresley Health Centre

Exhall Woods

Beaumont Rd

Piece Road

Garlands

Central

Synkere

Croft

Mercers

New Road

Mow

Bunson's Wood

West Av

Boulevard

3

Bennetts Road

Central Boulevard

Blackberry La

Winding House Lane

II

efield Road

84

Blackberry Lane

Cloverdale Close

Fallowfields

Keresley

Lacyfields Wy

Wentworth

Birkdale

Oatlands Close

Houldsworth Crs

Durham Close

4

Watery

Lane

President Kennedy Comprehensive School & Community College

Rookery Lane

Meadow Road

Bentley

Gospel Oak Road

Nunts Park Av

Hall Brook Road

Brookford Av

Bantam Rd

Elphin Cl

Nunts Lane

Highway

Parkville Cl

Forge Wy

Roland Mt

Avenue Surgery

5

Bennetts Road

Albert Crs

Farm Close

Broome Cft

Parkville

Roland

Parkgate Road

PO

Penny

Park

Edward Road

Lane

Holy Family RC J&I School

Parkgate Primary School

Chesholme Rd

Berkett Rd

Hallam Rd

Morland Rd

Blenheim

Romford Road

Holbrooks

Health Centre

A · · B · **22** · C · D

Sandpits

TAMWORTH RD

Cardinal Newman RC School &

Keresley Brook Rd

Keresley Cl

Paxmead

Leacres

Foreland Wy

Glentworth Av

Surgery

Headington Av

Malmesbury Road

Beake Avenue

Cawnpore Rd

Deerhurst

Rotherham Road

Alderney

Leeder Close

Foxglove Close

Holbrook Avenu

Langlodge Rd

E   F   **6**   G   H

COVENTR...

The Furl
Farm

38   39

Top   Road

I

Coventry Way

85

Road

Spring Rd   Top   Road

Park   Chapel   2
Farm   La   **Barnacle**

†

Lower   Road   Wood

M69

Shilton Lane   Chris Lan   3

Coventry   Way   84

ds

4

Coventry   Way

Grove   Road

Shilton Lane   **Ansty**   A...
H...

Meadow Close

The
RW

Brookfield
Farm   5   B4065

Woodway Lane

Centenary Way   2 83065   B4065

non

38   39   HI...LEY ROAD

E   F   **25**   G   H

E   F   G   H

BIRMINGHAM

22

Geary's Heath

I

Forest Hall

Golf Course

Stonebridge Golf Club

The Somers

2

Somers Road

BIRMINGHAM ROAD

A45

Maxstoke Lane

B4104

Maxstoke

Warwickshire County

Solihull

Molands Bridge

A452

HAMPTON LANE

B4102

North Warwickshire Golf Club

Heath Farm

3

18

Golf Course

KENILWORTH ROAD

Cornets End Lane

4

Hornbrook Farm

281

Cornets End

5

Mercote Mill Farm

E   F   G   H

22

23

Park Farm

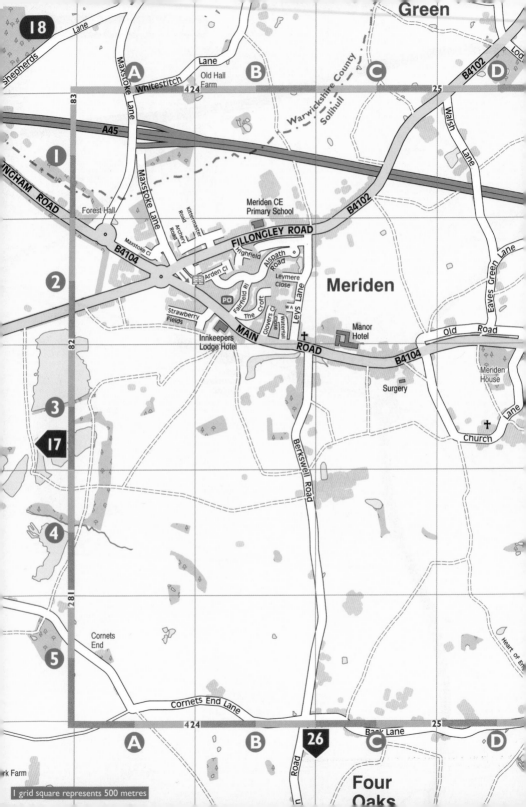

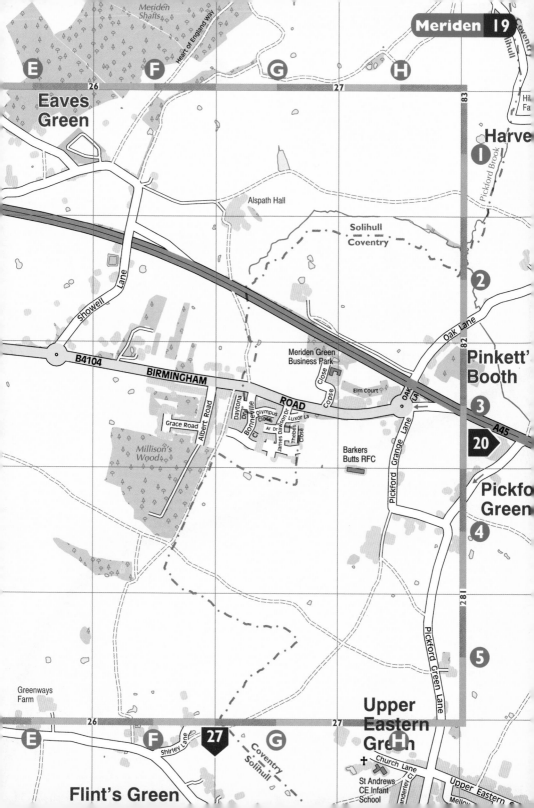

Meriden Shafts

Heart of England Way

E   F   G   H

Eaves Green

Harve

Pickford Brook

I

Alspath Hall

Solihull
Coventry

2

Showell Lane

B4104   BIRMINGHAM   ROAD

Meriden Green Business Park

Close

Copse

Elm Court

OAK LA

Pinkett' Booth

Oak Lane

3

A45

20

Grace Road

Albert Road

Daytona Dr

Bonneville Cl

Olympus
Close

Ar Dr

James Dawson Dr

Thebes

Luxor La

Millison's Wood

Barkers Butts RFC

Pickford Grange Lane

Pickfo Green

4

Greenways Farm

Pickford Green Lane

5

Upper Eastern Green

E   F   **27**   G   H

Shirley Lane

Coventry
Solihull

Church Lane

St Andrews CE Infant School

Upper Eastern

Flint's Green

20

Ⓐ 428 Ⓑ **10** Ⓒ 29 Ⓓ

Coventry
Solihull

Hill Fields
Farm

Harvest Hill Lane

Harvest Hill

Pickford Brook

Oak Lane

Haw

Hawke

Washbrook Lane

Ⓘ

Alton Hall
Farm

②

Oak Lane

Brick Hill Lane

**Pinkett's
Booth**

Pickford
Farm

OAK LA

③ A45

19

Pickford

Pickford Grange Lane

BIRMINGHAM ROAD

Windmill
Industrial
Estate

Birmingham Road

The Windmill

Wo
Close

Harvey
Close

④

**Pickford
Green**

CV5

Windmill Village
Golf & Leisure Club

Halifax Cl

Cameron C

Mackenzie
Alvesley
Croft

Pickford Green Lane

⑤

Golf Course

DUNCHURCH HIGHWAY

Ridge Ct

High
Beech

Rye Hill

Oxford Drive

Birch
Close

Larkfield Way

Fairfax C
Fairways Cl

Woodridge Avenue

Ⓐ 428 Ⓑ **28** Ⓒ 29 Ⓓ

ore
Lane

Under

Mello

Juniper
Close

New Ash Dr

Greenland Ct

Greenland
Greenland
AV

Cherrywood

Peregrine

Birch
Close

Harpende
Drive

Rebeck Drive

Park Hill La

Defro
Dr

Beaumaris

1 grid square represents 500 metres

E F H G H

30 31 B4098

TAMWORTH ROAD

Sandpits Lane

I Cardinal New RC School & Community C

Ted Pitts Lane

Burton Cl

Freshfield Close

Carvell Close

Saunton Close

Marystow Lane

Wn's Way

Wyevale Garden Centre

Brownshill Green

Brownshill

Waste **2** Keresley Grange Primary Sch

Long Lane

North Brook Road

North Brook Road

Green

Fairbourne Wy

Brownshill Ct

Map Rd

Kelmscot

Green

3

22

Brackley Close

Jaguar Daimler Heritage Centre

M

Works

Allesley

Northbrook Sports Club

North Brook Road

Coundon

Overslade Crescent

Swi Rd

Birchi Rd

Norma Place

4 Duncroft

B4076

Northfield Farm

Lane

Eversleigh Rd

Hollyfast Primary School

Coundon Court School & Community College

Hollyfast

Coundon

Christ the King RC Junior Sch

Ruff Lane

Town Fields

Anglesey Close

Ln C Wardens

The Wardens

Av

Avenue

Lion Fields Av

Ramsay Crs

Whitelaw Crs

Staircase

River Sherbourne

Rossiyn Av

Shornc Rd

Haynestone Road

William

Kendon Av

Shorncliffe Road

Clipstone Rd

Pk

Branksome

Caveston Road

Woodlose Av

Westhill Road

5

PO

Packington Avenue

PO

wn Clos

Church Walk

Rectory Lane

Claremont Wk

Birmingham Rd

Cem

COUNDON WEDGE DRIVE

Three Spires Special School

Kingsbury Road

Ruslin Close

Tarlington Road

Dallington Rd

Newington Cl

Rowington

Bevecote Cl

Forfield

Denbigh Rd

Newhaven

Welgarth Av

Courtland Av

Road

Christ RC

FORD WAY A4114

The bridal Path

Allesley Hotel

N Gra

30

E F **29** ooklands Grange Hotel G H Road

Allesley Old Rd

HOLYHEAD ROAD

Sherbourne Fields Special School

Tiverton Special School

Donnington Road

Clayton Road

Chelveston

Byfield Road

Coundon Primary School

Evenlode Avenue

Lilac Av

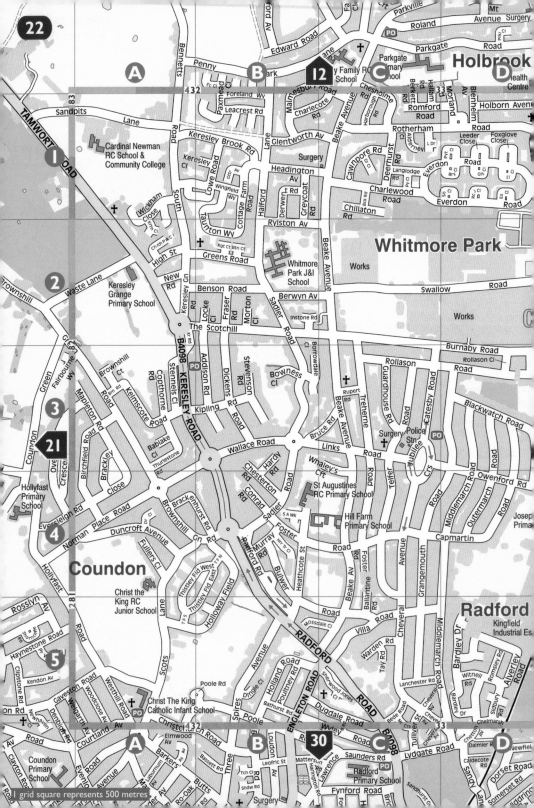

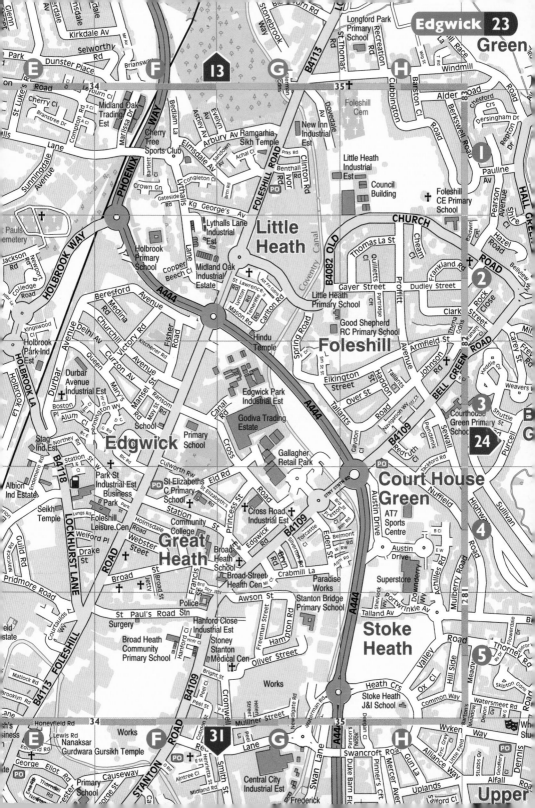

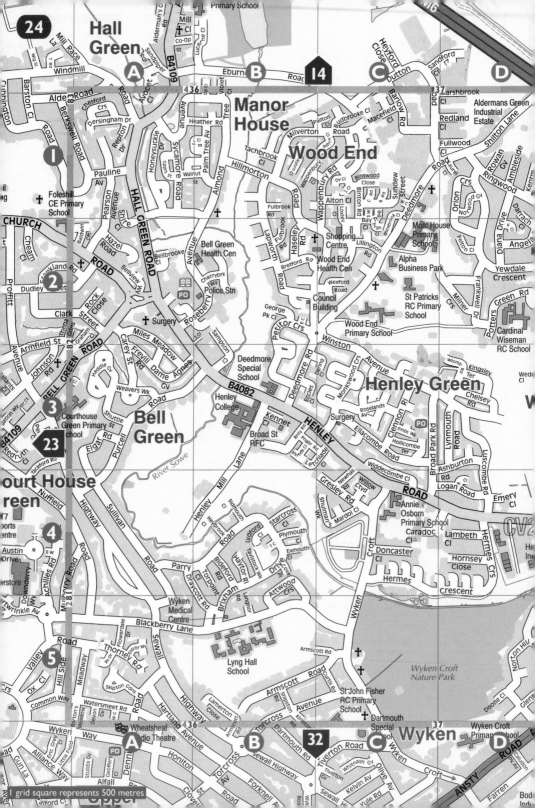

This page is a street map covering Hall Green, Manor House, Wood End, Bell Green, Henley Green, and Wyken areas.

Grid reference markers: 24, 14, A, B, C, D (top); I, 2, 3, 23, 4, 5 (left); A, B, 32, C, D (bottom)

Key place names and labels visible:

- Hall Green
- Manor House
- Wood End
- Henley Green
- Bell Green
- Wyken
- Wyken Croft Nature Park
- Aldermans Green Industrial Estate

Schools and buildings:
- Primary School
- Foleshill CE Primary School
- Bell Green Health Cen
- Bellbrooke CI
- Police Stn
- Deedmore Special School
- Henley College
- Broad St RFC
- Courthouse Green Primary School
- St Patricks RC Primary School
- Wood End Primary School
- Moat House Primary School
- Cardinal Wiseman RC School
- Alpha Business Park
- Council Building
- Shopping Centre
- Wood End Health Cen
- Annie Osborn Primary School
- St John Fisher RC Primary School
- Dartmouth Special School
- Wyken Croft Primary School
- Wyken Medical Centre
- Lyng Hall School
- Wheatsheaf Radio Theatre
- Surgery

Roads and streets (selection):
Mill Race La, Windmill Rd, Barston CI, Berkswell Road, Alder Road, B4109, B4082, Hall Green Road, Bell Green Road, Henley Road, Hillmorton Road, Wappenbury Rd, Deedmore Rd, Mill Lane, Sewall Highway, Hartland Avenue, Mulberry Road, Sullivan Road, Thorney Rd, Armscott Rd, Wyken Croft, Ansty Road, Eburn Road, Tachbrook, Fulbrook Rd, Haseley Rd, Lapworth Rd, Winston Avenue, Ellacombe Road, Clennon Rd, Broad Park Rd, Lynmouth Road, Luscombe Rd, Ashburton, Logan Road, Emery CI, Torcross Avenue, Dartmouth Rd, Tiverton Road, Whitnash Gv, Olive Av, Kelvin Av, Yule Rd

River Sowe

1 grid square represents 500 metres

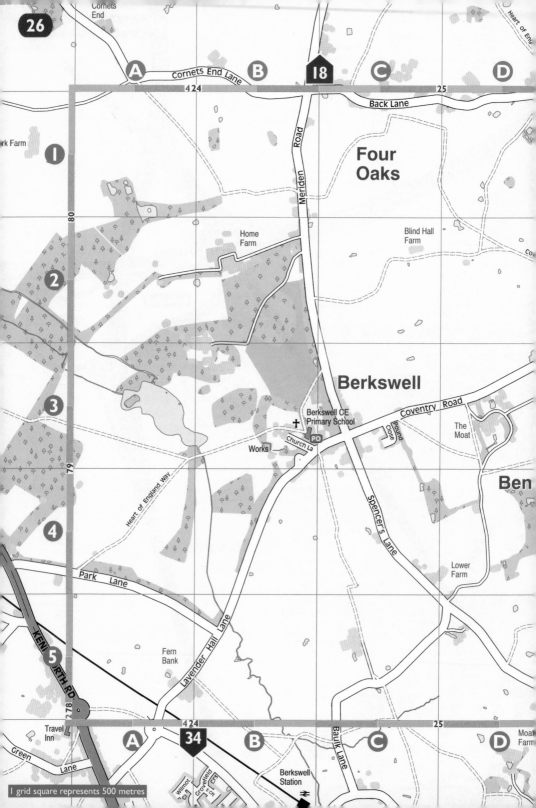

A Cornets End Lane B 18 C D

Cornets
End

4 24 Back Lane 25

Meriden Road

Four
Oaks

1 rk Farm 80

Home
Farm

Blind Hall
Farm

co

2 79

3 Berkswell

Berkswell CE
Primary School Coventry Road The
Moat

Church La PO Pound Close

Works Ben

Heart of England Way

4 Lower
Farm

Park   Lane

Lavender Hall Lane

Spencers Lane

5 KENILWORTH RD B 4101

Fern
Bank

Travel
Inn

Green Lane

4 24 25

A 34 B Bauk Lane C D Moat Farm

Willmor Grovefield Crs Berkswell
Station

I grid square represents 500 metres

E F **19** G **H**

Upper Eastern Green

Shirley Lane

Coventry Solihull

Flint's Green

† St Andrews CE Infant School

Church Lane

Manderley Cl

Hockley Lane

William

Bree Road

Upper Eastern Green

Mellowship Road

Holmes Dr

Eastern Green Junior Sch

Despard Road

I

Morgans Rd

Orchard Dr

Garrick Close

o'Thrnt Cl

Hockley

Frederick

Lynd'ns Cl

Kenthurst Cl

2

Sutton

Oldthorn Cl

Nova Cft

Broad Lane

Broad Lane Trading Estate

Farrcr

Broad Lane

Hill House Farm

Coventry Solihull

Works

Banner Lane

3

28

Wickmans Dr

Glendale Wy

Fow Oak

High Oak

Pheasant

Tilehurst Dr

The Hurst

Beech

4

Oak Way

Brck Dr

Asp

Rough Close

Benton Green Lane

Victoria Farm

Maureen Cl

Dvrx Cl

Ensign Cl

Wd

Cromes

Ashfield

Goodman Way

Edgehill Place

Wn Pl

Smmn Wy

Patricia Close

stowe Pl

Ireton Cl

anyard

5

B4101

Grendon Cl

278

PO

Hathaway Rd

een

Coventry Way

E **35** F

Spencer's Lane

TANNERS' LANE

G

Coventry Solihull

H

Nailcote Avenue

Conway Avenue

Station Avenue

Rex Cl

Trevor

Reeves Green

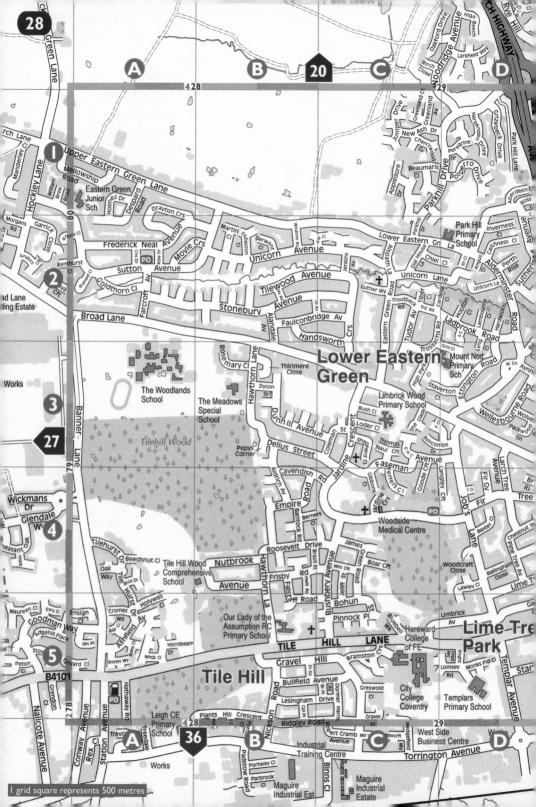

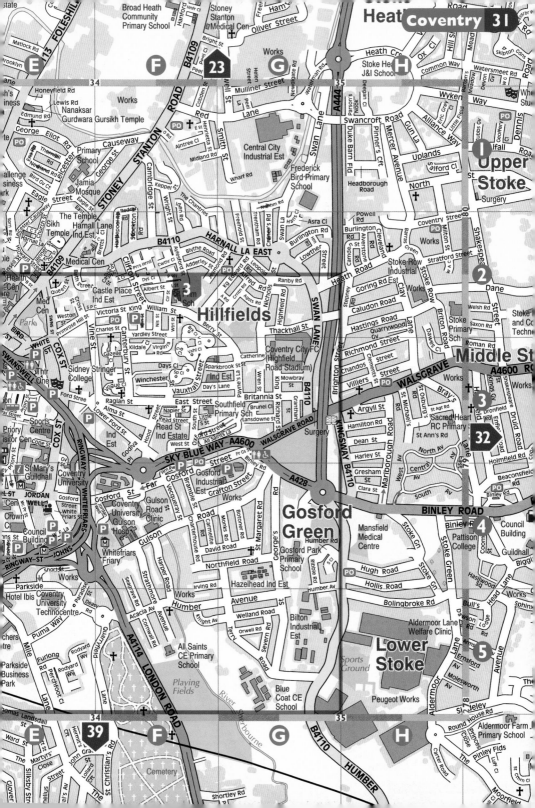

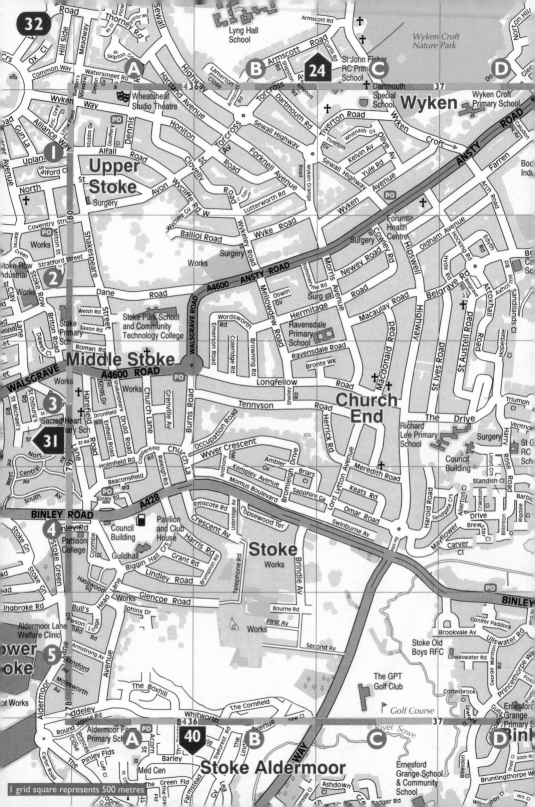

ANSTY

Closter Cft

House La

Rowcroft Rd

Farber Road

Fitzroy Cl

Walsgrave
Health
Centre

E

F

25

G

A46

H

38

Walsgrave
General Hospital

River Sowe

Coventry
Warwickshire County

I

39

80

Dorchester

Tollard
Cl

Cranborne

Blandford
Cl

Corfe Cl

Cha

Wareham Gn

Way

Pearl Hyde
Primary
School

Abbotsbury Cl

Fontmell Cl

Sturminster Cl

Bridport Close

Works

Dalton Gdns

Ennerdale

Marnhull

Wimborne
Dr

Wimborne Drive

Studland

Tarrant

Wormwell

Dorchester

Way

2

A46

Westmorland
Road

Keswick Wk

B4082

Superstore

B4082

Coombe
Pool

B4082

Combe Abbey
Country Park

The
Woodlands

3

befarm

Fieldside

Bridgeacre
Gardens

Abbeydale

Royston Cl

Coombe Pk Road

Gainford Rise

Faygate

Clifford
Bridge Primary
School

Bracadale Cl

Dunvegan Cl

Brinklow
Rd

Porchester

B4027

79

B4027

4

CLIFFORD BRIDGE ROAD

Colebrook Cl

Mill La

Portree Av

Burnside

Coombe
Ct

Camville

Tynley
Close

Hunters

BRINKLOW ROAD

Harvesters
Cl

278

Old Lodge
Farm

5

28

Harry
Weston
Rd

Eastwood

Bus Vlg

Kelway

Kenwin

Skipworth Road

Chelney
Wk

Hargrave

Virtleton Cl

Hepworth Road

Hume

Twickenham Wy

Harry
Weston
Road

Braddock

Orchard Ct

Brewers

BRANDON ROAD

Alvin

Kerris Wy

Winchat

Ibex Cl

Sheldrake
Close

Middlefield Drive

Kings Pk

Murrayfield

Dowley Cft

Ellis
Dr

Homeward
Way

Kgshm

Cl

Binley
Business
Park

Wilson Gn

B4082

E

41

38

A428

F

Skipworth
Rd

Kynner
Wy

Kynner Way

Broad Street
Old

RFC

G

39

A46

H

Superstore

Travel Inn

Brandon

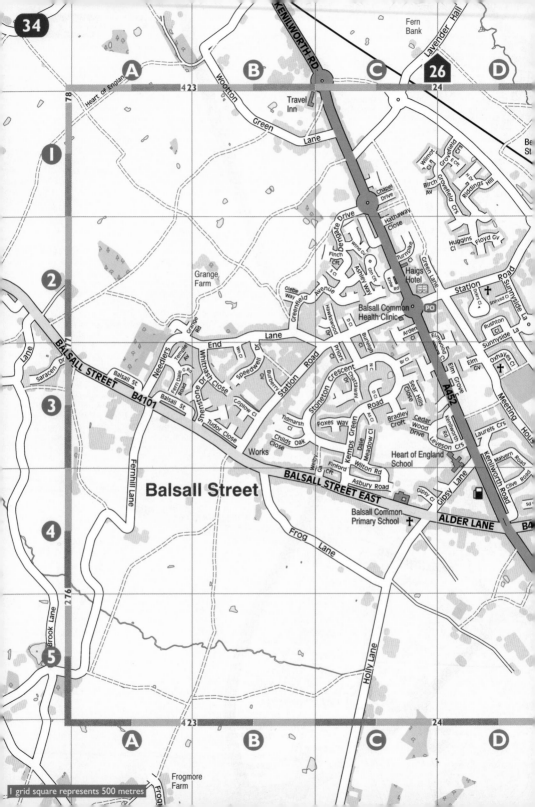

E   F   G   27   H

25   26   78

Moat House Farm

Spencer's Lane

Coventry Way

Reeves G

Truggist Lane

Hodgett's Lane

Carol Green

Works

Lant Cl

ALL ON

Nailcote Hall Hotel

NAILCOTE LANE

2

Beechwood

B4101

77

3

36

Coventry Way

Old Waste Lane

WASTE LANE

Hodgett's Lane

4

EY LANE

Catchems Corner

Wellfield Cl

Hob Lane

276

Berkswell Windmill

Beanit Farm

5

Windmill Lane

E   F   G   H

25   26

The Firs

Hob Lane

Bu

CE

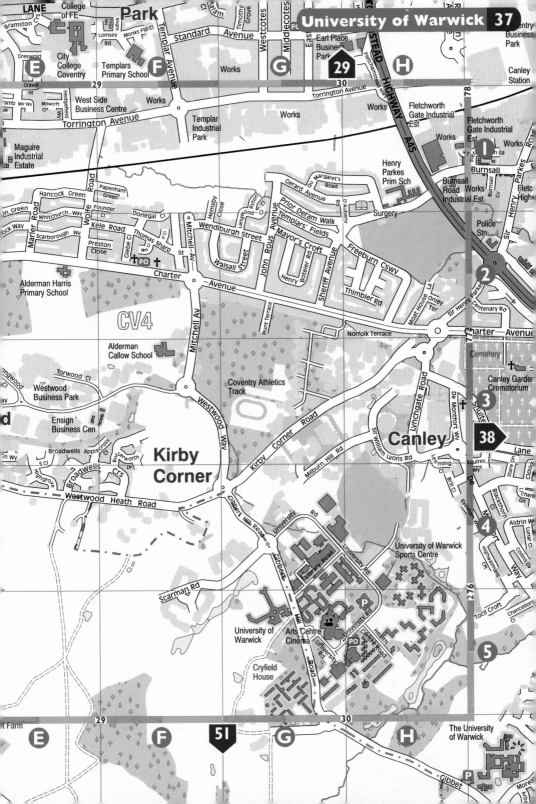

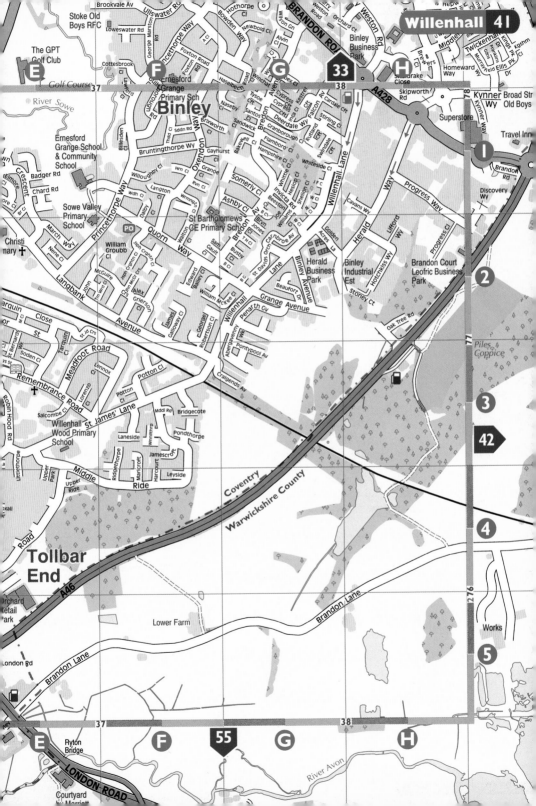

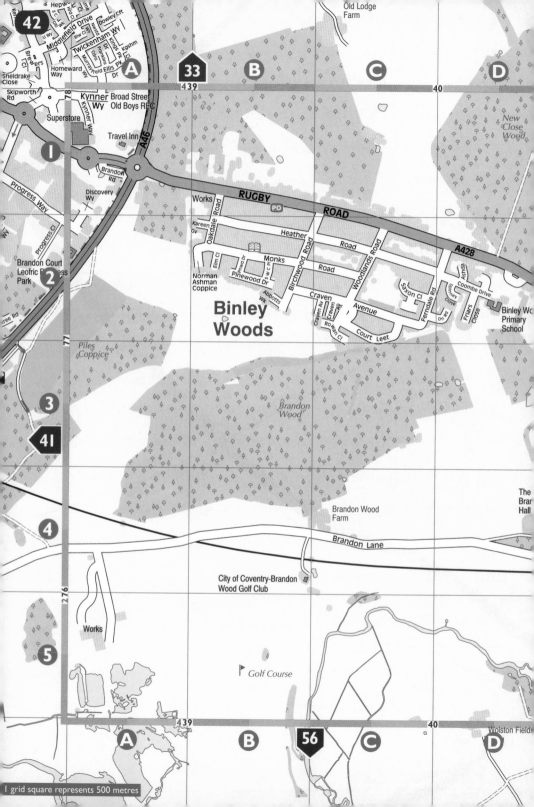

42

Hepw
Kid Cl
Middlefield Drive
Twickenham Wy
Dowley Cft
Kings Pk
Ellis Cft
Kgshm
Cl
33 **A** **B** **C** **D**
439 40
78 Kynner Broad Street
Wy Old Boys RFC
Superstore Kynner Way
New
Close
Wood
Travel Inn
Brandon
Rd
1
Discovery
Wy
Progress Way Works RUGBY ROAD
PO A428
Kareena
Gv Heather
Oakdale Road Road
Brandon Court Elm Cl
Leofric Business Phwd Dr Monks Birchwood Road
Park **2** Pinewood Dr Road Woodlands Road
Norman Abbotts Saxton Cl Ashta
Ashman Craven Ferndale Rd Coombe Drive
77 Coppice Av Avenue Friars Binley W
Binley Craven Cl Court Leet Primary
Woods Rowan Cl School
Piles
Coppice
Brandon
Wood
3
41
The
Brar
Hall
4
Brandon Wood
Farm
Brandon Lane
276
City of Coventry-Brandon
Wood Golf Club
Works
5
Golf Course
439 40
A **B** **56** **C** Wolston Fields **D**

I grid square represents 500 metres

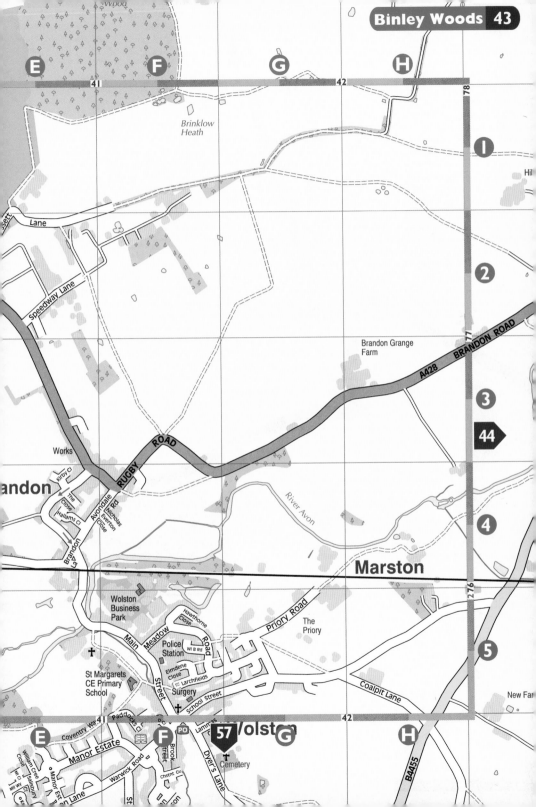

E F G H

41 42 78

Brinklow
Heath

I

Hil

Lane

2

Speedway Lane

Brandon Grange
Farm

A428 BRANDON ROAD 77

3

44 ▶

Works

ROAD

RUGBY Rd

andon

Kirby Cl

The Close

Hallams Cl

Avondale

Nicholas

Etterton Close

Brandon La

River Avon

4

276

Marston

Wolston
Business
Park

Hawthorne Close

Priory Road

The
Priory

Meadow

Road

5

Main

Police
Station

WI B Rd

Elmdene
Close

Larchfields

New Far

St Margarets
CE Primary
School

Street

Surgery

School Street

Coalpit Lane

B4455

E F G H

Coventry Wa 41

Paddocks Cl

PO

57 **/olst** n

Manor Estate

William Cree

Salisbury

Lammas

Brook treet

Dyer's Lane

Cemetery

Chstnt Gv

Manor Est

Mill Wy

M

Warwick Road

42

44

A 443 B B4455 C 44 D

Abbey Hall Farm

Coventry Way

1

QUEENS ROAD

Hill Farm

2

Bretford

Kings N

BRANDON ROAD

A428

River Avon

3

43

A428

Vicarage Farm

COVENTRY ROAD

4

The Grange

B4455

Chur Busi Cent

276

5

New Farm

Limestone

A 443 B **58** C Limest... Hall 44 D

B4455

1 grid square represents 500 metres

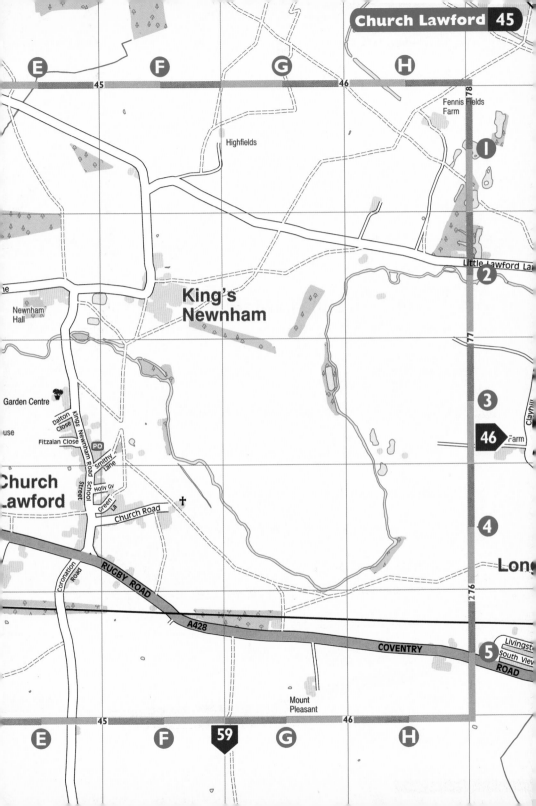

E F G H

45 46 78

Fennis Fields Farm

Highfields

I

Little Lawford La

2

77

King's Newnham

Newnham Hall

Garden Centre

Dalton Close

Kings Newnham Road

Fitzalan Close

PO

Smithy Lane

3

Clayhill

46 Farm

School Street

Holly Gv

Church Lawford

Green La

†

4

Church Road

Coronation Road

RUGBY ROAD

Long

A428

276

COVENTRY

Livingst

South View

5

ROAD

Mount Pleasant

E F G H

45 59 46

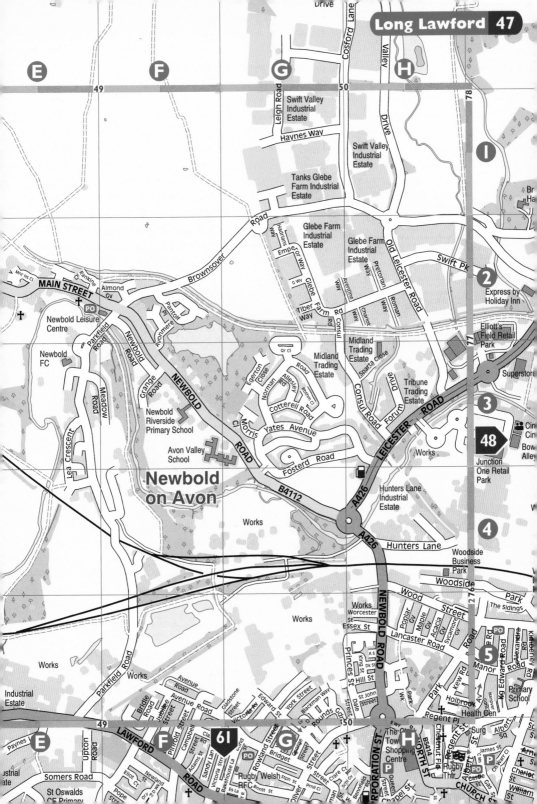

Brownsover

1 grid square represents 500 metres

Newton

The Leyes

E   F   G   H

The Hollies
The Paddock
The Orchards
Pilgrims Lane
Little London Lane
Main St

Watling Crs

54   78

River

I

2 more Farm

77

Newton Road

Buckwell Lane

3

Cemetery

Newton Road

Road

North Road

The Elms
Paddock

Church St

Buckwell Lane

Manor Farm

Clifton upon Dunsmore CE Primary School

Robertson Cl
Heafield Cl

Lilbourne Road

Main Street

PO

Whiley Cl
Allans La
Allans Ct
Orwell Cl

Everard Close

Clifton upon Dunsmore

4

Road

South

Shuttleworth Road

Road

276

The Kent

5

Clifton Hall

E   F   G   H

53   54

53

Dun

Dunsmore

Home Farm

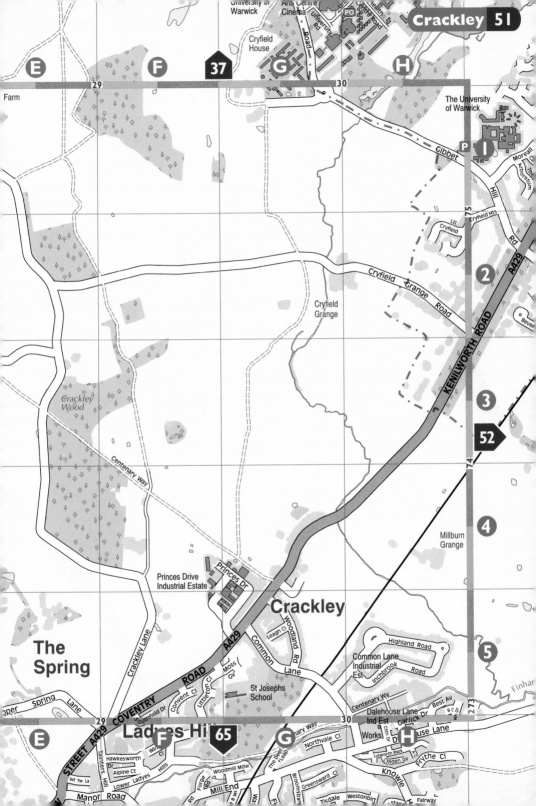

52

A The Galliards
Rivercroft
Heylcroft
Cft
B KENILWO
Bishop Ullathorne RC
Comprehensive School
38
C Gretna
D Coventry
Warwickshire Co

431
Abberton Wy
32

The University of Warwick
P
Heritage Cft
Moreall Meadow
Cassandra Ct
Poppyfield Ct
The Spinney

1

Arboretum
The Ct
Moreall Meadow
Cassandra Ct

75

Cryfield Hts
Leighton Cl
Wainbody Wood Special School

Ltl Cryfield

2
Grange Road
Marshfield Dr
Gibbet Hill

A429

Beverly Dr
Stoneleigh Road

KENILWORTH ROAD

Wainbody Wood Farm

King's Hill Lane

3

51

74

Finham Brook

Westley Bridge

4
Milburn Grange

CV8

Dalehouse Lane

land Road
5
Road

Finham Brook

Best Av
B C
Wn Dr
arlick Dr
ehouse Lane
Kingswood Farm

Frythe Cl
A
431
B
66
C
32
D

Centenary Way

Golf Course

Fairway

1 grid square represents 500 metres

A **B** **42** **C** **D**

439 40

1

Wolston Fie
Farm

Redland Lane

Church Rd

2

Church Road

Ryton-on-
Dunsmore

Chapel La

C Cl

Works

Centenary Way

Bagshaw Cl

PO

Handley's

oden's Av

3

High Street

Fetherston Crs

Holly Drive

Poplar Gv

Lea Wk

Cedar Av

Holly Dr

55

Wolston Lane

Ryton Gardens

LEAMINGTON RD A445

LONDON ROAD

A45

Mann's Cl

Grange Farm

A45

4

LEAMINGTON RD

Works

5

273 439 40

Freeboard

A **B** **C** Ryton
Heath **D** Plott

OXFORD ROAD

1 grid square represents 500 metres

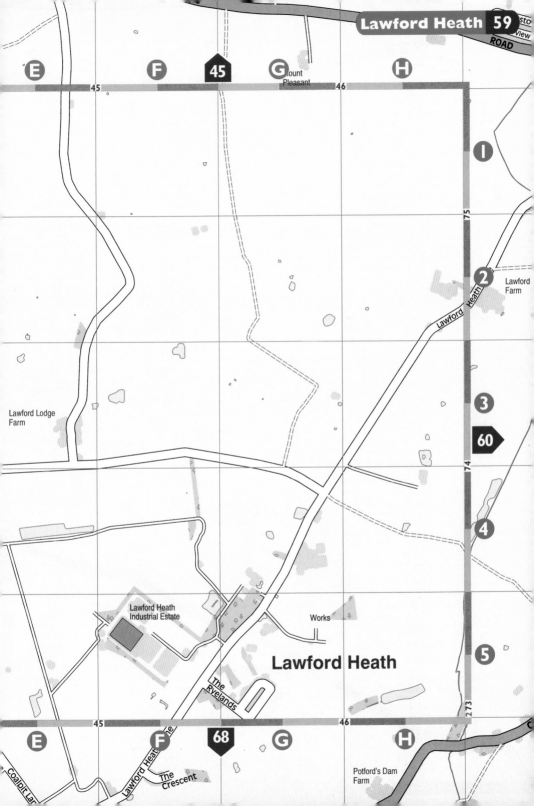

ROAD

E   F   **45**   G Mount Pleasant   H

I

75

Lawford Heath **2** Lawford Farm

3

60

74

4

Lawford Lodge Farm

Lawford Heath Industrial Estate

Works

Lawford Heath

The Ryelands

5

273

E   F   **68**   G   H

Lawford Heath The Crescent

Coalpit Lane

Potford's Dam Farm

60
Livingstone Avenue
South View Road
The Green
Green
ROAD
Back
Lane
46
428 RUGBY ROAD 48
Briars Close

A
447
B
C
D

I

75

Lawford Heath Lane

Bilton Lane

Lodge Farm Campsite

2
Lawford Hill Farm

Lawford Heath Lane

Bilton Lane

Henry Hinde Junior School

Wilson Road
Kenneth Drive
Keyes Dr
Freema Road
Madden Place
Anson Cl

Mulberry Road
Apple Gv
Birch Dr
Rowan Dr
Larch Cl
Lestock Close
Lilac Wy
Cornwallis Road
Barrington Road
Dreyer Close
Evans R
Cunningham
Cunningham Way Nth
Bla

Acorn Dr
Elder
L Dr
Pear Tree Way
Cowan
Keppel
Frobisher
Wych-elm Cl
Rdny
Henry Hinde Infant School
Ditton
Ne

3

74

59
D

Lawford Lane
Bilton High School
Montgomery Drive
Pipewell
Hy Cl
pin Cl
Chshr
Cl Cl
on Cl

Francis Dr
Joyce Wy
enhall Rd
Judith Wy
Gerard Road
Alicia
Chshr Cl
Chshr
Winwick Pl
Surgery
PO

4
Brudenell Cl
Planter
Cave
Trussell Wy
Durrell Dr
Clement Way
Turchil Rd
Monks Wy
Noble Dr
Calvestone Rd
Gold Cl
Kairs Dr
Edwin
COVENTRY ROAD
MAIN STREET
Bilton Infant School

B

5
273

COVENTRY ROAD
A4071
Cawston
Cawston Lane
Lime Tree Avenue
Alwyn Road
Scotts Close

A
447
B
69
Work
Cawston House
C
48
D

1 grid square represents 500 metres

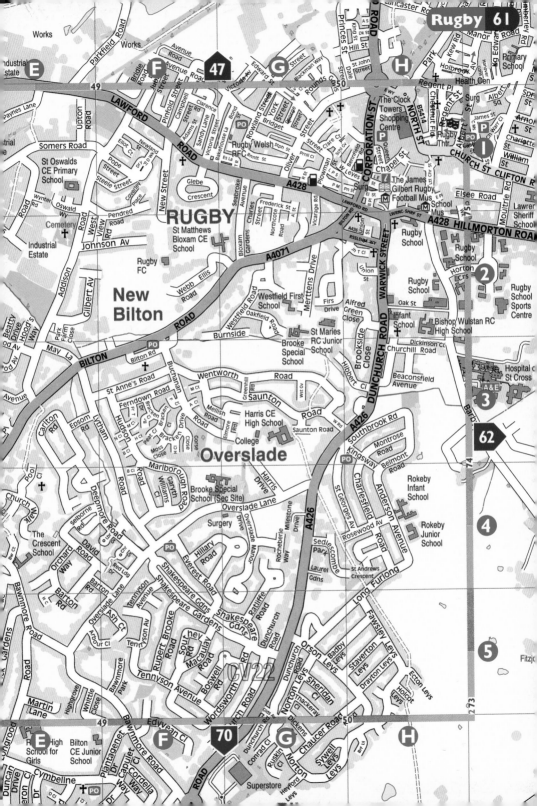

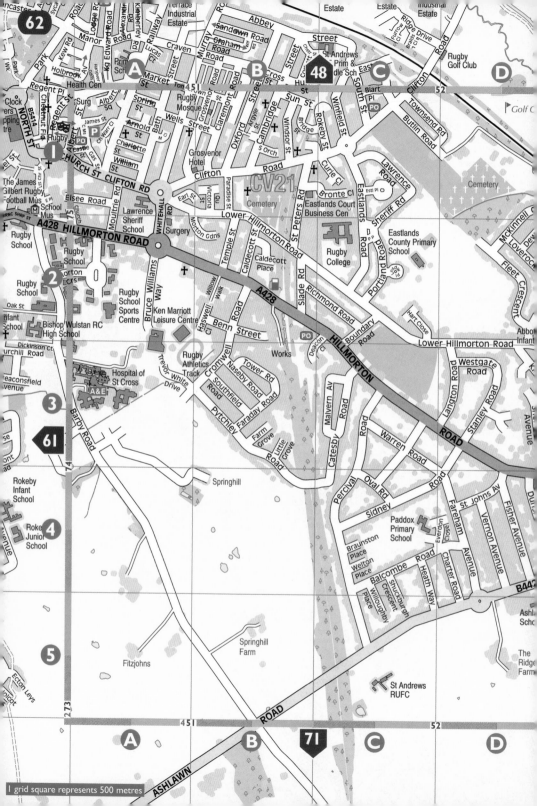

E   F   49   G   H

I
53   54
75
2
3
74
4
Moors Lane
CRICK
5
273

Kent
Hall
The Kent
Home Farm
Hillmorton Lane
Oxford Canal
The Locks

Road
Abbots Farm
Junior School
Unnell Rd
-orton Road
Waverley Road
Kent Lane
Gibson Drive
The Lane
Robert Hill Close
Pine Grove
Brindley Road
Gainsborough Crs
Bonnington Close
Eden Road
Vere Road
Phipps Av
Perkins
Dyson Close
Jenkins Rd
Jackson Rd
Lever Rd
School Street
Constable Road
Fox Cl
Landseer
Reynolds
Bromwich Road
land Av
Kirkby Rd
Lyndhurst Road
Pettiver Crs
Coton
Featherbed
Wigston Rd
School Gdns
Pl
Turner Cl
Lower Street
Hillmorton
fields Avenue
Paddox
Deerings Road
Roper Cl
Wesley Rd
Deane Road
Fenwick Cl
Cemetery
Watts Lane
Hillmorton Primary School
Mellor Rd
HC
Packwood Av
Myers Road
Oxford Canal Path
Hoskyn Close
Walford Pl
Elms Drive
Rathbone Cl
Gatehouse Cl
High Street
Horne Close
Bell Wk
Archer's Spinney
Browning Road
ASHLAWN ROAD
PO
HIGH STREET A428
Chamberlain Road
Eastwood Grove
Leys Road
Lennon Cl
RC
English Martyrs RC Primary School
Fellows Way
Duffy Pl
Barley Cl
Vale Cl
Cockerill's Meadow
Bucknill Crescent
Astley Place
Foresters Place
Kilworth Road
Leys Road
CRICK
Westwood Road
Hillmorton Manor Hotel & Restaurant
Moat Farm Drive
B4038 KILSBY LANE
Barby Lane

E   F   G   H
53   54
B

Stoneleigh
Grange

53

E   F   G   H

COVENTRY

Birmingham

B4113

Hall Cl

Avon Close

Stoneleigh Cl

Road

Stoneleigh

Walkers Orchard

Centenary Way

Vicarage
Road

Church La

33   34   73

I

STONELEIGH ROAD

Stoneleigh Deer Park
Golf Club

Cloud Bridge

River Avon

2

Golf Course

72

3

Centenary Way

Stoneleigh Deer Park
Business Village

Stareton

4

271

5

STONELEIGH ROAD

E   F   G   H

33   Stone House
Farm   34

LEICEST LANE   A445

Furzenhill
Farm

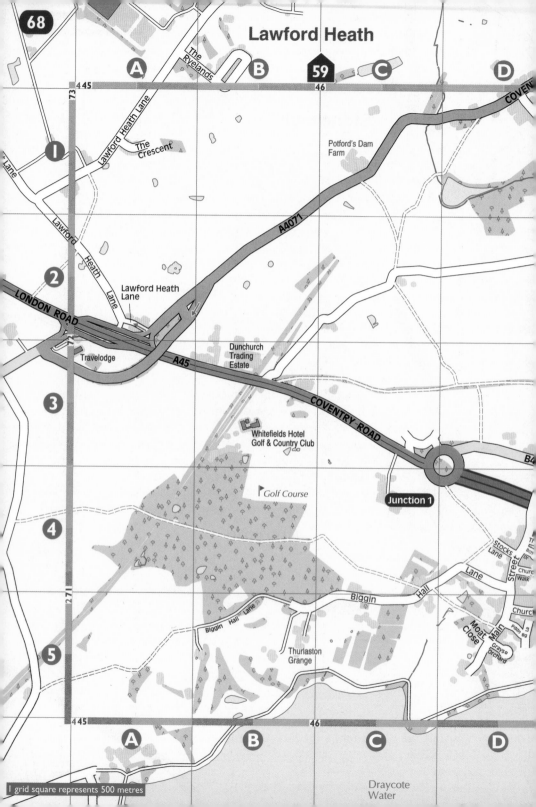

Lawford Heath

68

59

A 445 73

COVEN

Lawford Heath Lane

The Ryelands

The Crescent

Potford's Dam Farm

A4071

LONDON ROAD

Lawford Heath Lane

Travelodge

A45

Dunchurch Trading Estate

COVENTRY ROAD

Whitefields Hotel Golf & Country Club

Golf Course

Junction 1

B4

Stocks Lane

Biggin Hall Lane

Thurlaston Grange

Biggin Hall Lane

Moat Close

Church Walk

Street

Main

Grays Orchard

Church

Draycote Water

271

46

A 445

Driv

Springhill Farm

The Ridgeway Farm

St Andrews RUFC

E

ROAD

F

62

52

G

H

Barby Lane

53

73

I

Warwickshire County

Northamptonshire County

Rains Brook

Onley Lane

Lower Rainsbrook Farm

2

72

3

oxford Canal Path

Onley Farm

Whitehall Farm

4

271

5

Barby Wood Farm

H M Young Offenders Institution

52

53

E

F

G

H

Alderman's Green 14 B4
Allesley 21 E3
Ansty 15 H5
Ash Green 12 D2
Baginton 54 A2
Balsall Common 34 D2
Balsall Street 34 A4
Barnacle 15 G2
Bedworth 5 G5
Bedworth Heath 4 C3
Beechwood 35 G3
Bell Green 24 A3
Benton Green 26 D4
Berkswell 26 C3
Bilton 60 D5
Bilton Fields 70 B1
Binley 41 F1
Binley Woods 42 B2
Black Bank 5 F4
Brandon 43 E4
Bretford 44 B2
Brownshill Green 21 F2
Brownsover 48 B2
Bulkington 7 F4
Burton Green 36 B5
Canley 37 H3
Carol Green 35 G1
Catchems Corner 35 F4
Cawston 60 B5
Chapel Fields 29 H4
Cheylesmore 39 H2
Church End 32 B3
Church Lawford 45 E4
Clifton upon Dunsmore 49 F4

Coalpit Field 6 A4
Collycroft 5 G1
Corley 11 E1
Corley Moor 10 B1
Coundon 21 H4
Court House Green 23 H4
Coventry 2 E7
Crackley 51 G5
Dunchurch 69 H4
Earlsdon 30 B5
Eaves Green 19 E1
Edgwick 23 F3
Exhall 14 A1
Finham 53 E1
Flint's Green 27 E1
Foleshill 23 G3
Four Oaks 26 C1
Foxford 13 G4
Gibbet Hill 52 B2
Goodyers End 4 B4
Gosford Green 3 K4
Great Heath 23 F4
Green Lane 38 D4
Hall Green 14 A5
Hampton in Arden 16 A4
Harvest Hill 20 A1
Hawkes End 20 D1
Henley Green 24 C3
Hillfields 3 F1
Hillmorton 63 E4
Hockley 27 G2
Holbrooks 12 D5
Hollyberry End 10 A4
Hollyhurst 6 B5

Kenilworth 64 D4
Keresley 12 A4
Keresley Newlands 12 C2
Kings Hill 53 E2
King's Newnham 45 F2
Kirby Corner 37 F3
Ladyes Hill 65 F1
Lawford Heath 59 C5
Lime Tree Park 28 D5
Little Heath 23 G2
Little Lawford 46 B2
Little Packington 9 F2
Longford 13 G4
Long Lawford 46 A4
Lower Eastern Green 28 B3
Lower Stoke 31 H5
Manor House 24 B1
Marston 43 H4
Meriden 18 C2
Middle Bickenhill 9 E5
Middle Stoke 31 H3
Mount Pleasant 5 F2
Neal's Green 13 E2
New Bilton 61 F2
Newbold on Avon 47 F4
Overslade 61 F3
Park Hill 65 H2
Pickford 20 B3
Pickford Green 20 A4
Pinkett's Booth 20 A3
Pinley 40 B2
Potter's Green 25 E2
Radford 22 D5
Reeves Green 35 H1

Rowley's Green ....
Rugby ....
Ryton-on-Dunsmore ....
St Johns ....
Spon End ....
The Spring ....
Stareton ....
Stivichall ....
Stoke ....
Stoke Aldermoor ....
Stoke Heath ....
Stonebridge ....
Stoneleigh ....
Thurlaston ....
Tile Hill ....
Toft ....
Tollbar End ....
Upper Eastern Green ....
Upper Stoke ....
Walsgrave on Sowe ....
Weston in Arden ....
Westwood Heath ....
Whitemoor ....
Whitley ....
Whitmore Park ....
Whoberley ....
Willenhall ....
Windy Arbour ....
Wolston ....
Wood End ....
Woodway Park ....
Wyken ....

USING THE STREET INDEX

Street names are listed alphabetically. Each street name is followed by its postal town or area locality, the Postcode District, the page number, and the reference to the square in which the name is found.

Standard index entries are shown as follows:

Abberton Wy *TLHL/CAN* CV4 ....**52** A1

Street names and selected addresses not shown on the map due to scale restrictions are shown in the index with an asterisk:

Abbey Cottages *COVS* CV3 * **41** G2

GENERAL ABBREVIATIONS

ACC................................ACCESS	CSWY..........................CAUSEWAY	GND..............................GROUND	MEM.............................MEMO
ALY..................................ALLEY	CT...................................COURT	GRA..............................GRANGE	MKT..............................MAR
AP.............................APPROACH	CTRL...........................CENTRAL	GRG..............................GARAGE	MKTS.............................MARI
AR.................................ARCADE	CTS................................COURTS	GT....................................GREAT	ML......................................N
ASS.......................ASSOCIATION	CTYD.......................COURTYARD	GTWY..........................GATEWAY	ML......................................
AV.................................AVENUE	CUTT...........................CUTTINGS	GV...................................GROVE	MNR...............................MAI
BCH.................................BEACH	CV....................................COVE	HGR...............................HIGHER	MS......................................
BLDS..........................BUILDINGS	CYN...............................CANYON	HL......................................HILL	MSN.............................MISS
BND..................................BEND	DEPT........................DEPARTMENT	HLS...................................HILLS	MT.....................................MO
BNK..................................BANK	DL.....................................DALE	HO...................................HOUSE	MTN..........................MOUNT
BR.................................BRIDGE	DM.....................................DAM	HOL..............................HOLLOW	MTS........................MOUNTA
BRK..................................BROOK	DR...................................DRIVE	HOSP..........................HOSPITAL	MUS..............................MUS
BTM................................BOTTOM	DRO.................................DROVE	HRB............................HARBOUR	MWY..........................MOTOR
BUS............................BUSINESS	DRY..............................DRIVEWAY	HTH..................................HEATH	N..NO
BVD...........................BOULEVARD	DWGS.........................DWELLINGS	HTS...............................HEIGHTS	NE...........................NORTH E
BY..................................BYPASS	E...EAST	HVN.................................HAVEN	NW........................NORTH W
CATH..........................CATHEDRAL	EMB.........................EMBANKMENT	HWY..............................HIGHWAY	O/P.............................OVERF
CEM.........................CEMETERY	EMBY.............................EMBASSY	IMP..............................IMPERIAL	OFF...................................OFF
CEN................................CENTRE	ESP.............................ESPLANADE	IN.......................................INLET	ORCH...........................ORCH
CFT..................................CROFT	EST.................................ESTATE	IND EST ....INDUSTRIAL ESTATE	OV......................................O
CH.................................CHURCH	EX...............................EXCHANGE	INF.............................INFIRMARY	PAL..............................PAL
CHA..................................CHASE	EXPY.........................EXPRESSWAY	INFO.......................INFORMATION	PAS..............................PASS
CHYD.......................CHURCHYARD	EXT............................EXTENSION	INT.........................INTERCHANGE	PAV..............................PAVIL
CIR..................................CIRCLE	F/O..............................FLYOVER	IS....................................ISLAND	PDE.................................PAR
CIRC...............................CIRCUS	FC........................FOOTBALL CLUB	JCT..............................JUNCTION	PH......................PUBLIC HO
CL......................................CLOSE	FK.....................................FORK	JTY....................................JETTY	PK......................................NO
CLFS................................CLIFFS	FLD....................................FIELD	KG.......................................KING	PKWY..........................PARKW
CMP..................................CAMP	FLDS.................................FIELDS	KNL...................................KNOLL	PL..PL
CNR................................CORNER	FLS..................................FALLS	L..LAKE	PLN...................................PL
CO...................................COUNTY	FLS....................................FLATS	LA.......................................LANE	PLNS.............................PL/
COLL...............................COLLEGE	FM......................................FARM	LDG................................LODGE	PLZ....................................PL
COM...............................COMMON	FT.......................................FORT	LGT..................................LIGHT	POL....................POLICE STAT
COMM.......................COMMISSION	FWY...............................FREEWAY	LK.......................................LOCK	PR......................................PR
CON..............................CONVENT	FY.......................................FERRY	LKS...................................LAKES	PREC.............................PRECI
COT.................................COTTAGE	GA..GATE	LNDG.............................LANDING	PREP....................PREPARAT
COTS...........................COTTAGES	GAL................................GALLERY	LTL....................................LITTLE	PRIM..............................PRIM.
CP......................................CAPE	GDN.................................GARDEN	LWR.................................LOWER	PROM.....................PROMENA
CPS..................................COPSE	GDNS.............................GARDENS	MAG........................MAGISTRATE	PRS..............................PRINC
CR......................................CREEK	GLD....................................GLADE	MAN............................MANSIONS	PRT......................................P
CREM......................CREMATORIUM	GLN.....................................GLEN	MD.....................................MEAD	PT..PC
CRS...............................CRESCENT	GN....................................GREEN	MDW............................MEADOWS	PTH......................................P

...........PIAZZA	SCH ....SCHOOL	SW ....SOUTH WEST
...........QUADRANT	SE................SOUTH EAST	TDG ....TRADING
...........QUEEN	SER ....SERVICE AREA	TER ....TERRACE
...........QUAY	SH ....SHORE	THWY ....THROUGHWAY
...........RIVER	SHOP ....SHOPPING	TNL ....TUNNEL
...........ROUNDABOUT	SKWY ....SKYWAY	TOLL ....TOLLWAY
...........ROAD	SMT ....SUMMIT	TPK ....TURNPIKE
...........RIDGE	SOC ....SOCIETY	TR ....TRACK
...........REPUBLIC	SP ....SPUR	TRL ....TRAIL
...........RESERVOIR	SPR ....SPRING	TWR ....TOWER
...........RUGBY FOOTBALL CLUB	SQ ....SQUARE	U/P ....UNDERPASS
...........RISE	ST ....STREET	UNI ....UNIVERSITY
...........RAMP	STN ....STATION	UPR ....UPPER
...........ROW	STR ....STREAM	V ....VALE
...........SOUTH	STRD ....STRAND	VA ....VALLEY

VIAD ....VIADUCT / VIL ....VILLA / VIS ....VISTA / VLG ....VILLAGE / VLS ....VILLAS / VW ....VIEW / W ....WEST / WD ....WOOD / WHF ....WHARF / WK ....WALK / WKS ....WALKS / WLS ....WELLS / WY ....WAY / YD ....YARD / YHA ....YOUTH HOSTEL

OSTCODE TOWNS AND AREA ABBREVIATIONS

H..........Bedworth
NEC..........Birmingham N.E.C.
/FDBR/MGN ....Chelmsley Wood/ Fordbridge/ Marston Green
..........Coventry
..........Coventry east

COVN ....Coventry north
COVS ....Coventry south
COVW ....Coventry west
CSHL/WTROR ....Coleshill/Water Orton
HIA/OLT ....Hampton in Arden/ Olton
KNWTH ....Kenilworth

LGN/SDN/BHAMAIR ....Lyndon Green/ Sheldon/ Birmingham Airport
LUTT ....Lutterworth
NUN ....Nuneaton
NUNW/HART ....Nuneaton west/ Hartshill

RCOVN/BALC/EX ....Rural Coventry north/ Balsall Common/Exhall
RLSN ....Royal Leamington Spa north
RRUGBY ....Rural Rugby
RUGBYN/HIL ....Rugby north/Hillmorton
RUGBYS/DCH ....Rugby south/Dunchurch
TLHL/CAN ....Tile Hill/Canley

ndex - streets

Abb - Ayn

A

rton Wy TLHL/CAN CV4 ...52 A1	
y Cottages COVS CV3 * ...41 G2	
ydale Cl COVS CV3 ...33 E3	
y End KNWTH CV8 ...65 E3	
y HI KNWTH CV8 ...65 E3	
y Rd COVS CV3 ...40 A3	
y St RUGBYN/HIL CV21 ...48 B5	
y Wy COVS CV3 ...40 A3	
tsbury Cl COVE CV2 ...33 F2	
tts La COV CV1 ...2 B2	
tts Wk COVS CV3 ...42 B2	
tts La RUGBYN/HIL CV21 ...63 E3	
corn Rd COVW CV5 ...29 H4	
deen Cl COVW CV5 ...28 D1	
gavenny Wk COVS CV3 ...41 G3	
ia Av COV CV1 ...3 G6	
ia Crs BDWTH CV12 ...6 A2	
ia Gv RUGBYN/HIL CV21 ...47 H5	
l Cl COVN CV6 ...23 G1	
les Rd COVN CV6 ...23 F1	
n Cl BDWTH CV12 ...4 B5	
WTH CV8 ...53 E5	
n Dr RUGBYS/DCH CV22 ...60 C3	
n St COVS CV3 ...40 C1	
n Rd COVN CV6 ...23 G4	
ns St RUGBYN/HIL CV21 ...61 F1	
se Dr COVS CV3 ...39 F1	
ck Dr KNWTH CV8 ...65 G2	
enbrooke Rd	
COVN/BALC/EX CV7 ...12 B1	
erley St COV CV1 ...31 F2	
son Rd COVN CV6 ...22 B3	
GBYS/DCH CV22 ...61 E2	
aide St COV CV1 ...31 F2	
nson Av RUGBYS/DCH CV22 ...65 H4	
iral Gdns KNWTH CV8 ...65 H1	
court Rd COVS CV3 ...39 H2	
ury Rd COVW CV5 ...38 B1	
dale Cl COVS CV3 ...14 A4	
ree Cl BDWTH CV12 ...5 G1	
WN CV6 ...31 F1	
ort Wy HIA/OLT B92 ...8 B5	
Cl RUGBYN/HIL CV21 ...48 A3	
dale Av COVW CV5 ...28 B2	
Higgs Wy TLHL/CAN CV4 ...36 B2	
ny Rd COVW CV5 ...30 B5	
rt Crs COVN CV6 ...12 C5	
rt Fearn Gdns COVN CV6 ...23 G2	
rt Rd COVW CV5 ...19 F3	
rt Sq RUGBYN/HIL CV21 ...62 A1	
rt St COV CV1 ...3 G1	
JGBYN/HIL CV21 ...61 H1	
on St KNWTH CV8 ...65 F2	
rt Rd COV CV1 ...30 D1	
ourne Rd COVW CV5 ...29 F2	
ury Ri COVW CV5 ...29 F2	
r La RCOVN/BALC/EX CV7 ...34 D4	
man's Green Rd COVE CV2 ...14 A5	
r Meadow Cl COVN CV6 ...13 E5	
minster Rd COVW CV5 ...28 D2	
moor La COVS CV3 ...40 B1	

Alderney Cl COVN CV6 ...22 C1	
Alder Rd COVN CV6 ...23 H1	
The Alders BDWTH CV12 ...4 D3	
Aldrich Av TLHL/CAN CV4 ...28 B4	
Aldrin Wy TLHL/CAN CV4 ...38 A4	
Alexander Rd BDWTH CV12 ...5 H2	
Alexandra Rd COV CV1 ...3 J1	
RUGBYN/HIL CV21 ...48 A5	
Alex Grierson Cl COVS CV3 ...41 F2	
Alfall Rd COVE CV2 ...32 A1	
Alfred Green Cl	
RUGBYS/DCH CV22 ...61 H2	
Alfred Rd COV CV1 ...31 G2	
Alfred St RUGBYN/HIL CV21 ...61 G2	
Alfriston Rd COVS CV3 ...39 F5	
Alice Cl BDWTH CV12 ...5 E4	
Alicia Cl RUGBYS/DCH CV22 ...60 B4	
Alison Sq COVE CV2 ...14 A4	
Allan Rd COVN CV6 ...30 A2	
Allans Cl RUGBY CV23 ...49 F4	
Allans La RUGGBY CV23 ...49 F4	
Allard Wy COVS CV3 ...40 D2	
Allerton Cl COVE CV2 ...32 D4	
Allesley Cft COVW CV5 ...20 D5	
Allesley Hall Dr COVW CV5 ...29 F1	
Allesley Old Rd COV CV1 ...30 B3	
COVW CV5 ...29 G2	
Allesley Rd RUGBYN/HIL CV21 ...47 G3	
Alliance Wy COVE CV2 ...31 H1	
Allied Cl COVN CV6 ...23 E1	
Allitt Gv KNWTH CV8 ...65 G2	
All Saints La COV CV1 ...3 H3	
All Saints Rd BDWTH CV12 ...5 H4	
Alma St COV CV1 ...3 C3	
Almond Gv RUGBYN/HIL CV21 ...47 F2	
Almond Tree Av COVE CV2 ...24 B1	
Alpine Ct KNWTH CV8 ...65 H1	
Alpine Ri COVS CV3 ...38 D4	
Alspath La COVW CV5 ...28 C2	
Alspath Rd RCOVN/BALC/EX CV7 ...18 B2	
Alton Cl COVE CV2 ...24 C1	
Alum Cl COVN CV6 ...23 E3	
Alverley Rd COVN CV6 ...22 D5	
Alverstone Rd COVE CV2 ...31 H2	
Alvin Cl COVS CV3 ...33 E5	
Alwyn Freeman Ct	
RCOVN/BALC/EX CV7 * ...12 B1	
Alwyn Rd RUGBYS/DCH CV22 ...60 D5	
Ambassador Rd	
CHWD/FDBR/MGN B37 ...8 A4	
Amberley Av BDWTH CV12 ...7 F3	
Ambler Gv COVE CV2 ...32 B3	
Ambleside COVE CV2 ...24 D1	
RUGBYN/HIL CV21 ...48 C2	
Ambleside Rd BDWTH CV12 ...5 F3	
Ambrose Cl RUGBYN/HIL CV21 ...48 B3	
Amersham Cl COVW CV5 ...29 E2	
Amherst Rd KNWTH CV8 ...64 D1	
Amos Jacques Rd BDWTH CV12 ...5 F1	
Amy Cl COVN CV6 ...13 G4	
Anchorway Rd COVS CV3 ...39 G5	
Anderson Av RUGBYS/DCH CV22 ...61 H4	
Anderton Rd BDWTH CV12 ...4 A4	
COVN CV6 ...14 A4	
Angela Av COVE CV2 ...24 D2	

Anglesey Cl COVW CV5 ...21 E4	
Angless Wy KNWTH CV8 ...65 E4	
Angus Cl COVW CV5 ...28 D2	
Anker Dr RRUGBY CV23 ...46 C4	
Anne Crs COVS CV3 ...40 D4	
Ansell Dr COVN CV6 ...13 H3	
Anson Cl RUGBYS/DCH CV22 ...60 B3	
Anson Wy COVE CV2 ...25 E3	
Ansty Rd COVE CV2 ...25 E5	
COVE CV2 ...32 B2	
Anthony Wy COVE CV2 ...32 B4	
Antrim Cl COVW CV5 ...20 D4	
Applecross Cl TLHL/CAN CV4 ...37 E3	
Appledore Dr COVW CV5 ...28 C1	
Apple Gv RUGBYS/DCH CV22 ...60 C2	
The Arboretum TLHL/CAN CV4 ...52 A1	
Arbour Cl KNWTH CV8 ...65 G4	
RUGBYS/DCH CV22 ...61 E5	
Arbury Av BDWTH CV12 ...23 F1	
COVN CV6 ...23 F1	
Archer Rd KNWTH CV8 ...64 D4	
Archers Spinney	
RUGBYN/HIL CV21 ...63 G4	
Archery Rd RCOVN/BALC/EX CV7 ...18 A2	
Arches La RUGBYN/HIL CV21 ...48 B4	
Arch Rd COVE CV2 ...32 D1	
Arden Cl RCOVN/BALC/EX CV7 ...18 B2	
RCOVN/BALC/EX CV7 ...34 C2	
RUGBYS/DCH CV22 ...69 H2	
Arden Ct HIA/OLT B92 * ...16 B4	
Arden Rd BDWTH CV12 ...7 F3	
KNWTH CV8 ...65 G4	
Arden St COVW CV5 ...30 A5	
Argyle St RUGBYN/HIL CV21 ...62 B1	
Argyll St COVE CV2 ...31 H3	
Ariel Wy RUGBYS/DCH CV22 ...69 H1	
Arkle Dr COVE CV2 ...25 E4	
Arlidge Crs KNWTH CV8 ...65 H2	
Armarna Dr COVW CV5 ...19 G3	
Armfield St COVN CV6 ...23 H3	
Armorial Rd COVS CV3 ...39 E3	
Armscott Rd COVE CV2 ...24 B5	
Armson Rd RCOVN/BALC/EX CV7 ...5 F4	
Armstrong Av COVS CV3 ...31 H5	
Armstrong Cl	
RUGBYS/DCH CV22 ...61 E1	
Arne Rd COVE CV2 ...25 F5	
Arnhem Cnr COVS CV3 ...41 E3	
Arnold Av COVS CV3 ...39 F4	
Arnold St RUGBYN/HIL CV21 ...62 A1	
Arnside Cl COV CV1 ...3 G1	
Arthingworth Cl COVS CV3 ...32 D5	
Arthur St COV CV1 ...31 G1	
RUGBYN/HIL CV21 ...65 F2	
Arundel Rd BDWTH CV12 ...7 F2	
COVS CV3 ...39 G3	
Asbury Rd RCOVN/BALC/EX CV7 ...34 C4	
Ascot Cl BDWTH CV12 ...5 G1	
COVS CV3 ...40 D3	
Ashbridge Rd COVW CV5 ...29 F2	
Ashburton Rd COVE CV2 ...24 D4	
Ashby Cl COVS CV3 ...41 G1	
Ashcombe Dr TLHL/CAN CV4 ...28 C3	
Ash Ct RUGBYS/DCH CV22 ...61 F5	
Ashcroft Cl COVE CV2 ...25 F3	

Ashcroft Wy	
RCOVN/BALC/EX CV7 ...25 G3	
Ashdale Cl COVS CV3 ...42 D2	
Ashdene Gdns KNWTH CV8 ...65 G3	
Ashdown Cl COVS CV3 ...41 E1	
Ash Dr KNWTH CV8 ...65 F3	
Ashfield Av TLHL/CAN CV4 ...28 A5	
Ashfield Rd KNWTH CV8 ...65 G4	
Ashford Dr BDWTH CV12 ...5 F2	
Ashfurlong Cl	
RCOVN/BALC/EX CV7 ...34 C3	
Ash Green La	
RCOVN/BALC/EX CV7 ...12 D2	
Ash Gv RCOVN/BALC/EX CV7 ...12 D1	
Ashington Gv COVS CV3 ...40 B4	
Ashington Rd BDWTH CV12 ...4 B4	
Ashlawn Rd RUGBYN/HIL CV21 ...63 E4	
RUGBYS/DCH CV22 ...70 A2	
Ashley Wy RCOVN/BALC/EX CV7 ...34 C2	
Ashman Av RRUGBY CV23 ...46 C4	
Ashmore Rd COVN CV6 ...30 C2	
Ashorne Cl COVE CV2 ...24 B1	
Ashow Cl KNWTH CV8 ...65 G3	
Ash Priors Cl TLHL/CAN CV4 ...29 E4	
Ash Tree Av TLHL/CAN CV4 ...28 D4	
Ashurst Cl COVN CV6 ...14 A3	
Ashwood Av COVN CV6 ...30 A1	
Ashwood Ct RUGBYN/HIL CV21 * ...47 G5	
Aspen Cl TLHL/CAN CV4 ...28 A5	
Aspen Dr COVN CV6 ...14 B2	
Asplen Ct KNWTH CV8 ...65 H3	
Asra Cl COVE CV2 ...31 G2	
Assheton Cl RUGBYS/DCH CV22 ...60 B4	
Asthill Cft COVS CV3 ...2 C7	
Asthill Gv COVS CV3 ...39 F1	
Astley Av COVN CV6 ...23 F1	
Astley Pl RUGBYN/HIL CV21 ...63 G5	
Aston Rd COVW CV5 ...30 A5	
Atherston Pl TLHL/CAN CV4 ...38 A3	
Athol Rd COVE CV2 ...25 F5	
Attoxhall Rd COVE CV2 ...32 D2	
Attwood Crs COVE CV2 ...24 B5	
Augustus Rd COV CV1 ...3 J1	
Austin Dr COVN CV6 ...23 H4	
Aventine Wy RUGBYN/HIL CV21 ...47 G2	
Avenue Rd KNWTH CV8 ...64 C1	
RUGBYN/HIL CV21 ...47 F5	
The Avenue COVS CV3 ...40 B3	
Avocet Cl COVN CV6 ...24 A1	
Avondale Rd COVW CV5 ...38 D1	
KNWTH CV8 ...43 E4	
Avonmere RUGBYN/HIL CV21 ...47 F3	
Avon Rd KNWTH CV8 ...64 D4	
Avon St COVE CV2 ...32 A1	
RRUGBY CV23 ...48 D5	
RUGBYN/HIL CV21 ...47 H5	
Awson St COVN CV6 ...23 G5	
Axholme Rd COVE CV2 ...32 D2	
Aylesford St COV CV1 ...31 F2	
Aynho Cl COVW CV5 ...28 D3	

B

Babbacombe Rd COVS CV3 ....39 G4
Bablake Cl COVN CV6 ....22 A3
Back La RCOVN/BALC/EX CV7 ......26 C1
   RRUGBY CV23 ....46 B5
Badby Leys RUGBYS/DCH CV22 ...61 G5
Badger Rd COVS CV3 ....41 E1
Baffin Cl RUGBYS/DCH CV22 ....61 F3
Baginton Rd COVS CV3 ....39 F4
Bagshaw Cl KNWTH CV8 ....55 H3
Bailey's La KNWTH CV8 ....41 B4
Bakehouse La RUGBYN/HIL .61 C1
Bakers La COVW CV5 ....29 H4
Baker St COVN CV6 ....14 A2
Bakewell Cl COVS CV3 ....41 G1
Balcombe Rd RUGBYS/DCH CV22 .62 C4
Baldwin Cft COVN CV6 ....24 A2
Ballantine Rd COVN CV6 ....22 C5
Ballingham Cl TLHL/CAN CV4 ....28 D4
Balliol Rd COVE CV2 ....32 A2
Balmoral Cl COVN CV6 ....24 D5
Balsall St RCOVN/BALC/EX CV7 ....34 A4
Balsall St East
   RCOVN/BALC/EX CV7 ....34 B4
Bankside Cl COVS CV3 ....40 A3
Banks Rd COVN CV6 ....30 B1
Bank St RUGBYN/HIL CV21 * 61 H1
Banner La TLHL/CAN CV4 ....28 A3
Bantam Gv COVN CV6 ....12 B5
Bantock Rd TLHL/CAN CV4 ....28 B4
Barbican Ri COVE CV2 ....32 D4
Barbridge Cl BDWTH CV12 ....7 F3
Barbridge Rd BDWTH CV12 ....7 E3
Barby La RUGBYN/HIL CV21 ....63 E5
Barby Rd RUGBYS/DCH CV22 ....61 H3
Bardley Dr COVN CV6 ....22 D5
Barford Cl COVS CV3 ....41 E1
Barford Rd KNWTH CV8 ....65 C4
Barker's Butts La COVN CV6 ....30 A2
Barley Cl RUGBYN/HIL CV21 ....63 F4
The Barley Lea COVS CV3 ....40 C1
Barley Pl COVS CV3 * 40 C1
Barlow Rd COVE CV2 ....14 C5
Barnack Av COVS CV3 ....39 E4
Barnacle La BDWTH CV12 ....7 H4
Barnfield Av COVN CV6 ....21 E4
Barnstaple Cl COVW CV5 * 28 C1
Barnwell Cl RUGBYS/DCH CV22 ....69 G3
Baron Leigh Dr TLHL/CAN CV4 * 36 C3
Baron's Cft COVS CV3 ....39 H2
Baron's Field Rd COVS CV3 ....39 G2
Barracks Wy COV CV1 * 2 D4
Barras Gn COVE CV2 ....31 H2
Barras La COV CV1 ....2 A3
Barretts La RCOVN/BALC/EX CV7 ..34 D3
Barrington Rd
   RUGBYS/DCH CV22 ....60 D2
Barrow Cl COVE CV2 ....25 C5
Barrowfield La KNWTH CV8 ....65 E3
Barrow Rd KNWTH CV8 ....65 E3
Barston Cl COVN CV6 ....13 H5
Bartholomew Ct COVS CV3 * 40 B3
Bartlett Cl COVN CV6 ....23 F1
Barton Rd BDWTH CV12 ....5 G1
   COVN CV6 ....23 G1
   RUGBYS/DCH CV22 ....61 E4
Bartons Ct COVE CV2 * 31 H2
Barton's Meadow COVE CV2 ....32 A1
Basford Brook Dr COVN CV6 ....13 G3
Basley Wy COVN CV6 ....13 E4
Bassett Rd COVN CV6 ....30 B1
Bateman's Acre South COVN CV6 ..30 B2
Bates Rd COVW CV5 ....38 B2
Bath St COV CV1 ....3 F1
   RUGBYN/HIL CV21 ....62 A1
Bathurst Cl RUGBYS/DCH CV22 ....61 F4
Bathurst Rd COVN CV6 ....22 B4
Bathway Rd COVS CV3 ....38 D5
Batsford Rd COVN CV6 ....30 A2
Battalion Ct COVN CV6 ....22 B2
Baulk La RCOVN/BALC/EX CV7 ......35 C1
Bawnmore Ct RUGBYS/DCH CV22 ..61 E4
Bawnmore Pk
   RUGBYS/DCH CV22 ....61 F5
Bawnmore Rd
   RUGBYS/DCH CV22 ....61 E4
Baxter Cl TLHL/CAN CV4 ....28 D4
Bayley La COV CV1 ....2 E4
Bayliss Av COVN CV6 ....13 H4
Bayton Rd RCOVN/BALC/EX CV7 ...13 H1
Bayton Wy RCOVN/BALC/EX CV7 ..14 B1
Bay Tree Cl COVE CV2 ....24 C2
Beacon Rd COVN CV6 ....13 E5
Beaconsfield Av
   RUGBYS/DCH CV22 ....61 H3

Beaconsfield Rd COVE CV2 ....32 A4
Beake Av COVN CV6 ....22 C5
Beamish Cl COVE CV2 ....25 F5
Beanfield Av COVS CV3 ....38 C5
Beatty Dr RUGBYS/DCH CV22 ....61 E2
Beauchamp Rd KNWTH CV8 ....64 D5
Beaudesert Rd COVW CV5 ....30 B5
Beaufort Dr COVS CV3 ....41 G2
Beaumaris Cl COVW CV5 ....28 C1
Beaumont Crs COVN CV6 ....30 B2
Beaumont Rd
   RCOVN/BALC/EX CV7 ....12 B2
Beausale Cft COVW CV5 ....28 D3
Beckbury Rd COVE CV2 ....25 E5
Beckfoot Cl RUGBYN/HIL CV21 .....48 C1
Beckfoot Dr COVE CV2 ....25 E2
Bede Rd BDWTH CV12 ....5 F1
   COVN CV6 ....30 C1
Bede Village BDWTH CV12 * 4 B5
Bedford St COV CV1 ....30 B4
Bedlam La COVN CV6 ....23 F1
Bedworth Cl BDWTH CV12 ....7 E3
Bedworth La BDWTH CV12 ....4 B1
Bedworth Rd BDWTH CV12 ....6 D3
   COVN CV6 ....13 H3
Beechcroft BDWTH CV12 ....5 E4
Beech Dr KNWTH CV8 ....65 G2
   RRUGBY CV23 ....68 D4
   RUGBYS/DCH CV22 ....60 D3
The Beeches BDWTH CV12 ....4 D3
Beechnut Cl TLHL/CAN CV4 ....28 A4
Beech Rd COVN CV6 ....30 C1
Beech Tree Av COVW CV5 ....29 E4
Beechwood Av COVW CV5 ....29 H5
Beechwood Ct
   RUGBYN/HIL CV21 * 47 G5
Beechwood Cft KNWTH CV8 ....65 E5
Beechwood Rd BDWTH CV12 ....5 H1
Beehive Hl KNWTH CV8 ....50 C5
Beeston Cl COVS CV3 ....41 G1
Belgrade Sq COV CV1 * 2 C3
Belgrave Dr RUGBYN/HIL CV21 .....48 C3
Belgrave Rd COVE CV2 ....32 D2
Belgrave Sq COVE CV2 ....32 D2
Bellairs Av BDWTH CV12 ....4 D4
Bellbrooke Cl COVE CV2 ....24 A2
Belle Vue Ter HIA/OLT B92 ....16 B5
Bell Dr RCOVN/BALC/EX CV7 ....13 F1
Bell Green Rd COVN CV6 ....23 H5
Bellview Wy COVN CV6 ....24 A2
Bell Wk RUGBYN/HIL CV21 ....63 F4
Belmont Rd COVN CV6 ....23 G4
   RUGBYS/DCH CV22 ....61 H4
Belvedere Rd COVW CV5 ....38 D1
Benedictine Rd COVS CV3 ....39 F3
Bennett Ct KNWTH CV8 * 57 E1
Bennetts Rd
   RCOVN/BALC/EX CV7 ....12 A3
Bennetts Rd South
   RCOVN/BALC/EX CV7 ....12 A5
Bennett St RUGBYN/HIL CV21 ....61 G1
Bennfield Rd RUGBYN/HIL CV21 ...61 H1
Benn Rd BDWTH CV12 ....7 E3
Benn St RUGBYS/DCH CV22 ....62 B2
Bennthall Rd COVN CV6 ....23 G1
Bentley Ct COVN CV6 ....12 D4
Bentley Rd RCOVN/BALC/EX CV7 ...5 F4
Benton Green La
   RCOVN/BALC/EX CV7 ....27 E4
The Bentree COVS CV3 ....40 C1
Beresford Av COVN CV6 ....23 F2
Berkeley Rd KNWTH CV8 ....64 D1
Berkeley Rd North COVW CV5 ....30 B5
Berkeley Rd South COVW CV5 ....38 D1
Berkett Rd COVN CV6 ....12 C5
Berkswell Rd COVN CV6 ....23 H1
Berners Cl TLHL/CAN CV4 ....28 B4
Berry St COV CV1 ....3 H2
Bertie Ct KNWTH CV8 * 65 F3
Bertie Rd KNWTH CV8 ....65 E3
Berwick Cl COVW CV5 ....29 E2
Berwyn Av COVN CV6 ....22 A3
Best Av KNWTH CV8 ....51 H5
Beswick Gdns RUGBYS/DCH CV22 ..61 E5
Bettman Cl COVS CV3 ....39 H3
Beverley Cl RCOVN/BALC/EX CV7 ..34 D2
Beverly Dr TLHL/CAN CV4 ....52 A2
Bevington Crs COVN CV6 ....29 H1
Bexfield Cl COVW CV5 ....20 D5
Biart Pl RUGBYN/HIL CV21 ....62 C1
Bickenhill La
   CHWD/FDBR/MGN B37 ....8 A1
Bickenhill Pkwy
   CHWD/FDBR/MGN B37 ....8 B2
Bideford Rd COVE CV2 ....24 B4
Bigbury Cl COVS CV3 ....39 H4
Biggin Hall Crs COVS CV3 ....32 A4

Biggin Hall La RRUGBY CV23 ....68 C5
Bilberry Rd COVE CV2 ....24 C1
Billesden Cl COVS CV3 ....41 F1
Billing Rd COVW CV5 ....29 G3
Billinton Cl COVE CV2 ....32 D4
Bilton La RRUGBY CV23 ....60 C2
Bilton Rd RUGBYS/DCH CV22 ....61 E3
Binley Av COVS CV3 ....41 G1
Binley Gv COVS CV3 ....41 G2
Binley Rd COV CV1 ....3 J3
   COVS CV3 ....31 H4
Binns Cl TLHL/CAN CV4 ....37 E1
Binswood Cl COVE CV2 ....24 C1
Binton Rd COVE CV2 ....24 C1
Birch Av RCOVN/BALC/EX CV7 ......34 C1
Birch Cl BDWTH CV12 ....6 A1
   COVW CV5 ....20 C5
Birch Dr RUGBYS/DCH CV22 ....60 C2
Birches La KNWTH CV8 ....65 F4
The Birches BDWTH CV12 ....7 E1
Birchfield Rd COVN CV6 ....22 A4
Birchgrave Cl COVN CV6 ....23 H4
Birchwood Rd COVS CV3 ....42 B2
Bird Grove Ct COV CV1 ....31 E1
Bird St COV CV1 ....2 E1
Birkdale Cl COVN CV6 ....12 C4
Birmingham Rd COVW CV5 ....20 C4
   KNWTH CV8 ....50 A3
   KNWTH CV8 ....53 E5
   RCOVN/BALC/EX CV7 ....9 H5
Birstall Dr RRUGBY CV23 ....48 C3
Bishop St COV CV1 ....2 D2
Bishops Wk COVW CV5 ....39 E1
Bishopton Cl COVW CV5 ....29 E1
Black Bank RCOVN/BALC/EX CV7 ...5 G4
Blackberry Cl RRUGBY CV23 ....48 C2
Blackberry La COVN CV6 ....24 A5
   RCOVN/BALC/EX CV7 ....12 D3
Blackburn Rd COVN CV6 ....13 G5
Blackfirs La
   CHWD/FDBR/MGN B37 ....8 C1
Black Horse Rd COVN CV6 ....14 A3
   RCOVN/BALC/EX CV7 ....13 H2
Blackman Wy RUGBYN/HIL CV21 ..47 G5
Black Prince Av COVS CV3 ....39 H3
Blackshaw Dr COVE CV2 ....25 E5
Blackthorn Cl TLHL/CAN CV4 ....38 A4
Blackthorne Rd KNWTH CV8 ....65 F4
Blackwatch Rd COVN CV6 ....22 D3
Blackwell Rd COVN CV6 ....23 F3
Blackwood Av
   RUGBYS/DCH CV22 ....61 E2
Blair Dr BDWTH CV12 ....4 C4
Blake Cl RUGBYS/DCH CV22 ....60 D2
Blandford Dr COVE CV2 ....33 E1
Bleaberry RUGBYN/HIL CV21 ....48 B2
Blenheim Av COVN CV6 ....12 D5
Bletchley Dr COVW CV5 ....29 E1
Blockley Rd BDWTH CV12 ....5 H1
Blondvil St COVS CV3 ....39 F2
Bloxam Gdns RUGBYS/DCH CV22 ..61 G2
Bloxam Pl RUGBYN/HIL CV21 ....61 H1
Bluebell Cl RRUGBY CV23 ....48 C1
Bluebell Dr BDWTH CV12 ....4 D3
Bluebell Wk TLHL/CAN CV4 ....28 C5
The Blundells KNWTH CV8 ....65 E5
Blyth Av RCOVN/BALC/EX CV7 ......34 D4
Blyth Cl BDWTH CV12 ....4 B4
Blythe Rd COV CV1 ....31 F2
Boar Cft TLHL/CAN CV4 ....28 C4
Bockendon Rd TLHL/CAN CV4 ....36 C5
Bodmin Rd COVE CV2 ....33 E1
Bodnant Wy KNWTH CV8 ....65 H1
Bohun St TLHL/CAN CV4 ....28 C5
Bolingbroke Rd COVS CV3 ....31 H5
Bolton Cl COVS CV3 ....39 H4
Bond St COV CV1 ....2 C3
   RUGBYN/HIL CV21 ....61 G1
Bonington Dr BDWTH CV12 ....5 F1
Bonneville Cl COVW CV5 ....19 G3
Bonnington Cl RUGBYN/HIL CV21 .63 G3
Borrowdale RUGBYN/HIL CV21 ......48 B1
Borrowdale Cl COVN CV6 ....22 B2
Boston Pl COVN CV6 ....23 E3
Boswell Dr COVE CV2 ....25 F4
Boswell Rd RUGBYS/DCH CV22 .....61 F5
Botoner Rd COV CV1 ....3 J4
Bott Rd COVW CV5 ....38 A1
Boughton Rd RUGBYN/HIL CV21 ...48 B3
Boundary Rd RUGBYN/HIL CV21 ...62 C3
Bourne Rd COVS CV3 ....32 B5
Bowater Ct COVS CV3 * 40 A3
Bowden Wy COVS CV3 ....32 D5
Bow Fell RUGBYN/HIL CV21 ....48 C2
Bowfell Cl COVW CV5 ....29 E2
Bowling Green La
   RCOVN/BALC/EX CV7 ....13 F1
Bowls Ct COVW CV5 ....30 A3
Bowness Cl COVN CV6 ....22 B3

The Boxhill COVS CV3 ....
Boyce Wy RRUGBY CV23 ....
Boyd Cl COVE CV2 ....
Bracadale Cl COVS CV3 ....
Bracebridge Cl
   RCOVN/BALC/EX CV7 ....
Bracken Cl RUGBYS/DCH CV22 ...
Bracken Dr RUGBYS/DCH CV22 ...
Brackenhurst Rd COVN CV6 ....
Brackley Cl COVN CV6 ....
Braddock Cl COVS CV3 ....
Brade Dr COVE CV2 ....
Bradley Cft RCOVN/BALC/EX CV7 ..
Bradney Gn TLHL/CAN CV4 ....
Bradnick Pl TLHL/CAN CV4 ....
Braemar Cl COVE CV2 ....
Brafield Leys RUGBYS/DCH CV22 ...
Braids Cl RUGBYN/HIL CV21 ....
Bramble St COV CV1 ....
Bramcote Cl BDWTH CV12 ....
Brampton Wy BDWTH CV12 ....
Bramston Crs TLHL/CAN CV4 ....
Bramwell Gdns
   RCOVN/BALC/EX CV7 ....
Brandfield Rd COVN CV6 ....
Brandon La KNWTH CV8 ....
   KNWTH CV8 ....
Brandon Rd COVS CV3 ....
   KNWTH CV8 ....
Branksome Rd COVN CV6 ....
Bransdale Av COVN CV6 ....
Bransford Av TLHL/CAN CV4 ....
Branstree Dr COVN CV6 ....
Brathay Cl COVS CV3 ....
Braunston Pl RUGBYS/DCH CV22 ..6
Brayford Av COVS CV3 ....
Bray's La COVE CV2 ....
Braytoft Cl COVN CV6 ....
Brazil St TLHL/CAN CV4 ....
Bredon Av COVS CV3 ....
Bree Cl COVW CV5 ....
Brentwood Av COVS CV3 ....
Bretford Rd COVE CV2 ....
Bretts Cl COV CV1 ....
Brewer Rd BDWTH CV12 ....
Brewers Cl COVS CV3 ....
Brewster Cl COVE CV2 ....
Briansway COVN CV6 ....
Briardene Av BDWTH CV12 ....
Briars Cl COVE CV2 ....
   RRUGBY CV23 ....
Brick Hill La COVW CV5 ....
The Bridal Pth COVW CV5 ....
Bridgeacre Gdns COVS CV3 ....
Bridgecote COVS CV3 ....
Bridgeman Rd COVN CV6 ....
Bridge St COVN CV6 ....
   RUGBYN/HIL CV21 ....
Bridget St RUGBYN/HIL CV21 ....
Bridge Vw KNWTH CV8 * ....
Bridle Brook La COVW CV5 1
Bridle Rd RUGBYN/HIL CV21..........
Bridport Cl COVE CV2 ....
Brierley Rd COVE CV2 ....
Brightmere Rd COVN CV6 ....
Brighton St COVE CV2 ....
Bright St COVN CV6 ....
Brightwalton Rd COVS CV3 ....
Brill Cl TLHL/CAN CV4 ....
Brindle Av COVS CV3 ....
Brindley Paddocks COV CV1 ....
Brindley Rd RCOVN/BALC/EX CV7 .1
   RUGBYN/HIL CV21 ....
Brinklow Rd COVS CV3 ....
Brisbane Cl COVS CV3 ....
Briscoe Rd COVN CV6 1
Bristol Rd COVW CV5 ....
Britannia St COVE CV2 ....
Briton Rd COVE CV2 ....
Brixham Dr COVE CV2 ....
Brixworth Cl COVS CV3 ....
Broadgate COV CV1 ....
Broadlands Cl COVW CV5 ....
Broad La COVW CV5 ....
   RCOVN/BALC/EX CV7 ....
Broadmere Ri COVW CV5 ....
Broad Park Rd COVE CV2 ....
Broad St COVN CV6 ....
Broad St Jetty COVN CV6 ....
Broadwater COVW CV5 ....
Broadway COVW CV5 ....
Broadway Man COVW CV5 * ....
Broadwells TLHL/CAN CV4 ....
Broadwells Ct TLHL/CAN CV4 * ....
Broadwells Crs TLHL/CAN CV4 .....
Brockenhurst Wy COVN CV6 1
Brockhurst Dr TLHL/CAN CV4 3
Bromleigh Dr COVE CV2 3
Bromley Cl KNWTH CV8 64

wich Cl COVS CV3......41 G1
wich Cl RUGBYN/HIL CV21...63 E3
e Cl RUGBYN/HIL CV21......62 C1
e Walk COVE CV2......32 B3
Cl COV CV1......3 H1
e Rd KNWTH CV8......65 G3
ford Av COVN CV6......12 B5
lea BDWTH CV12......5 E3
time Dr RRUGBY CV23......48 D1
lyn Rd COV CV1......23 E5
shaw Vw COVE CV2......25 E3
side Av COVW CV5......29 F3
WTH CV8......64 D3
side Cl RUGBYS/DCH CV22...61 H3
st KNWTH CV8......57 F1
vale Cl COVS CV3......32 D5
Vw RUGBYS/DCH CV22......69 F4
n Cl RUGBYS/DCH CV22......61 F1
e Cft COVN CV6......12 C5
field Pl COVW CV5......30 B4
field Rd COVW CV5......30 A5
ybank KNWTH CV8......65 G1
ett Rd COVN CV6......30 A2
ning Rd COVE CV2......32 B2
GBYN/HIL CV21......63 C4
nshill Ct COVN CV6......22 A3
nshill Green Rd COVN CV6...21 H2
VW CV5......21 H2
n's La COVW CV5......21 E3
nsover La
GBYN/HIL CV21......48 A2
nsover Rd
GBYN/HIL CV21......47 F2
e Rd COVN CV6......22 B3
OVN/BALC/EX CV7......13 G1
e Williams Wy
GBYS/DCH CV22......62 A2
enell Cl RUGBYS/DCH CV22...60 B4
el Cl COVE CV2 *......3 J3
swick Cl RUGBYN/HIL CV21...48 B3
swick Rd COV CV1......2 A5
tingthorpe Wy COVS CV3 ....41 F1
ton Cl COVS CV3......33 G5
nston Cl COVE CV2......24 C1
nt Rd RCOVN/BALC/EX CV7 ..13 H1
pton Rd COVS CV3......32 B4
Jones Cl COVS CV3......41 G2
rt COVN CV6......23 G4
y Cl BDWTH CV12......4 D4
euch Cl RUGBYS/DCH CV22...69 G3
anan Rd RUGBYS/DCH CV22 .61 F3
fast Cl COVS CV3......39 H4
hold Dr COVW CV5......29 E1
ingham Ri COVW CV5......29 E2
land Rd COVN CV6......22 C2
nill Crs RUGBYN/HIL CV21 ..63 G4
well La RRUGBY CV23......49 G3
rooke Cl COVE CV2......24 C1
ngton Rd BDWTH CV12......6 A3
WTH CV12......7 G5
ield Av TLHL/CAN CV4......28 B5
nore Gv KNWTH CV8......65 F5
s Head La COVS CV3......31 H5
d COV CV1......2 D2
e Rd COVN CV6......22 B4
ick Cl COVS CV3......33 C5
agues La COVS CV3......13 E3
erry Gv
OVN/BALC/EX CV7......34 B3
ury Cl BDWTH CV12......5 H1
es COV CV1......2 D2
igh Cl RCOVN/BALC/EX CV7...34 C2
Rd COVE CV2......31 H2
aby Rd COVN CV6......22 D3
ham Rd COVS CV3......40 B3
sall Gv COVW CV5......38 A1
sall Rd COVW CV5......38 A1
side COVS CV3......33 F4
GBYS/DCH CV22......61 F2
s Rd COVE CV2......32 A3
s Wk BDWTH CV12......5 H4
ow Hill La
OVN/BALC/EX CV7......11 G1
on Cl COVW CV5......21 F2
es COVS CV3......39 G4
bery Av TLHL/CAN CV4......28 C5
Cl TLHL/CAN CV4......28 C3
elton Cl COV CV1......3 F7
her's La COVW CV5......21 F5
hers Rd HIA/OLT B92......16 B5
s KNWTH CV8......51 H5
ers Crs RCOVN/BALC/EX CV7..5 F4
ers Leap RUGBYN/HIL CV21 ..48 C4
Rd COVN CV6......12 D4
GBYN/HIL CV21......62 C1
ermere RUGBYN/HIL CV21 ..48 C3
ermere Cl COVS CV3......41 G2
erworth Dr TLHL/CAN CV4 ..37 F3

Butt La COVW CV5......21 E4
Butts COV CV1......2 A5
Butts Rd COV CV1......2 A4
Byfield Rd COVW CV6......29 H1
Byron Av BDWTH CV12......6 A3
Byron St COV CV1......2 E1
Bywater Cl COVS CV5......39 E4

C

Cadden Dr COVW CV5......29 E4
Cadman Cl BDWTH CV12......5 H2
Caesar Rd KNWTH CV8......64 D4
Caithness Cl COVW CV5......28 D2
Caldecote Rd COVN CV6......30 D1
Caldecott Cl RUGBYN/HIL CV21..62 B2
Caldecott St RUGBYN/HIL CV21..62 B2
Calder Cl BDWTH CV12......7 E3
COVS CV3......39 H2
Calmere Cl COVE CV2......25 E3
Caludon Park Av COVE CV2......32 D1
Caludon Rd COVE CV2......31 H2
Calvert Cl COVS CV3......39 G3
Calvestone Pl
RUGBYS/DCH CV22 *......60 B5
Calvestone Rd
RUGBYS/DCH CV22......60 B5
Calvestone Sq
RUGBYS/DCH CV22 *......60 C4
RUGBYN/HIL CV21......62 B1
Cambridge St COV CV1......31 F1
Camden St COVE CV2......31 H2
Cameron Cl COVW CV5......20 D4
Campbell St RUGBYN/HIL CV21..61 F1
Campion Cl COVS CV3......39 G3
Campion Wy RRUGBY CV23......48 C1
Campling Cl BDWTH CV12......7 E3
Camville COVS CV3......33 F4
Canal Rd COVN CV6......23 F3
Canalside COVN CV6......14 A2
Canberra Rd COVE CV2......14 B4
Canford Cl COVS CV3......53 F1
Canley Ford COVW CV5......38 B2
Canley Rd COVW CV5......38 A1
Cannas Ct TLHL/CAN CV4 *......38 A1
Cannocks La TLHL/CAN CV4......38 A3
Cannon Cl TLHL/CAN CV4......38 B3
Cannon Hill Rd TLHL/CAN CV4..38 A3
Cannon Park Rd TLHL/CAN CV4..38 A4
Canon Dr RCOVN/BALC/EX CV7..13 E2
Canon Hudson Cl COVS CV3......40 D3
Canterbury St COV CV1......3 L1
Cantlow Cl COVW CV5......28 D3
Capmartin Rd COVN CV6......22 C4
Capulet Cl COVS CV3......40 D3
RUGBYS/DCH CV22......70 A1
Caradoc Cl COVE CV2......24 C4
Cardale Cft COVS CV3......41 G1
Cardigan Rd BDWTH CV12......4 B4
Carding Cl COVW CV5......28 C2
Carey St COVN CV6......24 A2
Cargill Cl COVN CV6......13 G3
Carlton Cl BDWTH CV12......7 E3
Carlton Gdns COVW CV5 *......38 D1
Carlton Rd COVN CV6......23 G2
RUGBYS/DCH CV22......61 E3
Carmelite Rd COV CV1......3 H4
Carnbroe Av COVS CV3......41 G2
Carnegie Cl COVS CV3......40 C4
Carsal Cl RCOVN/BALC/EX CV7..13 G2
Carter Rd COVS CV3......40 B1
Carthusian Rd COVS CV3......39 F1
Cartmel Cl COVN CV6......22 D2
Carvell Cl COVW CV5......21 E2
Carver Cl COVE CV2......32 D4
Cascade Cl COVS CV3......39 H3
Cashmore Rd BDWTH CV12......4 A4
KNWTH CV8......65 H3
Cash's La COV CV1......23 E5
Casia Gv KNWTH CV8......65 H5
Caspian Wy COVE CV2......25 F3
Cassandra Cl TLHL/CAN CV4......52 A1
Castle Cl COVS CV3......39 G3
Castle Gn KNWTH CV8......64 C3
Castle Hill KNWTH CV8......64 C3
Castle Ms RUGBYN/HIL CV21..62 A1
Castle Pl COV CV1 *......31 F2
Castle Rd KNWTH CV8......64 C3
Castle St COV CV1......3 G1
RUGBYN/HIL CV21......61 H1
Catesby Rd COVN CV6......22 C3
RUGBYS/DCH CV22......61 H1
Catherine St COV CV1......3 J2
Cavans Wy COVS CV3......41 H4

Cave Cl RUGBYS/DCH CV22......60 B4
Cavendish Rd TLHL/CAN CV4......28 A4
Cawnpore Rd COVN CV6......22 C1
Cawston La RUGBYS/DCH CV22..60 B5
Cawston Wy RUGBYS/DCH CV22..60 D4
Cawthorne Cl COV CV1......31 F2
Cecily Rd COVS CV3......39 G2
Cedar Av KNWTH CV8......56 A3
Cedars Av COVN CV6......29 H1
Cedars Rd RCOVN/BALC/EX CV7..5 G4
Cedar Wood Dr
RCOVN/BALC/EX CV7......34 C3
Cedric Cl COVS CV3......40 D4
Celandine RRUGBY CV23......48 C1
Celandine Rd COVE CV2......24 C1
Celandine Wy BDWTH CV12......4 D3
Centaur Rd COVW CV5......30 A4
Centenary Rd TLHL/CAN CV4......38 A2
Centenary Wy KNWTH CV8......51 F3
Central Av COVE CV2......31 H4
Central Bvd RCOVN/BALC/EX CV7..12 C3
Chace Av COVS CV3......40 C4
Chaceley Cl COVE CV2......25 F3
Chadwick Cl COVW CV5......29 E4
Chalfont Cl BDWTH CV12......5 F3
COVW CV5......29 E2
Challenge Cl COV CV1......31 E2
Chamberlaine St BDWTH CV12..5 G1
Chamberlain Rd
RUGBYN/HIL CV21......63 G4
Chancellors Cl TLHL/CAN CV4......38 A5
Chandos St COVE CV2......31 H3
The Chantries COV CV1......31 F1
Chapel Dr RCOVN/BALC/EX CV7..34 C1
Chapel Farm Cl COVS CV3......40 D3
Chapel La KNWTH CV8......55 H1
RCOVN/BALC/EX CV7......15 G2
Chapel St BDWTH CV12......5 G2
COV CV1......2 C2
RRUGBY CV23......46 B5
RUGBYN/HIL CV21......61 H1
Chapel Yd COVE CV2 *......31 H2
Chard Rd COVS CV3......41 E1
Chariot Wy RUGBYN/HIL CV21..47 H2
Charity Rd RCOVN/BALC/EX CV7..12 A1
Charlecote Rd COVN CV6......22 B1
Charles Eaton Rd BDWTH CV12..5 E2
Charlesfield Rd
RUGBYS/DCH CV22......61 H4
Charles Lakin Cl
RCOVN/BALC/EX CV7......15 H3
Charles St COV CV1......3 G1
RUGBYS/DCH CV22......61 G2
Charles Warren Cl
RUGBYN/HIL CV21......62 A1
Charlewood Rd COVN CV6......22 C1
Charlotte St RUGBYN/HIL CV21..62 A1
Charminster Dr COVS CV3......39 G5
Charter Av TLHL/CAN CV4......36 C2
TLHL/CAN CV4......37 H2
Charterhouse Rd COV CV1......3 H4
Charter Rd RUGBYS/DCH CV22..62 D4
Charwelton Dr
RUGBYN/HIL CV21......48 D3
Chatham Cl COVS CV3 *......40 D1
Chatsworth Gv KNWTH CV8......65 H2
Chatsworth Wk COVS CV3......39 H4
Chattaway Dr
RCOVN/BALC/EX CV7......34 C3
Chaucer Rd RUGBYS/DCH CV22..70 A1
Chauntry Pl COV CV1......2 E2
Cheadle Cl COVN CV6......13 H4
Cheam Cl COVN CV6......23 H2
Chelmarsh COVN CV6......30 D1
Chelney Wk COVS CV3......33 F5
Chelsey Rd COVE CV2......24 D3
Cheltenham Cl BDWTH CV12......5 G1
Cheltenham Cft COVE CV2......25 E4
Chelveston Rd COVN CV6......29 H1
Chelwood Gv COVE CV2......25 E2
Chenies Cl COVW CV5......29 E3
Chepstow Cl COVS CV3......40 D4
Chequer St BDWTH CV12......7 F5
Cheriton Cl COVW CV5......29 G2
Cherrybrook Wy COVE CV2......24 B2
Cherry Cl COVN CV6......23 E1
Cherry Gv RUGBYS/DCH CV22..61 F4
Cherry Orch KNWTH CV8......65 F2
Cherry Wk KNWTH CV8......65 F2
Cherrywood Gv COVW CV5......28 C1
Cherwell Wy RRUGBY CV23......46 C5
Chesford Crs COVN CV6......24 A1
Cheshire Cl RUGBYS/DCH CV22..60 D4
Chesholme Rd COVN CV6......12 C5
The Chesils COVS CV3......39 F3
Chester Rd RCOVN/BALC/EX CV7..9 F4
Chester St COV CV1......2 A2
RUGBYN/HIL CV21......48 B5
Chesterton Rd COVN CV6......22 B3

Chestnut Av KNWTH CV8......65 E4
Chestnut Fld RUGBYN/HIL CV21..61 H1
Chestnut Gv KNWTH CV8......57 F1
TLHL/CAN CV4......28 D4
Chestnut Rd BDWTH CV12......6 A1
The Chestnuts COVW CV12......4 D3
Chestnut Tree Av TLHL/CAN CV4..28 D4
Cheswick Cl COVN CV6 *......23 H4
Chetton Av COVN CV6......30 D1
Chetwode Cl COVW CV5......29 E2
Cheveral Av COVN CV6......22 C5
Cheveral Rd BDWTH CV12......5 F2
Cheylesmore COV CV1......2 D5
Chicory Dr RRUGBY CV23......48 C1
Chideock Hl COVS CV3......38 D3
Chiel Cl COVW CV5......28 C2
Childs Oak Cl
RCOVN/BALC/EX CV7......34 B3
Chillaton Rd COVN CV6......22 C1
Chiltern Leys COVN CV6......30 B2
The Chilterns COVW CV5......29 E2
Chingford Rd COVN CV6......13 H4
Christchurch Rd COVN CV6......22 A5
Church Cl KNWTH CV8......56 A4
Churchill Av COVN CV6......23 F2
KNWTH CV8......65 F1
Churchill Rd RUGBYS/DCH CV22..61 H3
Church La COVE CV2......32 A3
COVW CV5......27 H1
KNWTH CV8......67 E1
RCOVN/BALC/EX CV7......11 F1
RCOVN/BALC/EX CV7......13 F1
RCOVN/BALC/EX CV7......18 D3
RCOVN/BALC/EX CV7......26 B3
RRUGBY CV23......68 D5
Church Park Cl COVN CV6......22 A4
Church Rd KNWTH CV8......54 A2
KNWTH CV8......55 H2
RRUGBY CV23......45 F4
Church St BDWTH CV12......7 F3
COV CV1......31 E2
RRUGBY CV23......49 F4
RUGBYN/HIL CV21......61 H1
Church Vw KNWTH CV8 *......56 A3
Church Wk COVW CV5......21 F5
RRUGBY CV23......68 D4
RUGBYN/HIL CV21......62 A1
RUGBYS/DCH CV22......61 E4
Church Wy BDWTH CV12......5 G2
Chylds Ct COVW CV5......28 D1
Clara St COVE CV2......31 H4
Clare Ct RUGBYN/HIL CV21......61 G1
Claremont Cl BDWTH CV12......7 E1
Claremont Rd RUGBYN/HIL CV21..62 B1
Claremont Wk COVW CV5......21 F5
Clarence Rd RUGBYN/HIL CV21..61 F1
Clarence St COV CV1......3 H1
Clarendon Rd KNWTH CV8......65 F4
Clarendon St COVW CV5......30 A5
Clarke's Av KNWTH CV8......65 F4
Clark St COV CV1......23 H2
Claverdon Rd COVW CV5......29 E3
Clayhill La RRUGBY CV23......46 A2
Clay La COVE CV2......31 H2
COVW CV5......10 B4
Clayton Rd COVN CV6......29 H1
Clements St COVE CV2......31 H3
Clement Wy RUGBYS/DCH CV22..60 B4
Clennon Ri COVE CV2......24 C3
Cleveland Rd BDWTH CV12......7 E2
COVE CV2......31 H2
Clifden Gv KNWTH CV8......65 H1
Clifford Bridge Rd COVE CV2......25 E5
Clifton Rd RUGBYN/HIL CV21..62 B1
Clifton St COV CV1......31 F2
Clinton Av KNWTH CV8......64 C1
Clinton La KNWTH CV8......64 C1
Clinton Rd COVN CV6......23 G1
Clipstone Rd COVN CV6......21 H5
Clive Rd RCOVN/BALC/EX CV7......34 C3
Cloister Cft COVE CV2......25 E5
The Close KNWTH CV8......43 E4
Cloud Br KNWTH CV8......67 H2
Cloud Gn TLHL/CAN CV4......38 A4
Clovelly Gdns COVE CV2......32 B4
Clovelly Rd COVE CV2......32 A1
Clover Cl RRUGBY CV23......48 C1
Cloverdale Cl
RCOVN/BALC/EX CV7......12 C4
Clyde Rd BDWTH CV12......5 H2
Coalpit Fields Rd BDWTH CV12..5 H3
Coalpit La RUGBYS/DCH CV22..43 H5
Coat of Arms Bridge Rd
COVS CV3......38 D3
Cobbs Rd KNWTH CV8......64 C1
Cobden St COVN CV6......31 F1
Cockerill's Meadow
RUGBYN/HIL CV21......63 F4
Colchester St COV CV1......3 G2

Colebrook Cl *COVS* CV3..............33 E4
Coleby Cl *TLHL/CAN* CV4..............36 C3
Coleman St *TLHL/CAN* CV4..............28 C3
Coleridge Rd *COVE* CV2..............32 B2
Coleshill Heath Rd
  CHWD/FDBR/MGN B37..............8 B1
Colina Cl *COVS* CV3..............40 D4
Colledge Rd *COVN* CV6..............23 E2
Collett Wk *COV* CV1..............2 A1
  KNWTH CV8 *..............65 E3
Colliery La *RCOVN/BALC/EX* CV7......5 G4
Collingwood Av
  RUGBYS/DCH CV22..............60 D3
Collingwood Rd *COVW* CV5..............30 B4
Collins Gv *TLHL/CAN* CV4..............38 A4
Columbia Gdns *BDWTH* CV12..............6 A3
Columbine Wy *BDWTH* CV12..............4 D4
Colyere Cl *RCOVN/BALC/EX* CV7 ...12 B2
Comet Rd *LGN/SDN/BHAMAIR* B26 ..8 A4
Common La *KNWTH* CV8..............51 G5
  RCOVN/BALC/EX CV7..............10 B1
Common Wy *COVE* CV2..............23 H5
Compton Rd *COVN* CV6..............23 E1
Comrie Cl *COVE* CV2..............25 E3
Concorde Rd
  LGN/SDN/BHAMAIR B26..............8 A4
Congleton Cl *COVN* CV6..............23 F1
Conifer Cl *BDWTH* CV12..............5 H1
Conifer Paddock *COVS* CV3..............32 D5
Coniston Cl *BDWTH* CV12..............7 F2
  RUGBYN/HIL CV21..............48 C3
Coniston Dr *COVW* CV5..............28 A2
Coniston Rd *COVW* CV5..............30 A5
Conrad Cl *RUGBYS/DCH* CV22..............70 B1
Conrad Rd *COVN* CV6..............22 B4
Constable Rd *RUGBYN/HIL* CV21....63 G3
Constance Cl *RCOVN/BALC/EX* CV7 ..5 E5
Consul Rd *RUGBYN/HIL* CV21..............47 H3
Convent Cl *KNWTH* CV8..............51 F5
Conway Av *TLHL/CAN* CV4..............36 C1
Cook Cl *COVN* CV6..............13 H4
  RUGBYN/HIL CV21..............48 B2
Cook St *COV* CV1..............2 D2
Coombe Cl *COVS* CV3..............33 F4
Coombe Dr *COVS* CV3..............42 D2
Coombe Park Rd *COVS* CV3..............33 E4
Coombe St *COVS* CV3..............32 A4
Co-operative St *COVE* CV2..............14 A5
Cope Arnolds Cl *COVN* CV6 *..............13 G4
Copeland *RUGBYN/HIL* CV21..............48 B2
Cope St *COV* CV1..............3 F3
Copland Pl *TLHL/CAN* CV4..............28 B5
Coplow Cl *RCOVN/BALC/EX* CV7 ..34 B3
Copperas St *COVE* CV2..............24 A1
Copper Beech Cl *COVN* CV6..............23 F2
Copperfield Rd *COVE* CV2..............32 A3
The Coppice *COVS* CV3..............40 C1
Copse Cl *COVW* CV5..............19 G3
The Copse *RCOVN/BALC/EX* CV7 ....5 F5
Copsewood Ter *COVS* CV3..............32 B4
Copthorne Rd *COVN* CV6..............22 A3
Copt Oak Cl *TLHL/CAN* CV4..............36 B2
Coral Cl *COVW* CV5..............29 F4
Corbetts Cl *HIA/OLT* B92..............16 C4
Corbett St *RUGBYN/HIL* CV21..............48 B5
Cordelia Wy *RUGBYS/DCH* CV22....70 A1
Corfe Cl *COV* CV2..............33 E1
Corinthian Pl *COVE* CV2 *..............24 C4
Corley Vw *RCOVN/BALC/EX* CV7 ..12 D1
Cornelius St *COVS* CV3..............39 G1
Cornets End La
  RCOVN/BALC/EX CV7..............17 F4
The Cornfield *COVS* CV3..............32 B5
Cornflower Dr *RRUGBY* CV23..............48 B1
Cornhill Gv *KNWTH* CV8..............65 H2
Corn Mdw *BDWTH* CV12..............5 H3
Cornwallis Rd *RUGBYS/DCH* CV22..60 C3
Cornwall Rd *COV* CV1..............3 G6
Coronation Rd *COV* CV1..............3 J1
  RRUGBY CV23..............45 E4
Coronel Av *COVN* CV6..............13 F4
Corporation St *COV* CV1..............2 C4
  RUGBYN/HIL CV21..............61 H1
Cotman Cl *BDWTH* CV12..............5 F1
Coton Park Dr *RRUGBY* CV23..............48 B1
Coton Rd *RUGBYN/HIL* CV21..............63 F4
Cotswold Dr *COVS* CV3..............53 F1
Cottage Farm Rd *COVN* CV6..............22 B2
Cottage Leap *RUGBYN/HIL* CV21...48 C5
Cotterell Rd *RUGBYN/HIL* CV21 ..47 G3
Cottesbrook Cl *COVS* CV3..............32 D5
Cotton Dr *KNWTH* CV8..............65 H1
Coundon Gn *COVN* CV6..............21 H3
Coundon Rd *COV* CV1..............2 A1
Coundon St *COV* CV1..............2 A2
Coundon Wedge Dr *COVW*.........21 F5
The Countess's Cft *COVS* CV3..............39 G2
Courtaulds Wy *COVN* CV6..............23 E5
Courthouse Cft *KNWTH* CV8 ....65 H3

Courtland Av *COVN* CV6..............30 A1
Court Leet *COVS* CV3..............42 C2
Court Leet Rd *COVS* CV3..............39 H2
Coventry Point *COV* CV1 *..............2 D4
Coventry Rd *BDWTH* CV12..............5 G4
  BDWTH CV12..............6 D5
  COVE CV2..............14 D2
  HIA/OLT B92..............9 F5
  KNWTH CV8..............53 H1
  KNWTH CV8..............53 H1
  RCOVN/BALC/EX CV7..............26 C5
  RRUGBY CV23..............44 C4
  RRUGBY CV23..............68 B3
  RUGBYS/DCH CV22..............60 C5
Coventry Rd Exhall
  RCOVN/BALC/EX CV7..............13 H1
Coventry St *COVE* CV2..............31 H2
Coventry Wy *BDWTH* CV12..............4 C3
  KNWTH CV8..............57 E1
  RCOVN/BALC/EX CV7..............26 D2
Cove Pl *COVE* CV2..............24 B4
Coverley Pl *RUGBYS/DCH* CV22....61 F1
Cowan Cl *RUGBYS/DCH* CV22..............60 C3
Cowley Rd *COVE* CV2..............32 C2
Cox Crs *RUGBYS/DCH* CV22..............69 G3
Cox St *COV* CV1..............3 F2
Cozens Cl *BDWTH* CV12..............5 F1
Crabmill La *COVN* CV6..............23 G4
Crackley Cottages *KNWTH* CV8 *..51 G4
Crackley Hl *KNWTH* CV8 *..............51 G4
Crackley La *KNWTH* CV8..............36 D5
Craigends Av *COVS* CV3..............41 F3
Crakston Cl *COVE* CV2..............32 D4
Cramper's Fld *COVN* CV6..............30 B1
Cranborne Cha *COVE* CV2..............33 E1
Craner's Rd *COV* CV1..............31 G2
Cranford Rd *COVW* CV5..............29 G2
Crathie Cl *COVE* CV2..............25 E5
Craven Av *COVS* CV3..............42 C2
Craven Rd *RUGBYN/HIL* CV21..............48 A5
Craven St *COVW* CV5..............30 A4
Crecy Rd *COVS* CV3..............39 H2
Crescent Av *COVS* CV3..............32 A4
The Crescent *HIA/OLT* B92..............16 C4
  RCOVN/BALC/EX CV7..............12 A2
  RRUGBY CV23..............68 A1
Cressage Rd *COVE* CV2..............25 F5
Crew La *KNWTH* CV8..............66 B2
Cricket Cl *COVW* CV5..............30 A3
Crick Rd *RUGBYN/HIL* CV21..............63 H5
Critchley Dr *RUGBYS/DCH* CV22....69 H4
Croft Flds *BDWTH* CV12..............5 G3
Croft Pool *BDWTH* CV12..............5 E3
Croft Rd *BDWTH* CV12..............5 E3
  COV CV1..............2 B4
The Croft *BDWTH* CV12..............7 E3
  COVN CV6..............13 G4
  RCOVN/BALC/EX CV7..............18 B2
  RUGBYN/HIL CV21 *..............63 F4
Cromarty Cl *COVW* CV5..............28 D1
Cromes Wd *TLHL/CAN* CV4..............28 A5
Cromwell La *TLHL/CAN* CV4..............36 B3
Cromwell Rd *RUGBYS/DCH* CV22 ..62 B3
Cromwell St *COVN* CV6..............23 G5
Crondal Rd *RCOVN/BALC/EX* CV7 ..14 A1
Croome Cl *COVN* CV6..............30 A2
Crosbie Rd *COVW* CV5..............29 H3
Cross Cheaping *COV* CV1..............2 D3
Cross Rd *COVN* CV6..............23 G3
  RCOVN/BALC/EX CV7..............12 A2
Cross St *COV* CV1..............3 F1
  RRUGBY CV23..............46 B4
  RUGBYN/HIL CV21..............48 B5
Crossway Rd *COVS* CV3..............39 E5
Crowmere Rd *COVE* CV2..............25 E4
Crown Gn *COVN* CV6..............23 F1
Crow Thorns *RUGBYN/HIL* CV21 ...48 B3
Croxhall St *BDWTH* CV12..............5 H3
Croydon Cl *COVS* CV3..............39 H3
Crummock Cl *COVN* CV6..............13 E5
Cryfield Grange Rd
  TLHL/CAN CV4..............51 H2
Cryfield Hts *TLHL/CAN* CV4..............52 A2
Cubbington Rd *COVN* CV6..............13 H5
Cuckoo La *COV* CV1..............2 E3
Culworth Cl *RUGBYN/HIL* CV21 ....48 D2
Culworth Rw *COVN* CV6..............23 F5
Cumbria Cl *COV* CV1..............30 B3
Cunningham Wy North
  RUGBYS/DCH CV22..............60 D3
Curie Cl *RUGBYN/HIL* CV21..............62 C1
Curriers Cl *TLHL/CAN* CV4..............36 C2
Curtis Rd *COVE* CV2..............24 C5
Curzon Av *COVN* CV6..............23 F3
Cymbeline Wy
  RUGBYS/DCH CV22..............69 H1
Cypress Cft *COVS* CV3..............41 G1

D

Dadleys Wd
  RCOVN/BALC/EX CV7 *..............10 C3
Daffern Rd *RCOVN/BALC/EX* CV7 ...5 F4
Daimler Rd *COVN* CV6..............30 D1
Daintree Cft *COVS* CV3..............39 F2
Dalby Cl *COVS* CV3..............41 F2
Dalehouse La *KNWTH* CV8..............65 H1
Dale Meadow Cl
  RCOVN/BALC/EX CV7..............34 C3
Dale St *RUGBYN/HIL* CV21..............47 H5
Daleway Rd *COVS* CV3..............53 E1
Dalkeith Av *RUGBYS/DCH* CV22....61 E5
Dallington Rd *COVN* CV6..............21 H5
Dalmeny Rd *TLHL/CAN* CV4..............36 C2
Dalton Cl *RRUGBY* CV23..............45 E3
Dalton Gdns *COVE* CV2..............33 E2
Dalton Rd *BDWTH* CV12..............5 E3
  COVW CV5..............39 E1
Dame Agnes Gv *COVN* CV6..............24 A3
Dane Rd *COVE* CV2..............32 A2
Daneswood Rd *COVS* CV3..............42 D2
Daphne Cl *COVE* CV2..............24 B1
Dark La *BDWTH* CV12..............4 C4
  COV CV1..............30 D2
Darnford Cl *COVE* CV2..............25 E4
Darrach Cl *COVE* CV2..............24 D1
Dartmouth Rd *COVE* CV2..............32 B1
Darwin Cl *COVE* CV2..............25 F5
Datchet Cl *COVW* CV5..............29 F2
D'Aubeny Rd *TLHL/CAN* CV4..............37 G1
Davenport Rd *COVW* CV5..............39 E1
Daventry Rd *COVS* CV3..............39 G2
  RRUGBY CV23..............70 A5
  RUGBYS/DCH CV22..............69 H5
David Rd *COV* CV1..............3 H5
  RCOVN/BALC/EX CV7..............13 G1
  RUGBYS/DCH CV22..............61 E4
Davies Rd *RCOVN/BALC/EX* CV7 ...13 G1
Dawes Cl *COVE* CV2..............31 H2
Dawlish Dr *COVS* CV3..............39 G4
Dawson Rd *COVS* CV3..............31 H5
Days Cl *COV* CV1..............3 H2
Day's La *COV* CV1..............3 H2
Daytona Dr *COVW* CV5..............19 G3
Deacon Cl *RUGBYS/DCH* CV22....62 B3
Deane Pde *RUGBYN/HIL* CV21 ....63 F4
Deane Rd *RUGBYN/HIL* CV21 ....63 F4
Deanston Cft *COVE* CV2..............25 E2
Dean St *COVE* CV2..............31 H3
Deans Wy *RCOVN/BALC/EX* CV7 ...13 G2
Deasy Rd *COV* CV1..............3 F6
De-Compton Cl
  RCOVN/BALC/EX CV7..............12 B1
Deedmore Rd *COVE* CV2..............24 C2
Deegan Cl *COVE* CV2..............23 H5
Deepmore Rd *RUGBYS/DCH* CV22..61 E4
Deerdale Wy *COVS* CV3..............41 G1
Deerhurst Rd *COVN* CV6..............22 C1
Deerings Rd *RUGBYN/HIL* CV21 ....63 H4
The Deer Leap *KNWTH* CV8..............65 G1
Delage Cl *COVN* CV6..............14 A4
Delamere Rd *BDWTH* CV12..............5 E3
Delaware Rd *COVS* CV3..............39 F4
Delhi Av *COVN* CV6..............23 E2
Delius St *TLHL/CAN* CV4..............28 B3
Dell Cl *COVS* CV3..............40 C4
De Montfort Rd *KNWTH* CV8..............64 D1
De Montfort Wy *TLHL/CAN* CV4 ...37 H3
Dempster Rd *BDWTH* CV12..............5 F1
Denbigh Rd *COVN* CV6..............21 H5
Dencer Dr *KNWTH* CV8..............65 H3
Denewood Wy *KNWTH* CV8..............65 H2
Dengate Dr *RCOVN/BALC/EX* CV7 ..34 C2
Denham Av *COVW* CV5..............29 E2
Dennis Rd *COVE* CV2..............32 A1
Denshaw Cft *COVE* CV2..............25 F3
Denton Cl *KNWTH* CV8..............64 C1
Dering Cl *COVE* CV2..............24 C3
Deronda Cl *BDWTH* CV12..............5 F2
Derry Cl *KNWTH* CV8..............57 F1
Dersingham Dr *COVN* CV6..............24 A1
Derwent Cl *COVW* CV5..............28 B2
  RUGBYN/HIL CV21..............48 B3
Derwent Rd *BDWTH* CV12..............5 F1
  COVN CV6..............22 B1
Despard Rd *COVW* CV5..............28 A1
Devereux Cl *TLHL/CAN* CV4..............27 H5
Devon Gv *COVE* CV2..............32 A5
Devoran Cl *RCOVN/BALC/EX* CV7 ...5 G5
Dewar Gv *RUGBYN/HIL* CV21 ....62 D2
Dew Cl *RUGBYS/DCH* CV22..............69 G4
Dewsbury Av *COVS* CV3..............39 E4
Dial House La *COVW* CV5..............28 C2
Diana Dr *COVE* CV2..............24 D2

Dickens Rd *COVN* CV6..............
  RUGBYS/DCH CV22..............
Dickinson Ct *RUGBYS/DCH* CV22...
Diddington La *HIA/OLT* B92..............
Didsbury Rd *RCOVN/BALC/EX* CV7
Digbey Cl *COVS* CV5..............
Dilcock Wy *TLHL/CAN* CV4..............
Dillam Cl *COVN* CV6..............
Dillotford Av *COVS* CV3..............
Dingle Cl *COVN* CV6..............
Dingley Rd *BDWTH* CV12..............
Discovery Wy *COVS* CV3..............
Ditton Cl *RUGBYS/DCH* CV22..............
Dockers Cl *RCOVN/BALC/EX* CV7 ..
Dodgson Cl *COVN* CV6..............
Doe Bank La *COV* CV1..............
Dogberry Cl *COVS* CV3..............
Dolomite Av *COVW* CV5..............
Doncaster Cl *COVE* CV2..............
Done Cerce Cl
  RUGBYS/DCH CV22..............
Donegal Cl *TLHL/CAN* CV4..............
Donnington Av *COVN* CV6..............
Doone Cl *COVE* CV2..............
Dorchester Wy *COVE* CV2..............
Dormer Harris Av *TLHL/CAN* CV4 .
Dorney Cl *COVW* CV5..............
Dorothy Powell Wy *COVE* CV2 ...
Dorset Rd *COV* CV1..............
Douglas Rd *RUGBYN/HIL* CV21 ..
Doulton Cl *COVS* CV2 *..............
Dove Cl *BDWTH* CV12..............
Dovecote Cl *COVN* CV6..............
Dovedale *RUGBYN/HIL* CV21..............
Dovedale Av *COVN* CV6..............
Dover St *COV* CV1 *..............
Dowley Cft *COVS* CV3..............
Downderry Wy *COVN* CV6..............
Downing Crs *BDWTH* CV12..............
Downton Cl *COVE* CV2..............
Dowty Av *BDWTH* CV12..............
Doyle Dr *COVN* CV6..............
Drake St *COVN* CV6..............
Draper Cl *KNWTH* CV8..............
Draper's Flds *COV* CV1..............
Draycott Rd *COVE* CV2..............
Drayton Crs *COVW* CV5..............
Drayton Leys *RUGBYS/DCH* CV22 .
Drayton Rd *BDWTH* CV12..............
Drew Crs *KNWTH* CV8..............
Dreyer Cl *RUGBYS/DCH* CV22..............
The Drive *COVE* CV2..............
  RUGBYS/DCH CV22..............
Dronfield Rd *COVE* CV2..............
Droylsdon Park Rd *COVS* CV3 ...
Druid Rd *COVE* CV2..............
Drummond Cl *COVN* CV6..............
Drury La *RUGBYN/HIL* CV21 *..............
Drybrooks Cl
  RCOVN/BALC/EX CV7..............
Dryden Cl *KNWTH* CV8..............
Dryden Pl *RUGBYS/DCH* CV22..............
Dryden Wk *RUGBYS/DCH* CV22..............
Dudley Rd *KNWTH* CV8..............
Dudley St *COVN* CV6..............
Duffy Pl *RUGBYN/HIL* CV21..............
Dugdale Rd *COVN* CV6..............
Duggins La *RCOVN/BALC/EX* CV7 .
Duke Barn Fld *COVE* CV2..............
Duke St *COVW* CV5..............
  RUGBYN/HIL CV21..............
Dulverton Av *COVW* CV5..............
Duncan Dr *RUGBYS/DCH* CV22..............
Dunchurch Cl
  RCOVN/BALC/EX CV7..............
Dunchurch Hwy *COVW* CV5..............
Dunchurch Rd
  RUGBYS/DCH CV22..............
Duncroft Av *COVN* CV6..............
Dunhill Av *TLHL/CAN* CV4..............
Dunnerdale *RUGBYN/HIL* CV21..............
Dunnose Cl *COVN* CV6..............
Dunrose Cl *COVE* CV2..............
Dunsmore Av *COVS* CV3..............
  RUGBYN/HIL CV21..............
Dunsmore Heath
  RUGBYS/DCH CV22..............
Dunster Pl *COVN* CV6..............
Dunsville Dr *COVE* CV2..............
Dunvegan Cl *COVS* CV3..............
  KNWTH CV8..............
Durbar Av *COVN* CV6..............
Durham Cl *RCOVN/BALC/EX* CV7 ..
Durham Crs *COVW* CV5..............
Durrell Dr *RUGBYS/DCH* CV22..............
Dutton Rd *COVE* CV2..............
Dyer's La *KNWTH* CV8..............
Dymond Rd *COVN* CV6..............
Dysart Cl *COV* CV1..............

.. Cl *RUGBYN/HIL* CV21 ....**63** E3
. St *TLHL/CAN* CV4 ....**28** B3

E

t Cl *COVN* CV6 ....**12** B5
St *COV* CV1 ....**31** E1
St East *COV* CV1 ....**31** E1
arl's Cft *COVS* CV3 ....**39** G2
ion Av North *COVW* CV5 ......**30** A5
ion Av South *COVW* CV5 ......**38** D1
ion St *COVW* CV5 ....**38** C1
. *BDWTH* CV12 ....**5** H3
V CV1 ....**2** E4
GBYN/HIL* CV21 ....**62** A1
v *BDWTH* CV12 ....**6** A3
VE CV2 ....**31** H3
ourne Cl *COVN* CV6 ....**21** H5
ar Park Rd *BHAMNEC* B40 ...**8** D4
otes *TLHL/CAN* CV4 ....**29** F5
rn Green Rd *COVW* CV5 ....**30** A5
eld Pl *RUGBYN/HIL* CV21.......**61** H1
nisgn Cl *COVW* CV5 ....**29** H2
nds Pl *RUGBYN/HIL* CV21 .....**62** C1
nds Rd *RUGBYN/HIL* CV21 ....**62** C1
igh Av *COVW* CV5 ....**38** C2
t *COV* CV1 ....**3** H3
GBYN/HIL* CV21 ....**48** C5
nion St *RUGBYS/DCH* CV22...**61** H4
Vy *BHAMNEC* B40 ....**8** D5
/OLT* B92 ....**9** F3
ood Gv *RUGBYN/HIL* CV21...**63** H4
a *RUGBYN/HIL* CV21 ....**61** H1
rpe Cl *COVE* CV2 ....**24** B2
Rd *COV* CV1 ....**2** C6
Green La
VN/BALC/EX* CV7 ....**18** D2
Vale Ter *COVS* CV3 ....**39** G2
e Cft *RCOVN/BALC/EX* CV7...**34** D1
e Cl *KNWTH* CV8 ....**65** F1
Crs *COVS* CV3 ....**33** E5
e Rd *COVE* CV2 ....**14** B5
s Cl *COVE* CV2 ....**24** B3
e Leys *RUGBYS/DCH* CV22 ...**61** H4
Wy *COVN* CV6 ....**23** H4
Miller Ct *BDWTH* CV12 * **5** F3
Cft *KNWTH* CV8 ....**65** G3
Rd *RCOVN/BALC/EX* CV7 .....**25** F2
GBYN/HIL* CV21 ....**63** E3
St *COVN* CV6 ....**23** G4
cote Cl *RUGBYN/HIL* CV21 ...**63** F3
ield Rd *COVE* CV2 ....**25** F3
ull Pl *TLHL/CAN* CV4 ....**27** H5
ck Rd *COVN* CV6 ....**23** G4
urgh Vls *KNWTH* CV8 * **54** A1
urgh Wy *RUGBY* CV23 ....**46** C4
ale Rd *COVE* CV2 ....**25** E3
w St *RUGBYN/HIL* CV21 ....**61** H1
berry Wy *COVE* CV2 ....**24** A5
Cl *RUGBYS/DCH* CV22 ....**60** C3
d *COVN* CV6 ....**23** F4
Ct *RUGBYS/DCH* CV22..........**61** F1
eth Wy *KNWTH* CV8 ....**64** D2
UGBY* CV23 ....**46** C4
gton St *COVN* CV6 ....**23** G3
mbe Rd *COVE* CV2 ....**24** C3
nan Gdns *COVN* CV6 ....**23** G3
here Rd *BDWTH* CV12 ....**5** F3
ark Dr *COVS* CV3 ....**33** G5
nk Rd *KNWTH* CV8 ....**64** D1
l *COVS* CV3 ....**42** B2
COVW* CV5 ....**19** H3
ene Cl *KNWTH* CV8 ....**43** F5
ene Rd *KNWTH* CV8 ....**65** G3
v *RCOVN/BALC/EX* CV7 ....**34** D3
urst Rd *COVN* CV6 ....**13** H4
dg *HIA/OLT* B92 * **16** B4
e Cl *COVS* CV3 ....**41** E1
e Rd *RUGBYS/DCH* CV22.......**61** G3

F

Fabian Cl *COVS* CV3 ....**41** E2
Fairbanks Cl *COVE* CV2 ....**25** F4
Fairbourne Wy *COVN* CV6 ....**21** H3
Faircroft *KNWTH* CV8 ....**65** E4
Fairfax St *COV* CV1 ....**2** E3
Fairfield Ct *COVS* CV3 ....**40** B2
Fairfield Ri *RCOVN/BALC/EX* CV7 ...**18** D2
Fairlands Pk *TLHL/CAN* CV4 .**38** B4
Fairmile Cl *COVS* CV3 ....**40** D1
Fairway Ri *KNWTH* CV8 ....**65** H1
Fairways Cl *COVW* CV5 ....**20** D5
Falcon Av *COVS* CV3 ....**41** G1
Falkland Cl *TLHL/CAN* CV4 ...**36** C2
Fallowfields *COVN* CV6 ....**12** D4
Falstaff Dr *RUGBYS/DCH* CV22 ...**69** H1
Falstaff Rd *TLHL/CAN* CV4 ...**28** B4
Fancott Dr *KNWTH* CV8 ....**64** D1
Faraday Rd *RUGBYS/DCH* CV22...**62** B3
Farber Rd *COVE* CV2 ....**25** F5
Farcroft Av *COVW* CV5 ....**28** A2
Fareham Av *RUGBYS/DCH* CV22 ...**62** D4
Far Gosford St *COV* CV1 ....**3** H4
Farlow Cl *COVN* CV6 * **23** H5
Farman Rd *COVW* CV5 ....**30** A4

Elmsdale Av *COVN* CV6 ....**23** F1
Elms Dr *RUGBYN/HIL* CV21 ...**63** E4
The Elms Paddock *RUGBY* CV23 ..**49** E4
The Elms *BDWTH* CV12 ....**4** D3
Elm Tree Av *TLHL/CAN* CV4 ..**28** D4
Elm Tree Ri *HIA/OLT* B92 ......**16** B5
Elm Tree Rd *BDWTH* CV12 ......**7** G3
Elmwood Av *COVN* CV6 ....**30** A1
Elmwood Cl *RCOVN/BALC/EX* CV7 ..**34** C3
Elphin Cl *COVN* CV6 ....**12** B4
Elsee Rd *RUGBYN/HIL* CV21 ..**61** H1
Elter Cl *RUGBYN/HIL* CV21 ...**48** C3
Eltham Rd *COVS* CV3 ....**39** H2
Elwy Cir *RCOVN/BALC/EX* CV7 ...**12** D1
Ely Cl *COVE* CV2 ....**25** F5
Embassy Wk *COVE* CV2 ....**24** C3
Emerson Rd *COVN* CV6 ....**32** B2
Emery Cl *COVE* CV2 ....**24** D4
Emperor Wy *RUGBYN/HIL* CV21 ..**47** G2
Empire Rd *TLHL/CAN* CV4 .....**28** D4
Empress Ar *COVE* CV2 * **32** A4
Emscote Rd *COVS* CV3 ....**32** B4
Ena Rd *COV* CV1 ....**31** E1
Endemere Rd *COVN* CV6........**23** E4
Enfield Rd *COVE* CV2 ....**32** A3
Engleton Rd *COVN* CV6 ....**30** B1
Ennerdale *RUGBYN/HIL* CV21 ...**48** B2
Ennerdale La *COVE* CV2 ....**33** E2
Ensign Cl *TLHL/CAN* CV4 ......**27** H5
Epsom Cl *BDWTH* CV12 ....**5** G1
Epsom Dr *COVS* CV3 ....**40** D3
Epsom Rd *RUGBYS/DCH* CV22 ...**61** E3
Erica Av *BDWTH* CV12 ....**4** D3
Eric Grey Cl *COVE* CV2 ....**31** H1
Erithway Rd *COVS* CV3 ....**39** E5
Ernest Richards Rd *BDWTH* CV12 ...**5** G1
Ernsford Av *COVS* CV3 ....**31** H5
Esker Dr *COVS* CV3 ....**39** H2
Eskdale *RUGBYN/HIL* CV21 ...**48** B1
Essex Cl *COVE* CV2 ....**29** E3
KNWTH CV8 ....**64** D5
Essex St *RUGBYN/HIL* CV21 ..**47** G5
Esterton Cl *COVN* CV6 ....**22** D1
Ethelfield Rd *COVE* CV2 ....**32** A3
Ettington Rd *COVW* CV5 ....**28** D3
Eustace Rd *BDWTH* CV12 ....**7** G4
Euston Crs *COVS* CV3 ....**40** D3
Evans Cl *BDWTH* CV12 ....**5** H1
Evans Rd *RUGBYS/DCH* CV22 ...**60** D2
Evelyn Av *COVN* CV6 ....**23** F1
Evenlode Crs *COVN* CV6 ....**30** A1
Everard Cl *RUGBY* CV23 ....**49** F4
Everdon Cl *RUGBYS/DCH* CV22 ...**62** D4
Everdon Rd *COVN* CV6 ....**22** C1
Everest Rd *RUGBYS/DCH* CV22 ...**61** F4
Eversleigh Rd *COVN* CV6 ......**21** H4
Evesham Wk *TLHL/CAN* CV4 .**37** H4
Evreux Wy *RUGBYN/HIL* CV21 ...**61** H1
Exeter Cl *COVS* CV3 ....**41** E1
Exhall Basin *COVN* CV6 * **14** A2
Exhall Gn *RCOVN/BALC/EX* CV7 ...**13** C1
Exhall Rd *RCOVN/BALC/EX* CV7 ...**12** A2
Exhibition Wy *BHAMNEC* B40 ...**8** B4
Exminster Cl *COVS* CV3 ....**39** H4
Exmouth Cl *COVE* CV2 ....**24** B4
Exton Cl *RCOVN/BALC/EX* CV7 ...**12** D1
Eydon Cl *RUGBYN/HIL* CV21 ..**48** D3

Farm Cl *COVN* CV6 ....**12** C5
Farmcote Rd *COVE* CV2 ....**14** A4
Farmer Ward Rd *KNWTH* CV8 ...**65** F4
Farm Gv *RUGBYS/DCH* CV22 ..**62** B5
Farm Pl *COVS* CV3 * **40** C1
Farm Rd *KNWTH* CV8 ....**64** D5
The Farmstead *COVS* CV3 .....**40** C1
Farndale Av *COVN* CV6 ....**13** E5
Farndon Cl *BDWTH* CV12 ....**7** E2
Farr Dr *TLHL/CAN* CV4 ....**29** E4
Farren Rd *COVE* CV2 ....**32** D1
Faseman Av *TLHL/CAN* CV4 ..**28** B2
Faulconbridge Av *COVW* CV5 ...**28** B2
Fawley Cl *COVS* CV3 ....**40** D3
Fawsley Leys *RUGBYS/DCH* CV22 ..**61** H5
Faygate Cl *COVS* CV3 ....**33** E3
Featherbed La *RUGBYN/HIL* CV21...**63** F3
Feilding Cl *COVE* CV2 ....**25** F5
Fellows Wy *RUGBYN/HIL* CV21 ...**63** E2
Felton Cl *COVE* CV2 ....**24** D1
Fenside Av *COVS* CV3 ....**39** G5
Fentham Cl *HIA/OLT* B92 ....**16** C5
Fentham Gn *HIA/OLT* B92 ......**16** B4
Fentham Rd *HIA/OLT* B92.......**16** B4
Fenwick Dr *RUGBYN/HIL* CV21 ...**63** F3
Fern Cl *COVE* CV2 ....**24** B1
RUGBY CV23 ....**48** C1
Fern Dale Rd
RCOVN/BALC/EX CV7 ....**34** A3
Ferndown Cl *COVW* CV5 ....**28** D3
Ferndown Ct *RUGBYS/DCH* CV22 ..**61** F3
Ferndown Rd *RUGBYS/DCH* CV22..**61** F3
Ferndown Ter
RUGBYS/DCH CV22 ....**61** F3
Fern Gv *BDWTH* CV12 ....**4** D3
Fernhill Cl *KNWTH* CV8 ....**64** D1
Fernhill La *RCOVN/BALC/EX* CV7 ..**34** A3
Ferrers Cl *TLHL/CAN* CV4 .....**28** B2
Ferrieres Cl *RUGBYS/DCH* CV22 ..**69** G4
Fetherston Crs *KNWTH* CV8 ...**55** H3
Fiddlers Gn *HIA/OLT* B92 ......**16** B4
Field Cl *KNWTH* CV8 ....**65** G2
Field Cottages *COVS* CV3 * ...**40** D1
Fieldfare Cl *RRUGBY* CV23 ....**48** B1
Fieldgate La *KNWTH* CV8 ....**50** D5
Fieldside La *COVS* CV3 ....**33** E3
Field Vw *KNWTH* CV8 ....**55** H2
Field View Cl *RCOVN/BALC/EX* CV7 ...**5** F5
Fife Rd *COVW* CV5 ....**30** A4
Fillongley Rd
RCOVN/BALC/EX CV7 ....**18** B2
Finch Cft *RCOVN/BALC/EX* CV7 ...**34** C2
Findon Cl *BDWTH* CV12 ....**7** F2
Finford Cft *RCOVN/BALC/EX* CV7 ...**34** C3
Fingal Cl *COVS* CV3 ....**40** D3
Fingest Cl *COVW* CV5 ....**29** E3
Finham Crs *KNWTH* CV8 ....**55** F1
Finham Green Rd *COVS* CV3 ..**53** E1
Finham Gv *COVS* CV3 ....**53** F1
Finham Rd *KNWTH* CV8 ....**65** G1
Finmere *RUGBYN/HIL* CV21 ...**48** B1
Finmore Cl *COVS* CV3 ....**39** E4
Fir Gv *TLHL/CAN* CV4 ....**28** D4
Firleigh Dr *BDWTH* CV12 ....**7** G3
Firs Dr *RUGBYS/DCH* CV22 ...**61** G2
First Av *COVS* CV3 ....**32** B5
First Exhibition Av *BHAMNEC* B40 ..**8** B4
The Firs *BDWTH* CV12 ....**4** D3
COVW CV5 ....**39** E1
RCOVN/BALC/EX CV7 * **18** A2
Fir Tree Av *TLHL/CAN* CV4 ....**28** D4
Fisher Av *RUGBYS/DCH* CV22 ..**62** D4
Fisher Rd *COVN* CV6 ....**23** F3
Fishponds Rd *KNWTH* CV8 ....**64** D4
Fishpool La *RCOVN/BALC/EX* CV7 ...**9** F2
Fitzalan Cl *RRUGBY* CV23 ......**45** E3
Fitzroy Cl *COVE* CV2 ....**25** G5
Fivefield Rd *RCOVN/BALC/EX* CV7...**11** H3
Flamboro' Cl *COVS* CV3 ....**41** G1
Flaunden Cl *COVW* CV5 ....**29** E3
Flecknose St *COVS* CV3 ....**40** D3
Fleet Crs *RUGBYN/HIL* CV21 ..**62** D2
Fleet St *COV* CV1 ....**2** C4
Fletchamstead Hwy *COVW* CV5 ..**29** F5
Fletchworth Ga *COVW* CV5 ...**38** A1
Florence Cl *RCOVN/BALC/EX* CV7 ...**5** E1
Flowerdale Dr *COVE* CV2 ......**24** A5
Floyd Gv *RCOVN/BALC/EX* CV7 ...**34** D2
Flude Rd *RCOVN/BALC/EX* CV7 ...**12** D2
Flynt Av *COVW* CV5 ....**20** D5
Foleshill Rd *COV* CV1 ....**2** D1
COVN CV6 ....**23** E3
Fontmell Cl *COVS* CV3 ....**33** F2
Ford St *COV* CV1 ....**3** F3
Fordwell Cl *COVW* CV5 ....**30** A3
Foreland Wy *COVN* CV6 ....**22** B1
Foresters Pl *RUGBYN/HIL* CV21 ...**63** G5

Forester's Rd *COVS* CV3 ....**39** H3
Forfield Rd *COVN* CV6 ....**29** H1
Forge Rd *KNWTH* CV8 ....**65** F1
Forge Wy *COVN* CV6 ....**12** D5
Forknell Av *COVE* CV2 ....**32** B1
Fornside Cl *RUGBYN/HIL* CV21...**48** C2
Forrest Rd *KNWTH* CV8 ....**64** D3
Forum Dr *RUGBYN/HIL* CV21 ..**47** H3
Fosseway Rd *COVS* CV3 ....**39** E5
Fosterd Rd *RUGBYN/HIL* CV21...**47** G4
Foster Rd *COVN* CV6 ....**22** C4
Founder Cl *TLHL/CAN* CV4 ....**37** E1
Four Pounds Av *COVW* CV5 ...**30** A3
Fowler Rd *COVN* CV6 ....**30** C1
Fow Oak *TLHL/CAN* CV4 ....**27** H4
Fox Cl *RUGBYN/HIL* CV21 ......**63** C5
Foxes Wy *RCOVN/BALC/EX* CV7...**34** C3
Foxford Crs *COVE* CV2 ....**14** A4
Foxglove Cl *BDWTH* CV12 ....**4** D4
COVN CV6 ....**22** D1
RRUGBY CV23 ....**48** D1
Foxons Barn Rd
RUGBYN/HIL CV21 ....**48** B3
Foxton Rd *COVS* CV3 ....**32** D5
Framlingham Gv *KNWTH* CV8 ...**65** H1
Frampton Wk *COVE* CV2 ....**33** E2
Frances Crs *BDWTH* CV12 ....**5** F2
Frances Rd *KNWTH* CV8 ....**53** H1
Franciscan Rd *COVS* CV3 ......**39** F1
Francis Dr *RUGBYS/DCH* CV22 ...**60** B3
Francis St *COVN* CV6 ....**23** F5
Frankland Rd *COVN* CV6 ....**23** H2
Franklin Gv *TLHL/CAN* CV4 ...**28** B5
Franklins Gdns *COVS* CV3 .....**33** G5
Frankpledge Rd *COVS* CV3 ....**39** H1
Frankton Av *COVS* CV3 ....**39** F2
Frankwell Dr *COVE* CV2 ....**24** D2
Fraser Rd *COVN* CV6 ....**22** B2
Frederick Neal Av *COVW* CV5 ...**28** A2
Frederick St *RUGBYS/DCH* CV22 ...**61** G1
Fred Lee Gv *COVS* CV3 ....**39** G5
Freeboard La *KNWTH* CV8 .....**56** D5
Freeburn Cswy *TLHL/CAN* CV4 ...**37** H2
Freehold St *COV* CV1 ....**31** G2
Freeman St *COVN* CV6 ....**23** G5
Freemantle Rd
RUGBYS/DCH CV22 ....**60** D2
Freshfield Cl *COVW* CV5 ....**21** F2
Fretton Cl *COVN* CV6 ....**23** G4
Frevill Rd *COVN* CV6 ....**24** A3
Friars Cl *COVS* CV3 ....**42** D2
Friars' Rd *COV* CV1 ....**2** D6
Frilsham Wy *COVW* CV5 ....**29** E2
Frisby Rd *TLHL/CAN* CV4 ......**28** B4
Friswell Dr *COVN* CV6 ....**23** G3
Frobisher Rd *COVS* CV3 ....**39** F4
RUGBYS/DCH CV22 ....**60** D3
Frog La *RCOVN/BALC/EX* CV7 ...**34** B4
Frogmere Cl *COVW* CV5 ....**21** F5
Frythe Cl *KNWTH* CV8 ....**65** H1
Fulbrook Rd *COVE* CV2 ....**24** B2
Fullers Cl *COVN* CV6 ....**22** A4
Fullwood Cl *COVE* CV2 ....**24** D1
Furlong Rd *COV* CV1 ....**3** F7
Furnace Cl *BDWTH* CV12 ....**5** H2
Furnace Rd *BDWTH* CV12 ....**6** A2
Furness Cl *RUGBYN/HIL* CV21 ...**48** C2
Furrow Cl *RUGBYN/HIL* CV21 ..**48** C5
Fynford Rd *COVN* CV6 ....**30** C1

G

Gables Cl *RUGBYS/DCH* CV22 ...**61** E4
Gabor Cl *RUGBYN/HIL* CV21 ..**48** B3
Gainford Ri *COVS* CV3 ....**33** E3
Gainsborough Crs
RUGBYN/HIL CV21 ....**63** G3
Gainsborough Dr *BDWTH* CV12...**5** F1
Galey's Rd *COVS* CV3 ....**39** G1
Gallagher Rd *BDWTH* CV12 .....**5** F3
The Galliards *TLHL/CAN* CV4 .**38** A5
Galmington Dr *COVS* CV3 ......**39** E4
Gardenia Dr *COVW* CV5 ....**20** D5
The Gardens *KNWTH* CV8 ......**65** F4
RRUGBY CV23 ....**68** D4
Gardner Wy *KNWTH* CV8 ....**65** F5
Garlands Cft
RCOVN/BALC/EX CV7 ....**12** B2
Garlick Dr *KNWTH* CV8 ....**65** H1
Garratt Cl *RRUGBY* CV23 ....**46** C4
Garrick Cl *COVW* CV5 ....**27** H2
Garth Crs *COVS* CV3 ....**40** D1
Garyth Williams Cl
RUGBYS/DCH CV22 ....**61** F4

Gas St RUGBYN/HIL CV21 ....62 A1
Gatehouse Rd RUGBYN/HIL CV21....63 F4
Gatehouse La BDWTH CV12..........5 F3
Gateside Rd COVN CV6.............23 F1
Gaulby Wk COVS CV3..............33 F5
Gaveston Rd COVN CV6............21 H5
Gaydon Cl COVN CV6.............23 H3
Gayer St COV CV1...............23 G2
Gayhurst Cl COVS CV3...........41 F1
Gaza Cl TLHL/CAN CV4...........28 D5
Gazelle Cl COV CV1.............3 C2
Gentian Wy RRUGBY CV23.........48 D1
Geoffery Cl COV CV2............32 A1
George Eliot Av BDWTH CV12.....6 A3
George Eliot Rd COV CV1........31 E1
George Hodgkinson Cl
  COVW CV5...................28 C3
George Marston Rd COVS CV3.....32 D5
George Park Cl COVE CV2........24 B2
George Robertson Cl COVS CV3...41 F2
George St COV CV1..............31 F1
  RUGBYN/HIL CV21.............61 G1
George St Ringway BDWTH CV12...5 G2
Gerard Av TLHL/CAN CV4.........37 G1
Gerard Rd RUGBYS/DCH CV22......60 B4
Gerard Rw RUGBYS/DCH CV22 *...60 B4
Gibbert Hill Rd TLHL/CAN CV4...37 G4
Gibbet Hill Rd TLHL/CAN CV4....51 H1
Gibbons Cl TLHL/CAN CV4........28 C4
Gibbs Cl COVE CV2..............25 G5
Gibson Crs BDWTH CV12..........5 F3
Gibson Dr RUGBYN/HIL CV21......63 E3
Gielgud Wy RCOVN/BALC/EX CV7..25 G3
Gilbert Av RUGBYN/HIL CV22.....61 E2
Gilbert Cl COV CV1.............3 H2
Giles Cl COVN CV6..............22 D1
Gillians Wk COVE CV2...........25 F3
Gilliquart Wy COV CV1..........3 F7
Gipsy Cl RCOVN/BALC/EX CV7.....34 C4
Gipsy La RCOVN/BALC/EX CV7.....34 D4
Girdlers Cl COVS CV3...........39 E4
Girtin Cl BDWTH CV12...........5 F1
The Glade RCOVN/BALC/EX CV7....28 C3
Gladiator Wy RUGBYN/HIL CV21...47 G2
Gladstone St RUGBYN/HIL CV21...47 F5
Glaisdale Av COVN CV6..........13 F5
Glaramara Cl RUGBYN/HIL CV21...48 C3
Glasshouse La KNWTH CV8........65 H2
Glebe Av BDWTH CV12............4 D4
Glebe Cl TLHL/CAN CV4..........37 F2
Glebe Crs KNWTH CV8............65 F4
  RUGBYN/HIL CV21.............61 G1
Glebefarm Gv COVS CV3..........33 E3
Glebe Farm Rd
  RUGBYN/HIL CV21.............47 G2
The Glebe RCOVN/BALC/EX CV7....11 F1
Glebe Wy RCOVN/BALC/EX CV7.....34 B2
Glencoe Rd COVS CV3............32 A5
Glendale Av KNWTH CV8..........65 F2
Glendale Wy TLHL/CAN CV4.......27 H4
Glendon Gdns BDWTH CV12........7 F2
Glendower Av COVW CV5..........29 G4
Gleneagles Rd COVE CV2.........24 D5
Glenfern Gdns KNWTH CV8........55 F1
Glenmore Dr COVN CV6...........13 G3
Glenmount Av COVN CV6..........13 G3
Glenn St COVN CV6..............13 E5
Glenridding Cl COVN CV6........13 G3
Glenroy Cl COVE CV2............24 D5
Glentworth Av COVN CV6.........22 B1
Gloster Dr KNWTH CV8...........65 E1
Gloucester St COV CV1..........2 A3
Glovers Cl RCOVN/BALC/EX CV7...18 D3
Glover St COVS CV3.............39 G1
Godiva Pl COV CV1..............3 G3
Gold Av RUGBYS/DCH CV22........60 C4
Golden Acres La COVS CV3.......41 G2
Goldsmith Av RUGBYS/DCH CV22...61 G5
Goldthorn Cl COVW CV5..........28 A2
Goodacre Cl RRUGBY CV23........49 F4
Goode Cft TLHL/CAN CV4.........28 C4
Goodman Wy TLHL/CAN CV4........27 H5
Goodwood Cl COVS CV3...........40 D3
Goodyers End La
  RCOVN/BALC/EX CV7...........4 C5
Gordon Cl BDWTH CV12...........5 C1
Gordon St COV CV1..............2 A6
Goring Rd COVE CV2.............31 H2
Gorse Cl RUGBYS/DCH CV22.......61 F3
Gorseway COVW CV5..............3 H3
Gorton Cft RCOVN/BALC/EX CV7...34 C2
Gosford St COV CV1.............3 J3
Gospel Oak Rd COVN CV6.........12 C4
Gosport Rd COVE CV2............23 F3
Gossett La KNWTH CV8...........43 E2
Grace Rd COVW CV5..............19 F3
Grafton Ct TLHL/CAN CV4 *......37 G2
Grafton St COV CV1.............3 H4
Graham Cl COVN CV6.............24 A3

Graham Rd RUGBYN/HIL CV21......48 B5
Granborough Cl COVS CV3........41 G1
Grange Av COVS CV3.............41 G2
  COVS CV3....................53 F1
  KNWTH CV8...................64 D1
Grangemouth Rd COVN CV6........22 C5
Grange Rd COVN CV6.............14 A4
  RCOVN/BALC/EX CV7...........34 A2
  RUGBYN/HIL CV21.............47 F5
Grange Wk COVN CV6 *...........14 A3
Granoe Cl COVS CV3.............41 F1
Grantham St COVE CV2...........3 K2
Grant Rd COVS CV3..............32 A4
  RCOVN/BALC/EX CV7...........5 F5
Grasmere Av COVS CV3...........38 C3
Grasmere Cl RUGBYN/HIL CV21....48 C3
Grasmere Rd BDWTH CV12.........5 F3
Grasscroft Dr COVS CV3.........39 H3
Gratton Cl COVS CV3............38 C3
Gravel Hl TLHL/CAN CV4.........28 C5
The Graylands COVS CV3.........39 F5
Grays Orch RRUGBY CV23.........68 D5
Grayswood Av COVW CV5..........29 G2
Great Borne RUGBYN/HIL CV21....48 B2
Great Central Wy
  RUGBYN/HIL CV21.............48 C5
Greenbank Rd
  RCOVN/BALC/EX CV7...........34 A3
Green Cl RRUGBY CV23...........46 A5
Greendale Rd COVW CV5..........29 G3
Greenfield Av
  RCOVN/BALC/EX CV7...........34 B2
Greenhill Rd RUGBYS/DCH CV22...61 G3
Greenland Av COVW CV5..........28 C1
Greenland Ct COVW CV5..........28 C1
Green La COVS CV3..............38 D3
  COVS CV3....................38 D5
  RCOVN/BALC/EX CV7...........10 A2
  RCOVN/BALC/EX CV7...........34 C2
  RRUGBY CV23.................45 E4
Greenleaf Cl COVS CV3..........28 D3
Greenodd Dr COVN CV6...........13 G3
Greensleeves Cl COVN CV6.......22 C1
Greens Rd COVN CV6.............22 B2
Greensward KNWTH CV8...........65 G1
The Greensward COVS CV3........33 F4
Greens Yd BDWTH CV12 *.........5 H2
The Green RRUGBY CV23..........46 B5
  RUGBYS/DCH CV22.............60 D4
Greenwood Cl RRUGBY CV23.......46 B4
Gregory Av COVS CV3............38 D3
Gregory Hood Rd COVS CV3.......39 G4
Grendon Cl TLHL/CAN CV4........27 H5
Grendon Dr RUGBYN/HIL CV21.....48 D2
Grenville Av COVE CV2..........32 A3
Grenville Cl RUGBYS/DCH CV22...60 D3
Gresham St COVE CV2............31 H4
Gresley Rd COVE CV2............24 C4
Greswold Cl TLHL/CAN CV4.......28 C5
Gretna Rd COVS CV3.............38 C5
Greville Rd KNWTH CV8..........64 D3
Greycoat Rd COVN CV6...........22 B1
Greyfriars La COV CV1..........2 D4
Greyfriars Rd COV CV1..........2 C5
Grimston Cl COVS CV3...........33 F4
Grindle Rd COVN CV6............13 G4
Grizebeck Dr COVW CV5..........28 D1
Grizedale RUGBYN/HIL CV21......48 B2
Grosvenor Rd COV CV1...........2 B6
  RUGBYN/HIL CV21.............62 B1
Grovefield Crs
  RCOVN/BALC/EX CV7...........34 D1
Grove La RCOVN/BALC/EX CV7.....12 A1
Grove Rd RCOVN/BALC/EX CV7.....15 H4
Grove St COV CV1...............3 F3
The Grove BDWTH CV12...........5 G2
  HIA/OLT B92.................16 B3
Guardhouse Rd COVN CV6.........22 C3
Guild Rd COVN CV6..............23 E4
Guilsborough Rd COVS CV3.......32 D5
Gulson Rd COV CV1..............3 G5
Gun La COVE CV2................31 H1
Gunton Av COVS CV3.............40 D4
Guphill Av COVW CV5............29 G4
Guphill La COVW CV5............29 G3
Gutteridge Av COVN CV6.........22 B1
Guy Rd KNWTH CV8...............65 E5

H

Haddon End COVS CV3............39 H3
Haddon St COVN CV6.............23 H3
Hadfield Cl RRUGBY CV23........49 F4

Hadleigh Rd COVS CV3...........53 F1
Hadrians Wy RUGBYN/HIL CV21....47 G2
Hales St COV CV1...............2 E2
Halford La COVN CV6............22 C5
Halfway La RUGBYS/DCH CV22.....69 F4
Halifax Cl COVS CV3............20 D4
Hallam Rd COVN CV6.............12 C5
Hallams Cl KNWTH CV8...........43 E4
Hall Brook Rd
  RCOVN/BALC/EX CV7...........12 B5
Hall Cl KNWTH CV8..............67 E1
The Hall Cl RUGBYS/DCH CV22....69 G4
Hall Dr KNWTH CV8..............53 H1
Hall Green Rd COVE CV2.........24 A1
Hall La COVE CV2...............25 E5
Hamilton Cl BDWTH CV12.........4 B4
Hamilton Rd COVE CV2...........31 H3
Hamlet Cl RUGBYS/DCH CV22......69 H1
Hammersley St BDWTH CV12.......4 D4
Hammond Rd COVE CV2............31 G2
Hampden Wy RUGBYS/DCH CV22.....60 D5
Hampshire Cl COVS CV3..........41 G1
Hampton La
  RCOVN/BALC/EX CV7...........17 G3
Hampton Rd COVN CV6............23 G5
Hanbury Rd BDWTH CV12..........5 H1
Hancock Gn TLHL/CAN CV4........37 F1
Handcross Gv COVS CV3..........38 D4
Handley's Cl KNWTH CV8.........55 H3
Handsworth Crs COVW CV5........28 B2
Hanford Cl COVN CV6............23 F5
Hanover Gdns RUGBYN/HIL CV21...48 A5
Hans Cl COV CV1................31 G2
Hanson Wy COVN CV6.............13 H4
Hanwood Cl COVW CV5............28 A2
Harbet Dr BHAMNEC B40..........8 C4
Harborough Rd COVN CV6.........22 C1
  RUGBYN/HIL CV21.............46 D1
Harcourt COVS CV3..............41 F4
Hardwick Cl COVW CV5...........28 D2
Hardwyn Cl COVS CV3............33 F5
Hardy Cl RUGBYS/DCH CV22.......60 D2
Hardy Rd COVN CV6..............22 B3
Harebell Wy RRUGBY CV23........48 C1
Harefield Rd COVE CV2..........32 A3
Harewood Rd COVW CV5...........29 F3
Harger Ct KNWTH CV8............65 E3
Hargrave Cl COVS CV3...........33 F5
Harington Rd COVN CV6..........30 B1
Harlech Cl KNWTH CV8...........65 H2
Harley St COVE CV2.............31 H3
Harmer Cl COVE CV2.............25 F4
Harnall La East COV CV1........31 F2
Harnall La West COV CV1........30 D2
Harnall Rw COV CV1.............3 H3
Harold Rd COVE CV2.............32 C4
Harpenden Dr COVW CV5..........28 D1
Harper Rd COV CV1..............3 G5
Harris Dr RUGBYS/DCH CV22......61 G4
Harrison Cl RUGBYN/HIL CV21....63 G4
Harrison Crs BDWTH CV12........5 F3
Harris Rd COVS CV3.............32 A4
Harrow Cl COVN CV6.............13 H4
Harry Rose Rd COVE CV2.........32 C3
Harry Truslove Cl COVN CV6.....22 B4
Harry Weston Rd COVS CV3.......33 F5
Hart Cl RUGBYN/HIL CV21........62 C2
Hartington Crs COVW CV5........29 H5
Hartland Av COVE CV2...........24 A5
Hartlepool Rd COV CV1..........31 F2
Hartridge Wk COVW CV5..........29 E2
Harvesters Cl COVS CV3.........33 F4
Harvest Hill La COVW CV5.......20 A1
Harvey Cl COVW CV5.............20 D4
Haselbech Rd COVS CV3..........33 E5
Haseley Rd COVE CV2............24 B3
Hasilwood Sq COVS CV3..........32 A4
Hastings Rd COVE CV2...........31 H2
Haswell Cl RUGBYS/DCH CV22.....62 B2
Hathaway Cl
  RCOVN/BALC/EX CV7...........34 C2
Hathaway Rd TLHL/CAN CV4.......28 A5
Hatters Ct BDWTH CV12..........5 H3
Haven Ct RUGBYS/DCH CV22 *.....61 F1
Havendale Cl COVN CV6..........30 C1
Hawkesbury La COVE CV2.........14 C3
Hawkeshead RUGBYN/HIL CV21.....48 C2
Hawkes Mill La COVW CV5........20 D1
Hawkesworth Dr KNWTH CV8.......65 F1
Hawkins Cl RUGBYS/DCH CV22.....61 F3
Hawkins Rd COVW CV5............30 B4
Hawkswood Dr
  RCOVN/BALC/EX CV7...........34 C2
Hawksworth Dr COV CV1..........30 B3
Hawlands RUGBYN/HIL CV21.......48 C3
Hawthorne Cl KNWTH CV8.........43 F5
Hawthorn La TLHL/CAN CV4.......28 B4
Hawthorn Wy RUGBYS/DCH CV22...60 C3

Haydock Cl COVN CV6............
Hayes Cl RUGBYN/HIL CV21.......
Hayes Green Rd
  RCOVN/BALC/EX CV7...........
Hayes La RCOVN/BALC/EX CV7.....
Hay La COV CV1.................
Haynestone Rd COVN CV6.........
Haynes Wy RUGBYN/HIL CV21......
Hayton Gn TLHL/CAN CV4.........
Haytor Ri COVE CV2.............
Hazel Gv BDWTH CV12............
Hazel Rd COVN CV6..............
Hazelwood Cl RUGBYS/DCH CV22...
Hazlemere Cl COVW CV5..........
Headborough Rd COVE CV2........
Headington Av COVN CV6.........
The Headlands COVW CV5.........
Healey Cl RUGBYN/HIL CV21......
Health Centre Rd TLHL/CAN CV4..
Hearsall Common COVW CV5.......
Hearsall La COVW CV5...........
Heath Av BDWTH CV12............
Heathcote St COVN CV6..........
Heath Crs COVE CV2 *...........
  COVN CV6....................
Heather Cl RUGBYS/DCH CV22.....
Heather Dr BDWTH CV12..........
Heather Rd COVE CV2............
  COVS CV3....................
Heathfield Rd COVW CV5.........
Heath Green Wy TLHL/CAN CV4....
The Heathlands RRUGBY CV23 *...
Heath Rd BDWTH CV12............
  COVE CV2....................
The Heath RUGBYS/DCH CV22......
Heath Wy RUGBYS/DCH CV22.......
Heckley Rd RCOVN/BALC/EX CV7...
Heddle Gv COVN CV6.............
Hedgefield Wy TLHL/CAN CV4.....
Hedgerow Wk COVN CV6...........
Heera Cl COVN CV6..............
Helen St COVN CV6..............
Hele Rd COVS CV3...............
Helmdon Cl RUGBYS/DCH CV22.....
Helvellyn Wy RUGBYN/HIL CV21...
Hemingford Rd COVE CV2.........
Hemsby Cl TLHL/CAN CV4.........
Hemsworth Dr BDWTH CV12........
Hendre Cl COVW CV5.............
Hen La COVN CV6................
Henley Mill La COVE CV2........
Henley Rd COVE CV2.............
Henley Wk COVE CV2 *...........
Henrietta St COVN CV6..........
Henry Boteler Rd TLHL/CAN CV4..
Henry St COV CV1...............
  KNWTH CV8...................
  RUGBYN/HIL CV21 *...........
Henson Rd BDWTH CV12...........
Hepworth Rd COVS CV3...........
Herald Av COVW CV5.............
Herald Wy COVS CV3.............
Herbert's La KNWTH CV8.........
Heritage Ct TLHL/CAN CV4.......
Hermes Crs COVE CV2............
Hermes Rd
  LGN/SDN/BHAMAIR B26.........
Hermitage Rd COVE CV2..........
Hermitage Wy KNWTH CV8.........
Hermit's Cft COVS CV3..........
Heronbank TLHL/CAN CV4.........
Herrick Rd COVE CV2............
Hertford Pl COV CV1............
Hertford St COV CV1............
Heslop Cl COVS CV3.............
Hewitt Av COVN CV6.............
Hexby Cl COVE CV2..............
Hexworthy Av COVS CV3..........
Heybrook Cl COVE CV2...........
Heycroft TLHL/CAN CV4..........
Heyford Cl COVE CV2............
Heyford Leys RUGBYS/DCH CV22...
Heyville Cft KNWTH CV8.........
Heywood Cl COVN CV6 *..........
Hibbert Cl RUGBYS/DCH CV22.....
Hidcote Rd KNWTH CV8...........
High Ash Cl RCOVN/BALC/EX CV7..
High Beech COVN CV6............
Highfield RCOVN/BALC/EX CV7....
Highfield Cl KNWTH CV8.........
Highfield Rd COVE CV2..........
Highgrove RUGBYS/DCH CV22......
  TLHL/CAN CV4................
Highland Rd COVW CV5...........
  KNWTH CV8...................
High Park Cl COVW CV5..........
High St BDWTH CV12.............
  COV CV1.....................
  COVN CV6....................

OLT B92 ...16 B5
TH CV8 ...56 A3
THE CV8 ...64 D2
3YN/HIL CV21 ...63 F4
ew Dr
N/BALC/EX CV7 ...12 D1
aymans Cft TLHL/CAN CV4 .38 A4
Rd TLHL/CAN CV4 ...38 A3
Rd RUGBYS/DCH CV22 ...61 F4
I Rd RUGBYS/DCH CV22 ...60 D3
y Dr COVS CV3 ...40 B4
CI BDWTH CV12... ...5 F1
ton La RRUGBY CV23 ...63 F2
ton Rd COVE CV2 ...24 B1
3YN/HIL CV21 ...62 C2
RCOVN/BALC/EX CV7 ...12 A2
ft COVE CV2 ...23 H5
OV CV1 ...2 B3
3YN/HIL CV21 ...47 H5
COV CV1 ...2 E3
Ct COVW CV5 * ...30 A4
Rd BDWTH CV12 ...4 C1
h CI RCOVN/BALC/EX CV7..25 C3
CI RUGBY/HIL CV21 ...48 B2
II Hwy COVE CV2 ...32 C2
y Rd COVE CV2 ...32 D2
y La COVW CV5 ...27 H1
t's La
N/BALC/EX CV7 ...35 C1
c CI KNWTH CV8 ...65 C2
h CI BDWTH CV12 ...5 F1
CI BDWTH CV12 ...5 F1
n Av COVN CV6 ...22 D1
ok Av RUGBY/HIL CV21 ...47 H5
ok La COVN CV6 ...22 D1
ok Rd RRUGBY CV23 ...46 C4
ok Wy COVN CV6 ...23 E2
Leys RUGBYS/DCH CV22...61 H5
I Rd COVN CV6 ...22 B5
mbe Ter COVE CV2 ...24 C3
a KNWTH CV8 ...50 D4
d COVS CV3 ...31 H4
ay Fld COVN CV6 ...22 B5
Crs COVN CV6 ...30 C1
ell Wy RUGBY/HIL CV21 ...48 B2
ank COVW CV5 * ...38 D1
sh La COVN CV6 ...13 H4
r KNWTH CV8 ...56 A3
st La RCOVN/BALC/EX CV7..11 F4
st Rd COVN CV6 ...21 H4
V RRUGBY CV23 ...45 E4
CAN CV4 ...29 F4
urst BDWTH CV12 ...5 E4
oft COVE CV2 ...25 E3
lk KNWTH CV8 ...53 H2
3YS/DCH CV22 ...60 D4
CI RUGBY/HIL CV21 ...48 B3
s Dr COVW CV5 ...28 A1
wood CI KNWTH CV8 ...65 C2
e Dr COVW CV5 ...32 A4
ale Rd COVN CV6 ...23 F4
ad Chambers COV CV1 * ...2 B3
ad Rd COV CV1... ...30 B3
ad Rd COVW CV5 ...29 C1
ad Rd COVW CV5 ...29 H2
k CI BDWTH CV12... ...5 E4
3YS/DCH CV22 ...60 D4
ll CI TLHL/CAN CV4 ...28 A5
eld La RUGBYS/DCH CV22..69 H3
ward Wy COVS CV3 ...33 F5
ourne CI COVW CV5 ...29 E3
ield Rd COV CV1 ...31 E1
suckle Dr COVE CV2 ...24 A1
Wy COVE CV2 * ...24 C2
h Rd COVE CV2 ...32 A1
t COV CV1 ...3 G3
Wy RUGBYS/DCH CV22...61 E3
RCOVN/BALC/EX CV7 ...12 A1
ale CI COVE CV2 ...32 D3
COV CV1 ...2 A4
s Rd COVN CV6 ...30 B2
CI COVW CV5 ...28 D2
am Dr TLHL/CAN CV4 ...28 A5
urch CV1 ...2 D7
an CI COVN CV6 ...23 F3
RUGBY/HIL CV21 ...63 F4
ghold CI COVS CV3 ...41 F1
d Rd COVS CV3 ...39 H3
ns Yd BDWTH CV12 * ...5 G1
shoe Rd COVN CV6 ...13 H4
d Rd COVS CV3 ...39 H3
Crs RUGBYS/DCH CV22...61 H2
y St BDWTH CV12 ...5 H3
CI RUGBY/HIL CV21 ...63 E4

Hospital La BDWTH CV12 ...4 A4
Hotchkiss Wy COVS CV3 ...41 H2
Hothorpe CI COVS CV3 ...33 E5
Houldsworth Crs COVN CV6...12 C4
Houston Rd RUGBYN/HIL CV21 ...48 B3
Hove Av COVW CV5 ...28 B2
Hovelands CI COVE CV2 ...24 B3
Howard CI COVW CV5 ...28 C2
RUGBYS/DCH CV22 ...69 H3
Howard St COV CV1 ...31 E2
Howat Rd RCOVN/BALC/EX CV7 ...12 A1
Howcotte Gn TLHL/CAN CV4 ...36 D2
Howells CI BDWTH CV12 ...4 C5
Howes La COVS CV3 ...53 F1
Howkins Rd RUGBYN/HIL CV21 ...48 B3
Howlette Rd TLHL/CAN CV4 ...28 B4
Huddesford Dr
RCOVN/BALC/EX CV7 ...34 D1
Hudson Rd RUGBYS/DCH CV22 ...61 F3
Huggins Rd RCOVN/BALC/EX CV7 ...34 D2
Hugh Rd COVS CV3 ...31 G4
Hulme CI COVS CV3 ...33 G5
Humber Av COV CV1 ...3 K5
Humber Rd COVS CV3 ...3 K5
Humphrey Burton's Rd
COVS CV3 ...39 F1
Humphrey-Davy Rd BDWTH CV12 ..4 C5
Hunters CI COVS CV3 ...33 F4
Hunters La RUGBYN/HIL CV21 ...47 H4
Hunter St BDWTH CV12 ...48 B5
Hunter Ter COVW CV5 ...37 H1
Huntingdon Rd COVW CV5 ...30 B5
Hunt Ter TLHL/CAN CV4 ...37 G2
Hurn Wy COVN CV6 ...14 A4
Hurst BDWTH CV12 ...5 G2
COVN CV6 ...13 H4
Hyde Rd COVE CV2 ...32 D2
KNWTH CV8 ...65 G2
Hypericum Gdns COVE CV2 ...32 B2

Ibex CI COVS CV3 ...33 E5
Ibstock Rd COVN CV6 ...13 H3
Iden Rd COV CV1 ...31 F1
Ilam Pk KNWTH CV8 ...65 H2
Ilford CI BDWTH CV12 ...5 E2
Ilford Dr COVS CV3 ...39 E4
Ilfracombe Gv COVS CV3 ...38 D4
Ilmer CI RUGBYN/HIL CV21 ...48 D2
Ilmington CI COVS CV3 ...39 E4
Inca CI COVS CV3 ...39 F4
Inchbrook Rd KNWTH CV8 ...51 H5
Ingram Rd COVW CV5 ...38 A1
Innis Rd COVW CV5 ...38 B2
Instone Rd COVN CV6 ...22 B2
International Dr
LGN/SDN/BHAMAIR B26 ...8 A4
International Sq
CHWD/FDBR/MGN B37 * ...8 A2
Inveraray CI KNWTH CV8 ...65 H3
Inverness CI COVW CV5 ...28 D2
Invicta Rd COVS CV3 ...41 C1
Ireton CI TLHL/CAN CV4 ...27 H5
Ironbridge Wy COVN CV6 ...14 A2
Ironmonger Rw COV CV1 ...2 D3
Irving Rd COV CV1 ...3 H6
Isambard Dr COVN CV6 ...13 C3
Ivor Rd COVN CV6 ...22 B2
Ivybridge Rd COVS CV3 ...39 G4
Ivy Farm La TLHL/CAN CV4 ...38 A3

Jacker's Rd COVN CV6 ...14 A4
Jacklin Dr COVS CV3 ...39 F5
Jackson CI RCOVN/BALC/EX CV7 ...12 B1
Jackson Rd COVN CV6 ...23 E2
RUGBY/HIL CV21 ...63 F3
Jacob Dr TLHL/CAN CV4 ...38 A3
Jacox Crs KNWTH CV8 ...65 H2
Jade CI COVN CV6 ...31 G2
Jamescroft COVS CV3 ...41 F3
James Dawson Dr COVW CV5 ...19 G3
James Galloway CI COVS CV3 ...41 F2
James Green Rd TLHL/CAN CV4 ...28 C4
James St RUGBYN/HIL CV21 ...62 A1
Jardine Crs TLHL/CAN CV4 ...28 C4
Jasmine Gv COVS CV3 ...40 D1

Jasmine PI COVS CV3 * ...40 D1
Jedburgh Gv COVS CV3 ...38 D5
Jeffrey CI BDWTH CV12 ...4 D5
Jeliff St TLHL/CAN CV4 ...28 C5
Jenkins Av COVW CV5 ...28 C2
Jenkins Rd RUGBYN/HIL CV21 ...63 F3
Jenner St COV CV1 ...31 E2
Jesmond Rd COV CV1 ...3 H1
Jim Forrest CI COVS CV3 ...41 C1
Joanna Dr COVS CV3 ...39 F5
Joan Ward St COVS CV3 ...39 G1
Job's La TLHL/CAN CV4 ...28 A4
Joe Obrien CI COVS CV3 ...40 D3
Joe Williams CI COVS CV3 ...41 G2
John Grace St COVS CV3 ...39 G1
John McGuire Crs COVS CV3 ...41 F2
John Nash Sq KNWTH CV8 ...65 E4
John O'Gaunt Rd KNWTH CV8 ...64 D4
John Rous Av TLHL/CAN CV4 ...37 G2
John Shelton Dr COVN CV6 ...12 D4
John Simpson CI KNWTH CV8 ...57 F1
Johnson Av RUGBYS/DCH CV22...61 G2
Johnson Rd BDWTH CV12... ...5 H1
COVN CV6 ...23 H3
John St BDWTH CV12 ...5 F3
John Thwaites CI
RUGBYS/DCH CV22 ...61 H2
Jonathan Rd COVE CV2 ...24 D3
Jones Rd RCOVN/BALC/EX CV7 ...5 F4
Jordan CI KNWTH CV8 ...65 G5
The Jordans COVW CV5 ...29 F2
Jordan Well COV CV1 ...2 E4
Joseph Creighton CI COVS CV3 ...41 F3
Joseph Luckman Rd BDWTH CV12 ..5 F1
Joyce Wy RUGBYS/DCH CV22 ...60 D4
Jubilee Crs COVN CV6 ...22 C4
Jubilee St RUGBYN/HIL CV21 ...61 F1
Jubilee Ter BDWTH CV12 * ...5 G1
Judd CI BDWTH CV12 ...5 E2
Judds La COVN CV6 ...13 F4
Judge CI RRUGBY CV23 ...46 B4
Judith Wy RUGBYS/DCH CV22 ...60 B4
Julian CI COVE CV2 ...25 E3
Juliet Dr RUGBYS/DCH CV22 ...69 H1
Junction One RUGBYN/HIL CV21 * ...47 H3
Junewood CI RUGBYN/HIL CV21 ...48 C2
Juniper CI BDWTH CV12 ...4 C3
Juniper Dr COVW CV5 ...28 C1

Kalfs Dr RUGBYS/DCH CV22 ...60 C4
Kanzan Rd COVE CV2 ...14 B4
Kareen Gv COVS CV3 ...42 B2
Karlingford CI COVW CV5 ...38 A1
Kathleen Av BDWTH CV12 ...4 D2
Kay CI RUGBYN/HIL CV21 ...48 D2
Keats Rd COVE CV2 ...32 C4
Kebull Gn TLHL/CAN CV4 ...36 D1
Keeling Rd KNWTH CV8 ...65 G2
Keenan Dr BDWTH CV12 ...4 C4
Keepers Wk BDWTH CV12 * ...4 C4
Kegworth CI COVN CV6 ...13 H4
Kele Rd TLHL/CAN CV4 ...37 E2
Kelmscote Rd COVN CV6 ...22 A3
Kelsey La RCOVN/BALC/EX CV7 ...34 D4
Kelsey's CI KNWTH CV8 ...57 E1
Kelvin Av COVE CV2 ...32 C1
Kelway COVS CV3 ...33 F5
Kempley Av COVE CV2 ...32 B4
Kemps Green Rd
RCOVN/BALC/EX CV7 ...34 C3
Kendal Ri COVW CV5 ...29 F2
Kendon Av COVN CV6 ...21 H5
Kendrick CI COVN CV6 ...13 H4
Kenilworth Rd COVS CV3 ...38 D3
RCOVN/BALC/EX CV7 ...16 D1
RCOVN/BALC/EX CV7 ...34 D3
TLHL/CAN CV4 ...51 H3
Kennedy Dr RUGBYS/DCH CV22 ...60 D3
Kennet CI COVE CV2 ...24 B3
Kenpas Hwy COVS CV3 ...38 D4
Kensington Rd COVW CV5 ...30 A5
Kent CI COVS CV3 ...39 H5
Kenthurst CI COVW CV5 ...27 H2
Kentmere CI COVE CV2 ...24 D1
The Kent RUGBYN/HIL CV21... ...63 E5
Keppel CI RUGBYS/DCH CV22 ...60 D3
Keppel St COV CV1 ...31 F1
Keresley Brook Rd COVN CV6 ...22 A1
Keresley CI COVN CV6 ...22 A1
Keresley Green Rd COVN CV6 ...22 A2
Keresley Rd COVN CV6 ...22 A2
Kerris Wy COVS CV3 ...33 F5

Kestrel Cft COVS CV3 ...41 G1
Keswick Dr RUGBYN/HIL CV21 ...48 B1
Keswick Wk COVE CV2 ...33 E2
Keviliok St COVS CV3 ...39 G3
Kew CI KNWTH CV8 ...65 H2
Kew Rd RUGBYN/HIL CV21 ...47 H5
Keyes Dr RUGBYS/DCH CV22 ...60 D2
Kilburn Dr COVW CV5 ...30 A3
Kildale CI COV CV1 ...3 G2
Kilderkin Ct COV CV1 ...3 F7
Kilsby La RUGBYS/DCH CV22 ...63 H5
Kilworth Rd RUGBYN/HIL CV21 ...63 G5
Kimberley CI COVW CV5 * ...28 C2
Kimberley Rd BDWTH CV12 ...5 G1
KNWTH CV8 ...53 H2
RUGBYN/HIL CV21 ...48 A5
Kimble CI COVW CV5 ...29 E2
Kineton Rd COVS CV3 ...24 B5
KNWTH CV8 ...65 G3
King Edward Rd COV CV1 ...3 H1
RUGBYN/HIL CV21 ...48 A5
Kingfield Rd COVN CV6 ...23 E5
King George's Av COVN CV6 ...23 F1
King Richard St COVE CV2 ...3 J2
Kingsbury Rd COVN CV6 ...21 G5
Kingscote Gv COVS CV3 ...38 D5
Kings Gdns BDWTH CV12 ...5 H3
Kings Gv COVE CV2 ...32 A3
King's Hill La COVS CV3 ...52 C3
Kingsholm CI COVS CV3 ...33 G5
Kingsland Av COVW CV5 ...30 A4
Kingsley Av RUGBYN/HIL CV21 ...62 D3
Kingsley Crs BDWTH CV12 ...7 E2
Kingsley Ter COVE CV2 ...24 D3
Kingsley Wk COVE CV2 ...25 E3
Kingsmead Ms COVS CV3 ...40 D3
Kings Newnham La
RRUGBY CV23 ...44 D2
Kings Newnham Rd
RRUGBY CV23 ...45 E3
Kings Park Dr COVS CV3 ...33 G5
Kingston Rd COVW CV5 ...30 A4
King St BDWTH CV12 ...5 H3
RUGBYN/HIL CV21 ...47 H5
Kingsway COVE CV2 ...31 G3
RUGBYS/DCH CV22 ...61 H3
Kingswood CI COVN CV6 ...23 E2
King William St COV CV1 ...3 G1
Kinman Wy RUGBYN/HIL CV21 ...48 B3
The Kintyre COVE CV2 ...25 G4
Kinver CI COVE CV2 ...24 D2
Kipling Rd COVN CV6 ...22 A3
Kirby CI COV CV1 ...23 E5
KNWTH CV8 ...43 E4
Kirby Corner Rd TLHL/CAN CV4...37 G4
Kirby Rd COVW CV5 ...30 A4
Kirkby CI RUGBYN/HIL CV21 ...48 D3
Kirkby Rd RUGBYN/HIL CV21 ...63 E4
Kirkdale Av COVN CV6 ...13 E5
Kirkstone RUGBYN/HIL CV21 ...48 C2
Kirkstone Rd BDWTH CV12 ...5 F3
Kirton CI COVN CV6 ...22 A2
Kitchener Rd COVN CV6 ...23 F2
Kittermaster Rd
RCOVN/BALC/EX CV7 ...18 A1
Knight Av COV CV1 ...3 H6
Knightlow Av COVS CV3 ...40 D4
Knightlow CI KNWTH CV8 ...65 H4
Knights Templar Wy
TLHL/CAN CV4 ...28 D5
Knoll Cft COVS CV3 ...39 F3
Knoll Dr COVS CV3 ...39 F3
Knowle HI KNWTH CV8 ...65 H1
Kynner Wy COVS CV3 ...42 A1

Laburnum Av COVN CV6 ...30 A1
KNWTH CV8 ...65 H3
Laburnum CI BDWTH CV12 ...4 D3
Laburnum Gv RUGBYS/DCH CV22 ...61 F4
Ladbrook Rd COVW CV5 ...28 D2
Ladyfields Wy
RCOVN/BALC/EX CV7 ...12 C4
Lady La COVN CV6 ...13 G4
Ladymead Dr COVN CV6 ...22 C1
Ladysmock RRUGBY CV23 ...48 C1
Lady Warwick Av BDWTH CV12...5 H3
Lakeside BDWTH CV12 ...5 F3
Lake View Rd COVW CV5 ...30 A2
Lambeth CI COVN CV6 ...24 D4
Lambourne CI COVW CV5 ...28 D2
Lamb St COV CV1 ...2 D2
Lamerton CI COVE CV2 ...24 B5

Lammas Ct KNWTH CV8 ....57 F1
Lammas House COVN CV6 * 30 B2
Lammas Rd COVN CV6 ....30 B2
Lancaster Pl KNWTH CV8 ....64 D5
Lancaster Rd RUGBYN/HIL CV21 ....47 H5
Lanchester Rd COVN CV6 ....22 C5
Lancia Cl COVN CV6 ....14 A4
Lancing Rd BDWTH CV12 ....7 F2
Landseer Cl RUGBYN/HIL CV21 ....63 C4
Laneside COVS CV3 ....41 F3
Langbank Av COVS CV3 ....40 D1
Langdale Av COVN CV6 ....13 C5
Langdale Cl RUGBYN/HIL CV21 ....48 B2
Langley Cft TLHL/CAN CV4 ....28 C3
Langlodge Rd COVN CV6 ....22 C1
Langnor Rd COVE CV2 ....24 B4
Langton Cl COVS CV3 ....41 F1
Langton Rd RUGBYN/HIL CV21 ....62 D3
Langwood Cl TLHL/CAN CV4 ....37 G2
Lansdowne Cl BDWTH CV12 ....5 F2
Lansdowne Rd RUGBYN/HIL CV21 ..62 C2
Lansdowne St COVE CV2 ....3 J3
Lant Cl RCOVN/BALC/EX CV7 ....36 A2
Lapwing Dr HIA/OLT B92 ....16 C4
Lapworth Rd COVE CV2 ....24 B2
Larch Cl RUGBYS/DCH CV22 ....60 C2
The Larches RCOVN/BALC/EX CV7 ..5 F5
Larchfields KNWTH CV8 ....43 F5
Larch Tree Av COVW CV5 ....28 D3
Larchwood Rd
    RCOVN/BALC/EX CV7 ....5 C5
Larkfield Wy COVW CV5 ....20 D5
Larkin Cl BDWTH CV12 ....7 E2
Larkin Gv COVE CV2 ....25 E5
Larkspur RRUGBY CV23 ....48 C1
Latham Rd COVW CV5 ....30 B4
Latimer Cl KNWTH CV8 ....65 E5
Lauderdale Av COVN CV6 ....13 E5
Lauderdale Cl RUGBYN/HIL CV21 ..46 C5
Laurel Cl COVE CV2 ....24 D1
Laurel Dr RUGBYS/DCH CV22 .....60 D3
Laurel Gdns RUGBYS/DCH CV22 ...61 G4
Laurels Crs RCOVN/BALC/EX CV7 ..34 D3
The Laurels BDWTH CV12 ....4 D3
Lavender Av COVN CV6 ....29 H1
Lavender Cl BDWTH CV12 ....4 D4
    RRUGBY CV23 ....48 D1
Lavender Hall La
    RCOVN/BALC/EX CV7 ....26 A5
Lawford Cl COVS CV3 ....32 D5
Lawford Heath La RRUGBY CV23 ..68 A2
Lawford La RUGBYS/DCH CV22 ....60 C3
Lawford Rd RUGBYN/HIL CV21 ....61 G1
Lawley Cl TLHL/CAN CV4 ....28 D4
The Lawns BDWTH CV12 ....4 C3
Lawrence Gdns KNWTH CV8 ....65 E1
Lawrence Rd RUGBYN/HIL CV21 ..62 C1
Lawrence Saunders Rd
    COVN CV6 ....30 C1
Lawrence Sheriff St
    RUGBYS/DCH CV22 ....61 H2
Lea Crs RUGBYN/HIL CV21 ....47 E4
Leacrest Rd COVN CV6 ....22 B1
Leafield Cl COVE CV2 ....25 E3
Leaf La COVS CV3 ....39 H4
Leagh Cl KNWTH CV8 ....51 C5
Leam Gn TLHL/CAN CV4 ....38 A4
Leamington Rd COVS CV3 ....39 F2
    KNWTH CV8 ....65 F5
Leas Cl BDWTH CV12 ....5 F2
Leasowe's Av COVS CV3 ....38 C5
Lea Wk KNWTH CV8 ....56 A3
Leeder Cl COVN CV6 ....22 D1
Leeming Cl TLHL/CAN CV4 ....37 H3
The Lee COVW CV5 ....29 F2
Le Hanche Cl
    RCOVN/BALC/EX CV7 ....12 B1
Leicester Cswy COV CV1 ....31 E2
Leicester Ct BDWTH CV12 ....7 F3
Leicester Rd BDWTH CV12 ....5 C1
    RUGBYN/HIL CV21 ....47 H3
Leicester Rw COV CV1 ....2 D1
Leicester St BDWTH CV12 ....5 G2
    BDWTH CV12 ....7 F3
Leigh Av COVS CV3 ....53 F1
Leigh Rd RUGBYN/HIL CV21 ....47 C1
Leigh St COV CV1 ....3 H1
Leighton Cl TLHL/CAN CV4 ....52 A2
Lennon Cl RUGBYN/HIL CV21 ......61 H5
Lennox Cl COVS CV3 ....41 E3
Lenton's La COVE CV2 ....14 C4
Leofric St COVN CV6 ....30 B1
Leopold Rd COV CV1 ....31 C2
Lesingham Dr TLHL/CAN CV4 ......28 B5
Lestock Cl RUGBYS/DCH CV22 ....60 D3
Letchlade Cl COVE CV2 ....24 B3
Leven Wy COVE CV2 ....25 F3
Lever Rd RUGBYN/HIL CV21 ....63 F3
Leveson Crs RCOVN/BALC/EX CV7 ..34 C3

Levy Cl RUGBYN/HIL CV21 ....61 G1
Lewis Rd COV CV1 ....31 E1
Leyburn Cl COVN CV6 ....13 E5
Leycester Rd KNWTH CV8 ....65 E5
Leyes La KNWTH CV8 ....65 H2
Leyland Rd BDWTH CV12 ....7 E3
    COVW CV5 ....29 G2
Leymere Cl RCOVN/BALC/EX CV7 .18 B2
Leyside COVS CV3 ....41 F4
Leys La RCOVN/BALC/EX CV7 ......18 B2
Leys Rd RUGBYN/HIL CV21 ....63 H5
Library Rd TLHL/CAN CV4 ....37 G4
Lichen Gn TLHL/CAN CV4 ....38 A4
Lichfield Rd COVS CV3 ....39 C1
Lifford Wy COVS CV3 ....41 H2
Light La COV CV1 ....2 C1
Lilac Av COVN CV6 ....30 A1
Lilac Cl RUGBYS/DCH CV22 ....60 C2
Lilbourne Rd RRUGBY CV23 ....49 F4
Lilley Cl COVN CV6 ....22 D1
Lillington Rd COVE CV2 ....24 C2
Limbrick Av TLHL/CAN CV4 ....28 D5
Lime Gv KNWTH CV8 ....65 F3
    TLHL/CAN CV4 ....29 E4
The Limes BDWTH CV12 ....4 D3
    RCOVN/BALC/EX CV7 * 12 A4
Limestone Hall La RRUGBY CV23 ..44 D5
Lime Tree Av RUGBYS/DCH CV22 ..60 C5
    TLHL/CAN CV4 ....28 D4
Linaker Rd COVS CV3 ....40 D4
Lincoln St COV CV1 ....31 E2
Lincroft Crs COVW CV5 ....29 G2
Lindale RUGBYN/HIL CV21 ....48 B1
Linden Lea BDWTH CV12 ....5 G2
The Lindfield COVS CV3 ....40 D1
Lindisfarne Dr KNWTH CV8 ....65 H3
Lindley Rd BDWTH CV12 ....4 C3
    COVS CV3 ....32 A4
Linford Wk COVE CV2 ....25 E2
Links Rd COVN CV6 ....22 C3
Linnell Rd RUGBYN/HIL CV21 ......62 D2
Linnet Cl COVS CV3 ....41 E4
Linstock Wy COVN CV6 ....14 A4
Linwood Dr COVE CV2 ....25 E2
Lion Fields Av COVW CV5 ....21 E5
Lismore Cft RCOVN/BALC/EX CV7 ..25 G4
Little Church St COV CV1 ....31 E2
    RUGBYN/HIL CV21 ....61 H1
Little Cryfield TLHL/CAN CV4 ....51 H2
Little Elborow St
    RUGBYN/HIL CV21 ....61 H1
Little Fld COVE CV2 ....31 H1
Little Gv RUGBYS/DCH CV22 ....62 B3
Little Lawford La RRUGBY CV23 ...45 H2
Little Park St COV CV1 ....2 E5
Little Pennington St
    RUGBYN/HIL CV21 ....61 G1
Little South St COV CV1 * 3 H3
Littlethorpe COVS CV3 ....41 E4
Littleton Cl KNWTH CV8 ....51 F5
Livingstone Av RUGBYN/HIL CV23 ..46 A5
Livingstone Rd COVN CV6 ....23 E4
Liza Cl RUGBYN/HIL CV21 ....48 B1
Lloyd Crs COVE CV2 ....32 D3
Lloyd Rd RUGBYN/HIL CV21 ....48 B3
Loach Dr COVE CV2 ....14 A4
Locke Cl COVN CV6 ....22 B2
Lockhart Cl KNWTH CV8 ....65 F3
Lockhurst La COVN CV6 ....23 E4
The Locks RRUGBY CV23 ....63 G3
Loder Cl TLHL/CAN CV4 ....28 C3
Lodge Rd COVS CV3 ....32 A5
    RUGBYN/HIL CV21 ....48 A5
Logan Rd COVE CV2 ....24 C4
Lole Cl COVN CV6 ....13 H4
Lollard Cft COVS CV3 ....39 C1
Lomsey Cl TLHL/CAN CV4 ....28 D5
London Rd COV CV1 ....3 G7
    COVS CV3 ....40 A2
    KNWTH CV8 ....55 E1
    KNWTH CV8 ....56 C3
    RRUGBY CV23 ....57 H5
Long Close Av COVW CV5 ....21 E5
Longfellow Rd COVE CV2 ....32 B3
Longford Rd
    RCOVN/BALC/EX CV7 ....13 H2
Longford Sq COVN CV6 ....13 G4
Long Furlong
    RUGBYS/DCH CV22 ....61 H5
Long La RCOVN/BALC/EX CV7 .....21 G1
Longrood Rd RUGBYS/DCH CV22 ..69 H1
Long St BDWTH CV12 ....7 G3
Longwood Cl TLHL/CAN CV4 ....37 E3
Lonscale Dr COVS CV3 ....39 E4
Lord Lytton Av COVE CV2 ....32 C4
Lord St COVW CV5 ....30 A4
Lorenzo Cl COVS CV3 ....41 E3
Loudon Av COVN CV6 ....30 B1
Lovell Cl RCOVN/BALC/EX CV7 .....5 F5

Lovell Rd BDWTH CV12 ....5 F2
Loverock Crs RUGBYN/HIL CV21 ..62 D2
Lower Eastern Green La
    COVW CV5 ....28 C2
Lower Ford St COV CV1 ....3 H4
Lower Hillmorton Rd
    RUGBYN/HIL CV21 ....62 B2
Lower Holyhead Rd COV CV1 ....2 B3
Lower Ladyes Hills KNWTH CV8 ..65 F1
Lowe Rd COVN CV6 ....22 B1
Lower Prec COV CV1 ....2 C4
Lower Rd RCOVN/BALC/EX CV7 ..15 G2
Lower St RUGBYN/HIL CV21 ....63 G4
Loweswater Rd COVS CV3 ....32 D5
Lowry Cl BDWTH CV12 ....5 F1
Lowther St COVE CV2 ....3 K1
Loxley Cl COVE CV2 ....24 C1
Lucas Ct RUGBYN/HIL CV21 ....48 A5
Lucerne Cl COVE CV2 ....14 B5
Lucian Cl COVE CV2 ....25 F4
Ludlow Rd COVW CV5 ....30 B4
Luff Cl COVS CV3 ....40 C1
Lulworth Pk KNWTH CV8 ....65 H1
Lumsden Cl COVE CV2 ....25 E3
Lunar Cl TLHL/CAN CV4 ....38 A4
Lunn Av KNWTH CV8 ....64 D4
Lupton Av COVS CV3 ....39 F3
Luscombe Rd COVE CV2 ....24 D3
Luther Wy COVW CV5 ....28 C2
Lutterworth Rd COVE CV2 ....32 B1
Luxor La COVW CV5 ....19 G3
Lydford Cl COVE CV2 ....24 B4
Lydgate Rd COVN CV6 ....30 C1
Lymesy St COVS CV3 ....39 G3
Lymington Cl COVN CV6 ....23 E3
Lymington Dr COVN CV6 ....14 A2
Lymore Cft COVE CV2 ....25 F3
Lynbrook Rd COVW CV5 ....30 A5
Lynchgate Ct TLHL/CAN CV4 * 37 H3
Lynchgate Rd TLHL/CAN CV4 ......37 H3
Lyndale Cl COVW CV5 ....29 F3
Lyndale Rd COVW CV5 ....29 F3
Lyndhurst Cl COVN CV6 ....14 A3
Lyndhurst Cft COVW CV5 ....27 H2
Lyndhurst Rd RUGBYN/HIL CV21 ..63 E3
Lyng Cl COVW CV5 ....28 D3
Lynmouth Rd COVE CV2 ....24 D3
Lynton Rd COVN CV6 ....23 G2
Lysander St COVS CV3 ....41 E3
Lythalls La COVN CV6 ....23 F1
Lytham Rd RUGBYS/DCH CV22 ...61 E3
Lyttleton Cl COVS CV3 ....33 F5

M

Macaulay Rd COVE CV2 ....32 C2
    RUGBYS/DCH CV22 ....61 F5
Macbeth Cl RUGBYS/DCH CV22 ..70 A1
Macdonald Rd COVE CV2 ....32 C3
Macefield Cl COVE CV2 ....24 C1
Mackenzie Cl COVW CV5 ....20 D4
Madden Pl RUGBYS/DCH CV22 ...60 D2
Madeira Cft COVW CV5 ....29 H4
Magnet La RUGBYS/DCH CV22 ....60 D4
Magnolia Cl COVS CV3 ....39 E4
Maidavale Crs COVS CV3 ....39 F4
Maidenhair Dr RRUGBY CV23 .....45 H1
Main Rd RCOVN/BALC/EX CV7 ....18 B2
Main St KNWTH CV8 ....43 F5
    RUGBY CV23 ....46 B5
    RRUGBY CV23 ....45 H1
    RRUGBY CV23 ....68 D5
    RUGBYN/HIL CV21 ....47 E2
    RUGBYS/DCH CV22 ....60 D4
Malam Cl TLHL/CAN CV4 ....28 D5
Mallory Wy RCOVN/BALC/EX CV7 .13 F3
Mallow Wy RRUGBY CV23 ....48 B1
Malmesbury Rd COVN CV6 ....22 B1
Malthouse La KNWTH CV8 ....64 D1
Malvern Av RUGBYS/DCH CV22 ...62 C3
Malvern Rd COVW CV5 ....29 H2
    RCOVN/BALC/EX CV7 ....34 D3
Manderley Cl COVW CV5 ....27 H1
Manfield Av COVE CV2 ....25 F4
Mann's Cl KNWTH CV8 ....56 A4
Manor Ct KNWTH CV8 * 65 F1
Manor Est KNWTH CV8 ....57 E1
Manor Hall Ms COVS CV3 ....40 D3
Manor House Cl
    RUGBYN/HIL CV21 ....47 E2
Manor House Dr COV CV1 ....2 C5
Manor Rd COV CV1 ....2 D6
    KNWTH CV8 ....65 E1
    RUGBYN/HIL CV21 ....48 A5

Manor Ter Flats KNWTH CV8 * ......
Manor Vw KNWTH CV8 * ....
Manse Cl RCOVN/BALC/EX CV7 ...
Mansel St COVN CV6 ....
Mantilla Dr COVS CV3 ....
Maple Av RCOVN/BALC/EX CV7 ...
Maplebeck Cl COVW CV5 ....
Maple Gv RUGBYN/HIL CV21 ....
The Maples BDWTH CV12 ....
Mapleton Rd COVN CV6 ....
Mapperley Cl COVE CV2 ....
March Wy COVS CV3 ....
Mardol Cl COVE CV2 ....
Margaret Av BDWTH CV12 ....
Margeson Cl COVE CV2 ....
Margetts Cl KNWTH CV8 ....
Marie Brock Cl TLHL/CAN CV4 .....
Marina Cl TLHL/CAN CV4 ....
Marion Rd COVN CV6 ....
Market End Cl BDWTH CV12 ....
Market St RUGBYN/HIL CV21 ....
Market Wy COV CV1 ....
Marlborough Rd COVE CV2 ....
    RUGBYS/DCH CV22 ....
Marlcroft COVS CV3 ....
Marler Rd TLHL/CAN CV4 ....
Marlissa Dr COVN CV6 ....
Marlow Cl COVW CV5 ....
Marlston Wk COVW CV5 ....
Marlwood Cl COVN CV6 ....
Marner Crs COVN CV6 ....
Marner Rd BDWTH CV12 ....
Marnhull Cl COVE CV2 ....
Marriners La COVW CV5 ....
Marriott Rd BDWTH CV12 ....
    COVN CV6 ....
Marshall Rd RCOVN/BALC/EX CV7 ..
Marshbrook Cl COVE CV2 ....
Marshdale Av COVN CV6 ....
Marshfield Dr TLHL/CAN CV4 ....
Marston La BDWTH CV12 ....
Martin Cl COVW CV5 ....
Martindale Rd
    RCOVN/BALC/EX CV7 ....
Martin La RUGBYS/DCH CV22 ......
Martins Rd BDWTH CV12 ....
The Martyrs' Cl COVS CV3 ....
Mary Herbert St COVS CV3 ....
Mary Slessor St COVS CV3 ....
Marystow Cl COVW CV5 ....
Mason Rd COVE CV2 ....
Masser Rd COVN CV6 ....
Matlock Cl RUGBYN/HIL CV21 ......
Matlock Rd COV CV1 ....
Matterson Rd COVN CV6 ....
Maudslay Rd COVW CV5 ....
Maureen Cl TLHL/CAN CV4 ....
Mavor Dr BDWTH CV12 ....
Mawnan Cl RCOVN/BALC/EX CV7 ..
Max Rd COVN CV6 ....
Maxstoke Cl
    RCOVN/BALC/EX CV7 ....
Maxstoke La
    RCOVN/BALC/EX CV7 ....
Maycock Rd COVN CV6 ....
Mayfield Cl BDWTH CV12 ....
Mayfield Dr KNWTH CV8 ....
Mayfield Rd COVW CV5 ....
Mayflower Dr COVE CV2 ....
May La RUGBYS/DCH CV22 ....
Maynard Av BDWTH CV12 ....
Mayor's Cft TLHL/CAN CV4 ....
May St COVN CV6 ....
McDonnell Dr
    RCOVN/BALC/EX CV7 ....
McKinnell Crs RUGBYN/HIL CV21 ..
McMahon Rd BDWTH CV12 ....
Meadfoot Rd COVS CV3 ....
Meadowcroft Cl TLHL/CAN CV4 ....
Meadow Dr HIA/OLT B92 ....
Meadow Ri
    RCOVN/BALC/EX CV7 * ....
Meadow Rd COVN CV6 ....
    KNWTH CV8 ....
    RUGBYN/HIL CV21 ....
Meadow St COV CV1 ....
Meadowsweet RRUGBY CV23 ......
Meadway COVE CV2 ....
Medhurst Cl RUGBYS/DCH CV22 ..
Medina Rd COVN CV6 ....
Medland Av COVS CV3 ....
Meeting House La
    RCOVN/BALC/EX CV7 ....
Melbourne Rd COVW CV5 ....
Melfort Cl COVS CV3 ....
Mellish Ct RUGBYS/DCH CV22 .....
Mellish Rd RUGBYS/DCH CV22 ....
Mellor Rd RUGBYN/HIL CV21 ....
Mellowdew Rd COVE CV2 ....

...ship Rd *COVW* CV5 ....27 H1
..e Av *BDWTH* CV12 ....4 C5
..e Cl *RCOVN/BALC/EX* CV7 ....5 F5
..YS/DCH CV22 ....61 F3
..V CV1 ....30 B3
..Av *COVE* CV1 ....31 H1
..Ct *RUGBYN/HIL* CV21 ....63 E4
s Meadow
..N/BALC/EX CV7 ....12 B2
..Av *KNWTH* CV8 ....64 D3
..e Rd *COVE* CV2 ....32 C4
..n Rd *HIA/OLT* B92 ....16 D4
..N/BALC/EX CV7 ....26 B1
..n St *COV* CV1 ....2 A2
..Cl *RRUGBY* CV23 ....48 B1
..ale Rd *COVW* CV5 ....29 H3
..elds Wy *COVE* CV2 ....25 F2
..d *BDWTH* CV12 ....6 D3
..s Dr *RUGBYS/DCH* CV22 ....61 G2
..on Av *TLHL/CAN* CV4 ....38 D3
..nes St *COVS* CV3 ....39 C3
..ws *BDWTH* CV12 ....5 G3
..TH CV8 ....64 D4
Blanning Pl
..N/BALC/EX CV7 * 34 C2
..lmas Rd *COVS* CV3 ....2 C7
..Cl *COVS* CV3 ....40 C1
..on Rd *COVW* CV5 ....38 D1
..Bickenhill La *HIA/OLT* B92 ....9 H4
..borough Rd *COV* CV1 ....2 B1
..cotes *TLHL/CAN* CV4 ....29 E5
..Field Dr *COVS* CV3 ....33 F5
..Ride *COVS* CV3 ....41 F3
..d Rd *COVN* CV6 ....31 F1
..n Hill Rd *TLHL/CAN* CV4 ....37 G4
..COV CV1 ....31 E5
..eadow *COVN* CV6 ....24 A2
..ne Dr *RUGBYS/DCH* CV22 ..61 G4
..e La *COVE* CV2 ....14 D2
..e Cl *COVW* CV5 ....21 E5
..Cl *COVW* CV5 ....5 F1
..nk Ms *KNWTH* CV8 ....65 E1
..k *RUGBYN/HIL* CV21 ....48 C2
..COVE CV2 ....14 A5
..TH CV8 ....57 E1
..n St *KNWTH* CV8 ....65 F1
..lum Wy *KNWTH* CV8 ....57 E1
..Cl *RUGBYS/DCH* CV22 ....69 G4
..Dale Cl *RUGBYN/HIL* CV21 ..48 B2
..se Cl *RUGBYS/DCH* CV22 ....69 G4
..ds Av *RUGBYN/HIL* CV21 ....63 E4
..COVS CV3 ....53 G1
..se Ct *COVN* CV6 ....23 G4
..BDWTH CV12 ....6 D2
..CV3 ....33 E4
..BY CV23 ....48 D4
..e La *COVN* CV6 ....13 G5
..RUGBYN/HIL CV21 ....48 B5
..BDWTH CV12 ....5 G2
..CV1 ....2 B1
..Cl *BDWTH* CV12 ....7 G3
..Crs *COVE* CV2 ....24 D2
..Wy *TLHL/CAN* CV4 ....37 E1
..Cl *BDWTH* CV12 ....6 A4
..st *COVE* CV2 ....31 H2
..on Rd *COVE* CV2 ....24 B1
..Rd *COV* CV1 ....2 A3
..d *COVE* CV2 ....24 D2
..la Cl *COVS* CV3 ....41 E2
..l Av *TLHL/CAN* CV4 ....37 F3
..Rd *BDWTH* CV12 ....5 H3
..COVS CV3 ....38 C3
..RRUGBY CV23 ....68 D3
..arm Dr *BDWTH* CV12 ....4 B5
..CV21 ....63 F5
..ouse La *TLHL/CAN* CV4 ....37 H2
..rl Av *COVS* CV3 ....39 G4
..s Br *RCOVN/BALC/EX* ..17 E2
..orth Av *COVS* CV3 ....31 H5
..Bvd *COVE* CV2 ....32 B4
..Cl *RUGBYS/DCH* CV22 ....60 B4
..nk's Cft *COVS* CV3 ....39 F2
..Field Cl *TLHL/CAN* CV4 ....28 D5
..Rd *COV* CV1 ....3 J4
..CV3 ....42 B2
..wood Crs *COVE* CV2 ....24 C3
..uth Cl *COVW* CV5 ....29 E3
..Cl *COVS* CV3 ....65 E1
..ue Rd *RUGBYS/DCH* CV22..69 H4
..Cl *COVS* CV3 ....39 H2
..mery Dr
..YS/DCH CV22 ....60 D3
..n St *COVS* CV3 ....41 E2
..ellier Cl *COVS* CV3 ....39 F3
..se Rd *RUGBYS/DCH* CV22 ..61 H1
..Cl *COVN* CV6 ....13 H4
..orfield *COVS* CV3 ....40 B1

Moorlands Av *KNWTH* CV8 ......65 E4
Moor St *COVW* CV5 ....30 A5
Moreall Mdw *TLHL/CAN* CV4 ....52 A1
Morgans Rd *COVW* CV5 ....27 H2
Morland Cl *BDWTH* CV12 ....7 G3
Morland Rd *COVN* CV6 ....12 D5
Morningside *COVW* CV5 ....39 E1
Morris Av *COVE* CV2 ....32 C2
Morris Rd *RUGBYN/HIL* CV21 ..47 G3
Morson Crs *RUGBYN/HIL* CV21..62 D1
Mortimer Rd *KNWTH* CV8 ....65 E5
Morton Cl *COVN* CV6 ....22 B2
Morton Gdns *RUGBYN/HIL* CV21 ..62 A2
Mosedale *RUGBYN/HIL* CV21 ....48 C2
Moseley Av *COVN* CV6 ....30 B2
Moseley Rd *KNWTH* CV8 ....65 G4
Moss Cl *RUGBYS/DCH* CV22 ....61 H5
Mossdale Cl *COVN* CV6 ....22 B5
Moss Gv *KNWTH* CV8 ....51 G5
Mottistone Cl *COVS* CV3 ....39 G3
Moultrie Rd *RUGBYN/HIL* CV21 ..62 A2
Mountbatten Av *KNWTH* CV8 ....65 H4
Mount Dr *BDWTH* CV12 ....5 F2
Mount Nod Wy *COVW* CV5 ......28 D3
Mount Pleasant Rd *BDWTH* CV12..5 F2
Mount St *COVW* CV5 ....30 A4
The Mount *COVS* CV3 ....39 G1
Mowbray St *COV* CV2 ....3 K2
Moyeady Av *RUGBYN/HIL* CV21..62 D4
Moyle Crs *COVW* CV5 ....28 A2
Much Park St *COV* CV1 ....2 E4
Mulberry Rd *COVN* CV6 ....23 H5
..RUGBYS/DCH CV22 ....60 C2
Mulliner St *COVN* CV6 ....30 A5
Murrayfield Wy *COVS* CV3 ....33 G5
Murrayian Cl *RUGBYN/HIL* CV21 ..62 A1
Murray Rd *COVN* CV6 ....22 A1
..RUGBYN/HIL CV21 ....48 B5
Myers Rd *RUGBYN/HIL* CV21 ....63 H4
Mylgrove *COVS* CV3 ....39 G5
Myrtle Gv *COVW* CV5 ....30 A5

Nailcote Av *TLHL/CAN* CV4 ......27 H5
Nailcote La *RCOVN/BALC/EX* CV7 ..35 H2
Napier St *COV* CV1 ....3 H3
Napton Gn *COVW* CV5 ....28 D3
Narberth Wy *COVE* CV2 ....25 E4
Nares Cl *RUGBYS/DCH* CV22 ....61 F3
Naseby Cl *COVS* CV3 ....41 G1
Naseby Rd *RUGBYS/DCH* CV22 ..62 B3
Navigation Wy *COVN* CV6 ....23 H3
Nayler Cl *RUGBYN/HIL* CV21 ....48 B5
Neal Ct *COVE* CV2 * 25 F3
Neale Av *COVW* CV5 ....20 D5
Neale Cl *BDWTH* CV12 ....7 F4
Needlers End La
..RCOVN/BALC/EX CV7 ....34 A3
Nelson St *COV* CV1 ....3 H1
Nelson Wy *RUGBYS/DCH* CV22 ..60 E3
Nene Cl *COVS* CV3 ....41 G2
Nesfield Gv *HIA/OLT* B92 ....16 C4
Nethermill Rd *COVN* CV6 ....30 D3
Newall Cl *RRUGBY* CV23 ....48 D4
New Ash Dr *COVW* CV5 ....28 C1
Newbold Cl *COVS* CV3 ....33 E5
Newbold Rd *RUGBYN/HIL* CV21 ..47 F3
..COVS CV3 ....38 C3
..RRUGBY CV23 ....68 D3
New Buildings *COV* CV1 ....2 E2
Newby Cl *COVS* CV3 ....39 H3
New Combe Cl
..RUGBYS/DCH CV22 ....69 G4
Newcombe Rd *COVW* CV5 ......30 B5
Newcomen Cl *BDWTH* CV12 ......4 C5
Newcomen Rd *BDWTH* CV12 ......4 C4
Newdegate Rd *BDWTH* CV12 ......5 F1
Newdigate Rd *COVN* CV6 ....31 G1
Newey Av *BDWTH* CV12 ....4 B5
Newey Dr *KNWTH* CV8 ....65 F5
Newey Rd *COVE* CV2 ....32 C2
Newfield Av *KNWTH* CV8 ....65 G4
Newfield Rd *COV* CV1 ....30 D1
New Green Pk *COVE* CV2 * 24 C4
Newhall Rd *COVE* CV2 ....25 E2
Newhaven Cl *COVN* CV6 ....21 H5
Newhouse Cft
..RCOVN/BALC/EX CV7 ....34 C3
Newington Cl *COVN* CV6 ....21 G1
Newland La *RCOVN/BALC/EX* CV7..12 C1
Newland Rd *COV* CV1 ....31 E1
Newland St *RUGBYS/DCH* CV22 ..61 F1
Newman Cl *BDWTH* CV12 ....5 F1
Newmarket Cl *COVN* CV6 ....14 A4
Newnham Rd *COV* CV1 ....31 G1

Newport Rd *COVN* CV6 ....23 E2
New Rd *COVN* CV6 ....22 A2
..RCOVN/BALC/EX CV7 ....12 C2
Newstead Wy *COVS* CV3 ....33 G5
New St *BDWTH* CV12 ....5 H3
..BDWTH CV12 ....7 F3
..KNWTH CV8 ....65 E1
..RUGBYS/DCH CV22 ....61 F1
Newton Cl *COVE* CV2 ....25 F3
Newton Manor La *RRUGBY* CV23 ..48 B1
Newton Rd *RRUGBY* CV23 ....49 F1
Newtown Rd *BDWTH* CV12 ....5 F3
New Union St *COV* CV1 ....2 D5
Nicholas Everton Cl *KNWTH* CV8..43 H4
Nicholls St *COV* CV1 ....3 J1
Nickson Rd *TLHL/CAN* CV4 ......36 D1
Nightingale La *COVW* CV5 ....38 A1
Niven Cl *COVW* CV5 ....20 D5
Noble Dr *RUGBYS/DCH* CV22 ....60 B4
Nod Ri *COVW* CV5 ....29 E3
Nolan Cl *COVN* CV6 ....13 E3
Nordic Drift *COVE* CV2 ....25 F5
Norfolk St *COV* CV1 ....2 A3
Norfolk Ter *TLHL/CAN* CV4 ......37 H2
Norman Ashman Coppice
..COVS CV3 ....42 B2
Norman Av *COVE* CV2 ....25 E2
Norman Place Rd *COVN* CV6 ......21 H4
Norman Rd *RUGBYN/HIL* CV21 ..47 G3
Northampton La
..RUGBYS/DCH CV22 ....69 G3
North Av *BDWTH* CV12 ....6 B3
..BHAMNEC B40 ....8 D3
..COVE CV2 ....31 H3
North Brook Rd *COVW* CV5 ......21 G3
Northcote Rd *RUGBYS/DCH* CV22..61 H2
Northey Rd *COVN* CV6 ....23 E3
Northfield Rd *COV* CV1 ....3 H4
North Rd *RRUGBY* CV23 ....49 E4
North St *COVE* CV2 ....31 H1
..RUGBYN/HIL CV21 ....61 H1
Northumberland Rd *COV* CV1 ....30 B3
Northvale Cl *KNWTH* CV8 ....65 G1
North Vw *RCOVN/BALC/EX* CV7..25 F2
Northway *BHAMNEC* B40 ....8 D3
Norton Gra *COVW* CV5 ....21 F5
Norton Hill Dr *COVE* CV2 ....24 B4
Norton Leys *RUGBYS/DCH* CV22 ..70 D1
Norwich Dr *COVS* CV3 ....39 E4
Norwood Gv *COVE* CV2 ....24 D1
Nova Cft *COVW* CV5 ....27 H2
Nuffield Rd *COVN* CV6 ....23 H4
Nuneaton Rd *BDWTH* CV12 ......5 G5
..BDWTH CV12 ....7 F2
Nunts La *COVN* CV6 ....12 C5
Nunts Park Av *COVN* CV6 ....12 C4
Nutbrook Av *TLHL/CAN* CV4 ......28 B4

Oak Cl *BDWTH* CV12 ....5 H1
..KNWTH CV8 ....54 A2
Oakdale Rd *COVS* CV3 ....42 B2
Oakey Cl *COVN* CV6 ....13 G4
Oakfield Rd *COVN* CV6 ....30 A1
..RUGBYS/DCH CV22 ....61 G2
Oakford Dr *COVW* CV5 ....20 C5
Oakham Crs *BDWTH* CV12 ....7 E3
The Oaklands *TLHL/CAN* CV4 ....28 D4
Oak La *COVW* CV5 ....19 H5
Oakmoor Rd *COVN* CV6 ....13 H5
Oaks Pl *COVN* CV6 ....13 H5
Oaks Rd *KNWTH* CV8 ....64 D5
The Oaks *BDWTH* CV12 ....5 E4
Oak St *RUGBYS/DCH* CV22 ......61 H2
Oak Tree Av *COVS* CV3 ....38 D4
Oak Tree Rd *COVS* CV3 ....41 H2
Oak Wy *TLHL/CAN* CV4 ....28 A4
Oakworth Cl *COVN* CV6 ....23 H5
Oatlands Cl *COVN* CV6 ....12 C4
Oban Rd *COVN* CV6 ....13 G3
Oberon Cl *RUGBYS/DCH* CV22 ..69 H1
Occupation Rd *COVE* CV2 ....32 B3
Oddicombe Cft *COVS* CV3 ....39 G4
Offa Dr *KNWTH* CV8 ....65 F2
Okehampton Rd *COVS* CV3 ......39 H4
Okement Gv *RRUGBY* CV23 ......46 C4
Olaf Pl *COVE* CV2 ....25 G4
Old Church Rd *COVN* CV6 ....23 G2
Old Crown Ms *COVW* CV5 ......14 C3
Oldfield Rd *COVW* CV5 ....29 G3
Oldham Av *COVE* CV2 ....25 F4
Old House La
..RCOVN/BALC/EX CV7 ....10 D1

Old Leicester Rd
..RUGBYN/HIL CV21 ....47 H2
Old Meeting Yd *BDWTH* CV12 * 5 G2
Old Mill Av *TLHL/CAN* CV4 ......38 A4
Old Rd *RCOVN/BALC/EX* CV7 ....18 D2
Old Station Rd *HIA/OLT* B92 ......16 A1
Old Waste La
..RCOVN/BALC/EX CV7 ....35 F3
Old Winnings Rd
..RCOVN/BALC/EX CV7 ....12 A1
Olive Av *COVE* CV2 ....32 C1
Oliver St *COVN* CV6 ....23 G5
..RUGBYN/HIL CV21 ....61 G1
Olivier Wy *RCOVN/BALC/EX* CV7..25 G3
Olton Av *COVW* CV5 ....28 B2
Olympus Cl *COVW* CV5 ....19 G3
Omar Rd *COVE* CV2 ....32 C4
Onley Gdns *RUGBYS/DCH* CV22 ..71 E2
Onley Ter *TLHL/CAN* CV4 ....37 H2
Oratory Dr *COVS* CV3 ....40 D3
Orchard Cl *COVS* CV3 ....33 E5
Orchard Crs *COVS* CV3 ....39 F1
Orchard Dr *COVW* CV5 ....27 H2
Orchard Wy *RUGBYS/DCH* CV22 ..61 E4
Orchid Wy *RRUGBY* CV23 ....48 C1
Ordnance Rd *COVN* CV6 ....31 F1
Orion Crs *COVE* CV2 ....24 D1
Orlando Cl *RUGBYS/DCH* CV22 ..69 H1
Orlescote Rd *TLHL/CAN* CV4 ....38 A3
Orpington Dr *COVN* CV6 ....13 E4
Orson Leys *RUGBYS/DCH* CV22 ..61 G5
Orton Rd *COVN* CV6 ....12 D5
Orwell Cl *RRUGBY* CV23 ....49 F4
Orwell Rd *COV* CV1 ....3 J6
Osbaston Cl *COVW* CV5 ....28 B2
Osborne Rd *COVW* CV5 ....38 D1
Oslo Gdns *COVE* CV2 ....25 G5
Osprey Cl *COVE* CV2 ....25 G5
Oswald Wy *RUGBYS/DCH* CV22 ..61 G1
Oswin Gv *COVE* CV2 ....32 B2
Othello Cl *RUGBYS/DCH* CV22 ..69 H2
Outermarch Rd *COVN* CV6 ......22 D4
Oval Rd *RUGBYS/DCH* CV22 ......62 C4
Overberry Cl *COVE* CV2 ....24 C1
Overdale Rd *COVW* CV5 ....29 F3
Overslade Crs *COVN* CV6 ....21 H4
Overslade La *RUGBYS/DCH* CV22..61 E5
Overslade Manor Dr
..RUGBYS/DCH CV22 ....61 G4
Over St *COVN* CV6 ....23 G4
Owenford Rd *COVN* CV6 ....22 D4
Ox Cl *COVN* CV6 ....23 H5
Oxendon Wy *COVS* CV3 ....41 F1
Oxford Canal Pth
..RUGBYN/HIL CV21 ....48 C2
Oxford Rd *KNWTH* CV8 ....55 G3
Oxford St *COV* CV1 ....3 H3
..RUGBYN/HIL CV21 ....B1
Oxhayes Cl *RCOVN/BALC/EX* CV7 ..34 D3
Oxley Dr *COVS* CV3 ....53 F1

Packington Av *COVW* CV5 ....21 E5
Packwood Av *RUGBYN/HIL* CV21 ..63 G4
Packwood Gn *COVW* CV5 ....28 D3
Paddocks Cl *KNWTH* CV8 ....57 F1
The Paddocks *BDWTH* CV12 ......7 E2
Paddox Cl *RUGBYN/HIL* CV21 ....63 E4
Padstow Rd *TLHL/CAN* CV4 ......36 D1
Page Rd *TLHL/CAN* CV4 ....36 D2
Paget Ct *COVE* CV2 ....14 A5
Pailton Cl *COVN* CV6 ....24 B1
Palermo Av *COVS* CV3 ....39 H3
Palmer La *COV* CV1 ....2 D3
Palmer's Cl *RUGBYN/HIL* CV21 ..63 G4
Palmerston Rd *COVW* CV5 ......38 C1
Palm Tree Av *COVE* CV2 ....24 B1
Pancras Cl *COVE* CV2 ....24 D2
Pandora Rd *COVE* CV2 ....24 D4
Pangbourne Rd *COVE* CV2 ......24 B3
Pangfield Pk *COVW* CV5 ....29 F2
Pantolf Pl *RUGBYN/HIL* CV21 ....47 F2
Papenham Gn *TLHL/CAN* CV4 ..37 F1
Paradise St *COV* CV1 ....3 F6
..RUGBYN/HIL CV21 ....62 B1
Paradise Wy
..RCOVN/BALC/EX CV7 ....25 F2
Paragon Wy *RCOVN/BALC/EX* CV7 ..25 G5
Parbrook Cl *TLHL/CAN* CV4 ......36 D1
Park Av *COVN* CV6 ....12 D5
Park Cl *KNWTH* CV8 ....65 G2
Park Ct *RUGBYN/HIL* CV21 * 47 H5

Parkend *RUGBYN/HIL* CV21 ......48 A2
Park Farm Cl *RUGBYS/DCH* CV22 ..61 E2
Parkfield Dr *KNWTH* CV8 ....65 G2
Parkfield Rd
  RCOVN/BALC/EX CV7 ....12 B2
  RUGBYN/HIL CV21 ....47 E3
Parkgate Rd *COVN* CV6 ....12 C5
Park Hl *KNWTH* CV8 ....65 G2
Parkhill Dr *COVN* CV5 ....28 C2
Park Hill La *COVW* CV5 * 20 D5
Parkland Cl *COVN* CV6 ....12 D5
The Park Paling *COVS* CV3 ....39 H3
Park Rd *BDWTH* CV12 ....5 G3
  COV CV1 ....2 D6
  KNWTH CV8 ....65 F1
  RUGBYN/HIL CV21 ....47 H5
Parkside *COV* CV1 ....3 F5
Parkstone Rd *COVN* CV6 ....23 G1
Park St *COVN* CV6 ....23 F4
Park View Cl
  RCOVN/BALC/EX CV7 ....13 H1
Parkville Cl *COVN* CV6 ....12 D5
Parkville Hwy *COVN* CV6 ....12 C5
Park Wk *RUGBYN/HIL* CV21 ....47 H5
Parkway *RCOVN/BALC/EX* CV7 ....25 G3
Park Wood La *TLHL/CAN* CV4 ....36 C2
Parnell Cl *RUGBYN/HIL* CV21 .....61 G1
Parrotts Gv *COVE* CV2 ....14 C3
Parry Rd *COVE* CV2 ....24 A4
Parson's Nook *COVE* CV2 ....31 H1
Partridge Cft *COVN* CV6 ....23 H2
Patrcia Cl *TLHL/CAN* CV4 ....27 H5
Patrick Br *HIA/OLT* B92 ....17 E4
Patterdale *RUGBYN/HIL* CV21 ....48 C2
Pauline Av *COVN* CV6 ....24 A1
Pavilion Wy *COVW* CV5 ....30 A3
Paxmead Cl *COVN* CV6 ....22 B1
Paxton Rd *COVN* CV6 ....30 B2
Paynell Cl *COVN* CV6 ....22 C1
Payne's La *COVE* CV2 ....3 J3
  RUGBYN/HIL CV21 ....61 E1
Peacock Av *COVE* CV2 ....25 E2
Pears Cl *KNWTH* CV8 ....65 E2
Pearson Av *COVW* CV5 ....24 A2
Pear Tree Wy *RUGBYS/DCH* CV22 ..60 C3
Peat Cl *RUGBYS/DCH* CV22 ....61 F3
Pebblebrook Wy *BDWTH* CV12 ....5 H3
Pebworth Cl *COVW* CV5 ....29 E3
Peckstone Cl *COV* CV1 ....3 F7
Peel Cl *COVN* CV6 ....12 C5
  HIA/OLT B92 ....16 C5
Peel La *COVN* CV6 ....31 G1
Peel St *COVN* CV6 ....23 G5
Pegmill Cl *COVS* CV3 ....40 A1
Pembroke Cl *BDWTH* CV12.........4 B4
Pembrook Rd *COVN* CV6 ....22 D1
Pembury Av *COVN* CV6 ....13 H5
Penarth Gv *COVS* CV3 ....41 G2
Pencraig Cl *KNWTH* CV8 ....65 G2
Pendenis Cl *COVN* CV6 ....23 H3
Pendigo Wy *BHAMNEC* B40 ....8 D5
Pendred Rd *RUGBYS/DCH* CV22 ..61 F2
Pennington Ms
  RUGBYN/HIL CV21 ....61 G1
Pennington St *RUGBYN/HIL* CV21 ..61 H1
Pennington Wy *COVN* CV6 ....23 F3
Penny Park La *COVN* CV6 ....12 A5
Penrose Cl *TLHL/CAN* CV4 ....37 F2
Penryhn Cl *KNWTH* CV8 ....65 H2
Pensilva Wy *COV* CV1 ....3 H1
Pepper La *COV* CV1 ....2 D4
Pepys Cnr *TLHL/CAN* CV4 ....28 B3
Perchfoot Cl *COV* CV1 ....3 F7
Percival Rd *RUGBYS/DCH* CV22 ..62 C4
Percy Crs *KNWTH* CV8 ....64 D5
Percy Rd *KNWTH* CV8 ....64 D5
Percy St *COV* CV1 ....2 A3
Peregrine Dr *COVW* CV5 ....28 D1
Perimeter Rd *BHAMNEC* B40 ......8 C5
Perkins Gv *RUGBYN/HIL* CV21 ...63 E3
Permian Cl *RUGBYN/HIL* CV21 ...48 B3
Pershore Pl *TLHL/CAN* CV4 ....38 B3
Perth Ri *COVW* CV5 ....28 D2
Peters Wk *COVN* CV6 ....13 H4
Petitor Crs *COVE* CV2 ....24 B2
Pettiver Crs *RUGBYN/HIL* CV21 ..37 H5
Peveril Dr *COVS* CV3 ....39 E4
Peyto Cl *COVN* CV6 ....22 D1
Pheasant Cl *BDWTH* CV12 ....4 C4
Pheasant Oak *TLHL/CAN* CV4 ....27 H4
Phipps Av *RUGBYN/HIL* CV21 ....63 E3
Phoenix Wy *COVN* CV6 ....23 E5
Pickard Cl *RUGBYN/HIL* CV21 ...48 D2
Pickford Grange La *COVW* CV5 ...19 H4
Pickford Green La *COVW* CV5 ....19 H5
Pickford Wy *COVW* CV5 ....21 E5
Pikers La *COVW* CV5 ....10 D5
Pilkington Rd *COVW* CV5 ....38 A1

Pilling Cl *COVE* CV2 ....25 E3
Pinders La *RUGBYN/HIL* CV21 * ..48 A5
Pine Gv *RUGBYN/HIL* CV21 ....63 F3
The Pines *BDWTH* CV12 ....4 D3
  TLHL/CAN CV4 * 36 C2
Pine Tree Av *TLHL/CAN* CV4 ......28 D4
Pine Tree Rd *BDWTH* CV12...........5 H1
Pinewood Dr *COVS* CV3 ....42 B2
Pinewood Gv *COVW* CV5 ....39 E1
Pinfold St *RUGBYN/HIL* CV21 .....61 F1
Pinley Flds *COVS* CV3 ....40 C1
Pinner's Cft *COVE* CV2 ....31 H1
Pinnock Pl *TLHL/CAN* CV4..........28 C5
Piper's La *KNWTH* CV8 ....65 F3
Pipewell Cl *RUGBYS/DCH* CV22 ..60 D3
Pipkin Ct *COV* CV1 ....3 G7
Plantagenet Dr
  RUGBYS/DCH CV22 ....70 A1
Planter Cl *RUGBYS/DCH* CV22 ...60 B4
Plants Hill Crs *TLHL/CAN* CV4 ....28 B5
Plexfield Rd *RUGBYS/DCH* CV22 ..60 D3
Pleydell Cl *COVS* CV3 ....40 D4
Plomer Cl *RUGBYS/DCH* CV22 ...60 D4
Plowman St *RUGBYN/HIL* CV21 ..61 G1
Plymouth Cl *COVE* CV2 ....24 B4
Poitiers Rd *COVS* CV3 ....39 G3
Polperro Dr *COVW* CV5 ....28 D1
Pomeroy Cl *TLHL/CAN* CV4.........36 C2
Pondthorpe *COVS* CV3 ....41 F3
Pontypool Av *COVS* CV3 ....41 G3
Pool Cl *RUGBYS/DCH* CV22 ....61 E4
Pool Cottages *KNWTH* CV8 * 53 H2
Poole Rd *COVN* CV6 ....22 B5
Poolside Gdns *COVS* CV3 ....38 D4
Pope St *RUGBYS/DCH* CV22 ......61 F1
Poplar Av *BDWTH* CV12 ....6 A3
  RUGBYN/HIL CV21 ....47 H5
Poplar Gv *KNWTH* CV8 ....56 A3
  RUGBYN/HIL CV21 ....47 H5
Poplar Rd *COVW* CV5 ....30 A5
Poppy Ct *COVS* CV3 * 41 E3
Poppy Dr *RRUGBY* CV23 ....48 D1
Poppyfield Ct *TLHL/CAN* CV4 .....52 A1
Porchester Cl *COVS* CV3 ....33 F4
Porlock Cl *COVS* CV3 ....39 H4
Porter Cl *TLHL/CAN* CV4 ....36 D1
Portland Pl *RUGBYN/HIL* CV21 ...62 C2
Portland Rd *RUGBYN/HIL* CV21 ..62 C2
Portree Av *COVS* CV3 ....33 E4
Portsea Cl *COVS* CV3 ....39 G3
Portway Cl *TLHL/CAN* CV4 ....36 D1
Portwrinkle Av *COVN* CV6 ....23 H5
Postbridge Rd *COVS* CV3 ....39 G4
Potters Green Rd *COVE* CV2 ....24 D2
Potters Rd *BDWTH* CV12 ....4 B4
Potton Cl *COVS* CV3 ....41 F3
Potts Cl *KNWTH* CV8 ....65 H5
Poultney Rd *COVN* CV6 ....22 B5
Pound Cl *RCOVN/BALC/EX* CV7 ..26 C3
Powell Rd *COVE* CV2 ....31 H2
Powis Gv *KNWTH* CV8 ....65 H2
Prentice Cl *RRUGBY* CV23 ....46 C4
Preston Cl *TLHL/CAN* CV4 ....37 E2
Pretorian Wy *RUGBYN/HIL* CV21 ..47 H2
Pridmore Rd *COVN* CV6 ....23 E4
Primrose Cl *RRUGBY* CV23 ....48 D1
Primrose Dr *BDWTH* CV12 ....4 D4
Primrose Hill St *COV* CV1 ....3 F1
Prince of Wales Rd *COVW* CV5 ...29 H3
Princes Cl *COVS* CV3 ....40 C1
Princes Dr *KNWTH* CV8 ....51 F4
Princess Dr *COVN* CV6 * 24 A2
Princess St *COVN* CV6 ....23 G4
Princes St *RUGBYN/HIL* CV21 ....47 G5
Princethorpe Wy *COVS* CV3 ....41 E2
Prince William Cl *COVN* CV6 ....21 H5
Prior Deram Wk *TLHL/CAN* CV4 ..37 G1
Priors Cl *RCOVN/BALC/EX* CV7 ..34 C3
Priorsfield Rd *KNWTH* CV8 ....50 C5
Priorsfield Rd North *COVN* CV6 ..30 B2
Priors Harnall *COV* CV1 ....31 F2
The Priors *BDWTH* CV12 ....5 H3
Priory Cl *COVW* CV5 * 30 B5
Priory Cft *KNWTH* CV8 ....65 E3
Priory Pl *COV* CV1 ....2 E3
Priory Rd *KNWTH* CV8 ....43 G5
  KNWTH CV8 ....65 E3
Priory Rw *COV* CV1 ....2 D3
Priory St *COV* CV1 ....2 E3
Privet Rd *COVE* CV2 * 24 A1
Proffitt Av *COVN* CV6 ....23 H2
Progress Cl *COVS* CV3 ....41 H2
Progress Wy *COVS* CV3 ....41 H1
Projects Dr *RUGBYN/HIL* CV21 ...48 A3
Prospect Wy *RUGBYN/HIL* CV21 ..48 B4
Providence St *COV* CV5 ....38 C1
Pudding Bag La *RRUGBY* CV23 ...68 D5
Puma Wy *COV* CV1 ....3 F6
Purcell Rd *COVN* CV6 ....24 A3
Purefoy Rd *COVS* CV3 ....39 G1

Purlieu La *KNWTH* CV8 ....64 B2
Pytchley Rd *RUGBYS/DCH* CV22 ..62 B3
Pyt Pk *COVW* CV5 ....29 F2

Q

The Quadrant *COV* CV1 * 2 C5
Quarry Cl *RUGBYN/HIL* CV21 .....47 G3
Quarryfield La *COV* CV1 ....3 G7
Quarry Rd *KNWTH* CV8 ....64 D1
Quarrywood Gv *COVE* CV2 ....31 H2
Queen Isabel's Av *COVS* CV3 ......39 G1
Queen Margaret's Rd
  TLHL/CAN CV4 ....37 G1
Queen Mary's Rd *COVN* CV6 ......23 E3
Queen Philippa St *COVS* CV3 ......39 G3
Queen's Cl *KNWTH* CV8 ....65 E4
Queensferry Cl
  RUGBYS/DCH CV22 ....60 D4
Queensland Av *COVW* CV5 ....30 A4
Queen's Rd *COV* CV1 ....2 A5
  KNWTH CV8 ....65 E4
  RRUGBY CV23 ....44 B2
Queen St *BDWTH* CV12 ....5 H3
  COV CV1 ....3 F1
  RUGBYN/HIL CV21 ....61 H1
Queen Victoria Rd *COV* CV1 ....2 B3
Queen Victoria St
  RUGBYN/HIL CV21 ....62 B1
Quilletts Cl *COVN* CV6 ....23 H2
Quinn Cl *COVS* CV3 ....40 C2
Quinton Pk *COVS* CV3 ....39 G2
Quinton Rd *COV* CV1 ....2 E7
Quorn Wy *COVS* CV3 ....41 F2

R

Radcliffe Rd *COVW* CV5 ....38 C1
Radford Rd *COVN* CV6 ....22 B5
Radnor Wk *COVE* CV2 ....25 E3
Raglan Gv *KNWTH* CV8 ....65 G2
Raglan St *COV* CV1 ....3 G3
Railway St *RRUGBY* CV23 ....46 B5
Railway Ter *BDWTH* CV12 * 5 H3
  RUGBYN/HIL CV21 ....48 A5
Rainsbrook Av
  RUGBYS/DCH CV22 ....62 D4
Raleigh Rd *COVE* CV2 ....32 A3
Ralph Rd *COVN* CV6 ....30 A1
Ramp Rd *CHWD/FDBR/MGN* B37 ..8 B4
Ramsay Crs *COVW* CV5 ....21 E4
Ranby Rd *COVE* CV2 ....1 J1
Randall Rd *KNWTH* CV8 ....65 E4
Randle St *COVN* CV6 ....30 C1
Rankine Cl *RUGBYN/HIL* CV21 ...47 E2
Rannock Cl *COVS* CV3 ....33 E4
Ransom Rd *COVN* CV6 ....23 F3
Ranulf Cft *COVS* CV3 ....39 F2
Raphael Cl *COVW* CV5 ....29 F3
Rathbone Cl
  RCOVN/BALC/EX CV7 ....12 B2
  RUGBYN/HIL CV21 ....63 F2
Ratliffe Rd *RUGBYS/DCH* CV22 ..61 G5
Raven Cragg Rd *COVW* CV5 ....38 B1
Ravenglass *RUGBYN/HIL* CV21 ...48 C2
Ravensdale Rd *COVE* CV2 ....32 B3
Ravensholt *TLHL/CAN* CV4 * 38 A3
Ravensthorpe Cl *COVS* CV3 ....41 F1
Rawnsley Dr *KNWTH* CV8 ....65 H1
Raymond Cl *COVN* CV6 ....13 G3
Raynor Crs *BDWTH* CV12 ....4 C4
Reading Cl *COVE* CV2 ....14 A5
Read St *COV* CV1 ....3 H3
Recreation Rd *COVN* CV6 ....13 H5
Rectory Cl *COVW* CV5 ....21 F5
  RCOVN/BALC/EX CV7 ....5 F4
Rectory Dr *RCOVN/BALC/EX* CV7 ....5 F4
Rectory La *COVN* CV6 ....21 F5
Redcap Cft *COVN* CV6 * 13 E4
Redcar Rd *COV* CV1 ....31 F2
Redesdale Av *COVN* CV6 ....30 A1
Redfern Av *KNWTH* CV8 ....65 F1
Redgrave Cl
  RCOVN/BALC/EX CV7 ....25 G3
Redland Cl *COVE* CV2 ....24 C1
Redland La *KNWTH* CV8 ....55 H1
Red La *COVN* CV6 ....31 F1
  KNWTH CV8 ....36 A5
  KNWTH CV8 ....50 C4
Red Lodge Dr *RUGBYS/DCH* CV22 ..61 H4
Redruth Cl *COVN* CV6 ....23 H3
Rees Dr *COVS* CV3 ....39 F5

Reeve Dr *KNWTH* CV8 ....
Regency Ct *COVW* CV5 ....
Regency Dr *COVS* CV3 ....
  KNWTH CV8 ....
Regent Pl *RUGBYN/HIL* CV21 .....
Regent St *BDWTH* CV12 ....
  COV CV1 ....
  RUGBYN/HIL CV21 ....
Regiment Ct *COVW* CV5 ....
Regina Crs *COVE* CV2 ....
Regis Wk *COVE* CV2 ....
Rembrandt Cl *COVW* CV5 ....
Remembrance Rd *COVS* CV3 ....
Renison Rd *BDWTH* CV12 ....
Renolds Cl *COVW* CV5 ....
Renown Av *COVW* CV5 ....
Repton Dr *COVN* CV6 ....
Reservoir Rd *RUGBYN/HIL* CV21 ..
Rex Cl *TLHL/CAN* CV4..................
Reynolds Cl *RUGBYN/HIL* CV21 ..
Reynolds Rd *BDWTH* CV12 ....
Ribble Cl *BDWTH* CV12 ....
Ribble Rd *COVS* CV3 ....
Richard Joy Cl *COVN* CV6 ....
Richards Cl *KNWTH* CV8 ....
Richmond Rd *RUGBYN/HIL* CV21..
Richmond St *COVE* CV2 ....
Riddings Hl *RCOVN/BALC/EX* CV7 ..
The Riddings *COVW* CV5 ....
Ridge Ct *COVW* CV5 ....
Ridge Dr *RUGBYN/HIL* CV21 ....
Ridgethorpe *COVS* CV3 ....
Ridgeway Av *COVS* CV3 ....
Ridgley Rd *TLHL/CAN* CV4 ....
Rigdale Cl *COVE* CV2 ....
Riley Cl *KNWTH* CV8 ....
Ringway Hill Cross *COV* CV1 ....
Ringway Queens *COV* CV1 ....
Ringway Rudge *COV* CV1 ....
Ringway St Johns *COV* CV1 ....
Ringway St Nicholas *COV* CV1 .....
Ringway St Patricks *COV* CV1 ......
Ringway Swanswell *COV* CV1 ......
Ringway Whitefriars *COV* CV1 ......
Ringwood Hwy *COVE* CV2 ....
Ripon Cl *COVW* CV5 ....
Risborough Cl *COVW* CV5 ....
River Cl *RCOVN/BALC/EX* CV7.....
River Ct *COV* CV1 * ....
Riverford Cft *TLHL/CAN* CV4 ....
Riverside Cl *COVS* CV3 ....
Robbins Ct *RUGBYN/HIL* CV21 ....
Robert Cl *COVS* CV3 ....
Robert Cramb Av *TLHL/CAN* CV4..
Robert Hill Cl *RUGBYN/HIL* CV21 ..
Robert Rd *RCOVN/BALC/EX* CV7 ..
Robertson Cl *RRUGBY* CV23 ....
Robin Hood Rd *COVS* CV3 ....
Robinson Rd *BDWTH* CV12 ....
Robotham Cl *RUGBYN/HIL* CV21 ..
Rochelene Wy
  RUGBYS/DCH CV22 ....
Rochester Rd *COVW* CV5 ....
Rock Cl *COVN* CV6 ....
Rocken End *COVN* CV6 ....
Rock La *RCOVN/BALC/EX* CV7 ....
Rocky La *KNWTH* CV8 ....
Rodhouse Cl *TLHL/CAN* CV4 ....
Rodney Cl *RUGBYS/DCH* CV22 ...
Rodway Dr *COVW* CV5 ....
Rodyard Wy *COV* CV1 ....
Rokeby St *RUGBYN/HIL* CV21......
Roland Av *COVN* CV6 ....
Roland Mt *COVN* CV6 ....
Rollason Cl *COVN* CV6 ....
Rollason Rd *COVN* CV6 ....
Rollasons Yd *COVN* CV6 * ....
Roman Rd *COVE* CV2 ....
Roman Wy *COVS* CV3 ....
  RUGBYN/HIL CV21 ....
Romford Rd *COVN* CV6 ....
Romsley Rd *COVN* CV6 ....
Ro-oak Rd *COVN* CV6 ....
Rookery La *COVN* CV6 ....
Roosevelt Dr *TLHL/CAN* CV4 ....
Roper Cl *RUGBYN/HIL* CV21 ....
Rosaville Crs *COVW* CV5 ....
Rose Av *COVN* CV6 ....
Roseberry Av *COVE* CV2 ....
Rose Cottages
  RUGBYN/HIL CV21 * ....
Rose Cft *KNWTH* CV8 ....
Rosegreen Cl *COVS* CV3 ....
Rosehip Dr *COVE* CV2 ....
Roseland Rd *KNWTH* CV8 ....
Roselands Av *COVE* CV2 ....
Rosemary Cl *COVN* CV6 ....
Rosemary Hl *KNWTH* CV8 ....
Rosemount Cl *COVE* CV2 ....

...ullion Cl
　...'N/BALC/EX CV7 .....5 G5
...ood Av RUGBYS/DCH CV22..61 G4
...COVW CV5 .....28 D1
...n AV COVN CV6 .....21 H5
...ham Rd COVW CV6 .....22 C1
...ay Av TLHL/CAN CV4 .....29 E4
...y Dr RUGBYS/HIL CV21 ...48 D2
...knowles Rd TLHL/CAN CV4..36 D5
...La KNWTH CV8 .....65 E5
...AV RRUGBY CV23 .....46 B4
...House Rd COVS CV3 .....40 B1
...s Gdns RUGBYN/HIL CV21 ...61 G1
...s HI KNWTH CV8 .....64 D5
...St RUGBYN/HIL CV21 .....61 G1
...Rd COV CV1 * 2 C4
...St RUGBYS/DCH CV22 .....42 C2
...y Dr RUGBYS/DCH CV22 ...60 D2
...Gv COVE CV2 .....24 D1
...wans BDWTH CV12 .....4 D3
...oft Rd COVE CV2 .....25 F5
...ngton Cl COVE CV6 .....21 G5
...ad St RUGBYN/HIL CV21 ...61 G1
...r Dr COVS CV3 .....40 C5
...La COVS CV3 .....55 E1
...r Rd KNWTH CV8 .....54 A1
...'s Green La COVN CV6 ...13 F4
...Cl RUGBYN/HIL CV21 .....48 B2
...w KNWTH CV8 * 54 A2
...t RUGBYN/HIL CV21 * 61 G1
...rs COVS CV3 .....40 D4
...Oak La
　...'N/BALC/EX CV7 .....12 D1
...Oak Rd BDWTH CV12 * 5 G1
...n Cl COVS CV3 .....33 H3
...s Cl COVW CV5 .....29 F3
...'d Rd COVN CV6 .....13 H4
...Rd BDWTH CV12 .....7 F3
...S 42 B1
...TH CV8 .....43 F4
...GBY CV23 .....45 F5
...GBY CV23 .....46 C5
...GBY CV23 .....49 E4
...CV22 .....69 H3
...BYS/DCH CV22 .....61 H2
...Gv TLHL/CAN CV4 * 52 A1
...glen Av COVS CV3 .....40 B3
...d Cft COVS CV3 .....41 C1
...Cl COVW CV5 .....21 E3
...BYN/HIL CV21 .....48 C3
...COVW CV5 .....20 D5
...elands RRUGBY CV23 .....59 F5
...eadow KNWTH CV8 .....50 D2
...ece Ringway BDWTH CV12...5 G2
...e Cl BDWTH CV12 .....4 B4
...n Av COVN CV6 .....22 B2
...Br KNWTH CV8 .....55 E1
...Cl TLHL/CAN CV4 .....37 G1

S

...gton Rd COVS CV3 .....41 F1
...Gdns BDWTH CV12 .....5 H3
...Rd COVN CV6 .....22 B2
...n Cl RRUGBY CV23 .....48 D1
...tha's Rd COVE CV2 .....31 H3
...es La COV CV1 * 2 D2
...rews Crs
　...BYS/DCH CV22 .....61 H4
...rew's Rd COVW CV5 .....38 C1
...s Rd RUGBYS/DCH CV22 ...61 F3
...s Rd COVE CV2 .....31 H3
...ustine's Wk COVN CV6 ...22 B4
...ell Rd COVE CV2 .....32 D3
...holemews Cl COVS CV3 ...33 F4
...aards Wk COVS CV3 .....41 E3
...erine's Cl COVS CV3 .....40 C1
...stian's Cft COVS CV3 .....39 G1
...stian's Rd COVS CV3 .....39 H1
...mba's Cl COV CV1 .....2 C1
...ds Orch COVS CV3 .....41 G2

St Elizabeth's Rd COVN CV6 .....23 F4
St Georges Av
　RUGBYS/DCH CV22 .....61 G4
St George's Rd COV CV1 .....3 K6
St Giles Rd RCOVN/BALC/EX CV7 .13 E2
St Helen's Wy COVW CV5 .....21 E1
St Ives Rd COVE CV2 .....32 C3
St James' La COVS CV3 .....40 D4
St John's Av KNWTH CV8 .....65 F4
　RUGBYS/DCH CV22 .....62 B4
St John's La RRUGBY CV23 .....46 B4
St Johns St COV CV1 .....2 E5
　KNWTH CV8 .....65 E4
St John St RUGBYN/HIL CV21 .....47 H5
St Jude's Crs COVS CV3 .....41 E2
St Lawrence's Rd COVN CV6 .....23 G2
St Leonard's Wk KNWTH CV8.....55 H3
St Luke's Rd COVN CV6 .....23 E1
St Margaret Rd COV CV1 .....3 J5
St Mark's Av RUGBYS/DCH CV22 ...60 D5
St Martin's Rd COVS CV3 .....53 F2
St Mary St COV CV1 .....2 E4
St Michael's Rd COV CV1 .....31 H3
St Nicholas Av KNWTH CV8 .....65 E4
St Nicholas St COV CV1 .....30 D2
St Osburg's Rd COVE CV2 .....31 H3
St Paul's Rd COVN CV6 .....23 F5
St Peter's Ct COV CV1 * 3 G1
St Peters Rd RUGBYN/HIL CV21 ...62 B2
St Thomas Ct COV CV1 * 2 A5
St Thomas' Rd COVN CV6 .....13 C5
St Thomas's Ct COV CV1 .....2 A5
Salcombe Cl COVS CV3 .....41 E3
Salford Cl COVE CV2 .....31 H1
Salisbury Av COVS CV3 .....39 F3
Salisbury Cl KNWTH CV8 .....57 E1
Salt La COV CV1 .....2 D4
Sam Gault Cl COVS CV3 .....41 F2
Sammons Wy TLHL/CAN CV4 .....28 A5
Sampson Cl COVE CV2 .....24 B2
Sanby Cl BDWTH CV12 .....5 F1
Sanders Rd COVN CV6 .....14 C5
Sandford Cl COVE CV2 .....14 C5
Sandford Wy RUGBYS/DCH CV22 .69 G4
Sandgate Crs COVE CV2 .....32 C4
Sandhurst Gv COVN CV6 .....30 C1
Sandilands Cl COVE CV2 .....32 D2
Sandown Av COVN CV6 .....23 F1
Sandown Rd RUGBYN/HIL CV21 ...48 B5
Sandpiper Rd COVE CV2 .....14 A5
Sandpits La RCOVN/BALC/EX CV7 .21 H1
Sandringham Cl TLHL/CAN CV4 ...37 E4
Sandwick Cl COVS CV3 .....41 G1
Sandy La COVN CV6 .....30 D1
　RUGBYN/HIL CV21 .....61 H1
Santos Cl COVS CV3 .....41 G1
Sapcote Gv COVN CV6 .....14 A4
Sapphire Ct
　RCOVN/BALC/EX CV7 * 25 G2
Sapphire Ga COVE CV7 .....32 C3
Saunders Av BDWTH CV12 .....5 G3
Saunton Cl COVW CV5 .....21 E2
Saunton Rd RUGBYS/DCH CV22 ...61 G3
Saville Gv KNWTH CV8 .....65 H1
Saxon Cl COVS CV3 .....42 C2
　RUGBYS/DCH CV22 .....60 B4
Saxon Rd COVE CV2 .....32 A2
Scafell RUGBYS/HIL CV21 .....48 C2
Scafell Cl COVS CV3 .....28 D2
Scarborough Wy TLHL/CAN CV4 ...37 E2
Scarman Rd KNWTH CV8 .....37 F5
Scholfield Rd
　RCOVN/BALC/EX CV7 .....12 B2
School Bell Ms KNWTH CV8 * 67 E1
School Cl COVS CV3 .....1 K5
Schoolfield Gv RUGBYN/HIL CV21 61 H1
School Gdns RUGBYN/HIL CV21...63 F3
School House La COVE CV2 .....25 F5
School La KNWTH CV8 .....65 E2
　RCOVN/BALC/EX CV7 .....13 F1
School Rd BDWTH CV12 .....7 F3
School St KNWTH CV8 .....43 F5
　RRUGBY CV23 .....45 E4
　RRUGBY CV23 .....46 B5
　RUGBYN/HIL CV21 .....63 F3
　RUGBYS/DCH CV22 .....69 G4
The Scotchill COVN CV6 .....22 A2
Scots Cl RUGBYS/DCH CV22 .....60 D5
Scots La COVN CV6 .....22 A5
Scott Rd KNWTH CV8 .....64 D4
Seabroke Av RUGBYS/DCH CV22...61 G1
Seaford Cl COVN CV6 .....14 A4
Seagrave Rd COV CV1 .....3 G5
Sealand Dr BDWTH CV12 .....5 E2
Sear Hills Cl
　RCOVN/BALC/EX CV7 .....34 C3
Seathwaite RUGBYN/HIL CV21 ...48 B2
Sebastian Cl COVS CV3 .....40 C4
Second Av COVS CV3 .....32 B5

Second Exhibition Av
　BHAMNEC B40 .....8 B4
Sedgemere Gv
　RCOVN/BALC/EX CV7 .....34 D4
Sedgemoor Rd COVS CV3 .....40 D2
Sedlescombe Pk
　RUGBYS/DCH CV22 .....61 G4
Seed Field Cft COVS CV3 .....39 G2
Sefton Rd TLHL/CAN CV4 .....38 B3
Selborne Rd RUGBYS/DCH CV22 ...61 H4
Selsey Cl COVS CV3 .....40 D5
Selside RUGBYS/HIL CV21 .....48 C3
Selworthy Rd COVN CV6 .....13 E5
Seneschal Rd COVS CV3 .....39 H2
Sephton Dr COVN CV6 .....14 B2
Severn Rd BDWTH CV12 .....6 D2
　COV CV1 .....3 J6
Sewall Hwy COVE CV2 .....24 A5
　COVN CV6 .....23 H3
Seymour Cl COVS CV3 .....40 D4
Seymour Rd RUGBYN/HIL CV21...48 B3
Shadowbrook Rd COVN CV6 .....30 B1
Shaftesbury Av
　RCOVN/BALC/EX CV7 .....12 B1
Shaftesbury Rd COVW CV5 .....38 C1
Shakespeare Av BDWTH CV12.....6 A3
Shakespeare Gdns
　RUGBYS/DCH CV22 .....61 F5
Shakespeare St COVE CV2 .....32 A3
Shakleton Rd COVW CV5 .....30 B4
Shanklin Rd COVS CV3 .....40 C5
Shapfell RUGBYN/HIL CV21 .....48 C2
Sharp Cl COVN CV6 .....22 D1
Sharpley Ct COVE CV2 * 25 F3
Sharratt Rd BDWTH CV12 .....5 E3
Sheldrake Cl COVS CV3 .....33 F5
Shelfield Cl COVW CV5 .....29 E3
Shelley Cl BDWTH CV12 .....6 A4
Shelley Rd COVE CV2 .....32 B3
Shellon Cl COVS CV3 .....41 G1
Shelton Sq COV CV1 .....2 C4
Shenstone Av RUGBYN/HIL CV21 .62 D3
Shenstone Dr
　RCOVN/BALC/EX CV7 .....34 B3
Shepherd Cl TLHL/CAN CV4 .....28 C3
Sherbourne Crs COVW CV5 .....29 H2
Sherbourne St COV CV1 .....30 B4
Sheridan Cl RUGBYS/DCH CV22 ...61 G5
Sheriff Av TLHL/CAN CV4 .....37 G2
Sheriff Rd RUGBYN/HIL CV21 .....62 C2
Sheriffs Orch COV CV1 .....2 C5
Sherington Av COVW CV5 .....29 F3
Sherlock Rd COVW CV5 .....29 G3
Sherwood Jones Cl COVN CV6.....22 C5
Shetland Cl COVW CV5 .....28 D2
Shevlock Wy COVN CV6 .....23 H5
Shillingstone Cl COVE CV2 .....33 F2
Shilton La BDWTH CV12 .....7 H3
　COVE CV2 .....24 D1
Shipston Rd COVE CV2 .....24 B5
Shirebrook Cl COVE CV2 .....24 C2
Shire Cl COVN CV6 .....24 A1
The Shires RRUGBY CV23 * 45 E3
Shirlett Cl COVN CV6 .....14 A4
Shirley La RCOVN/BALC/EX CV7 ...27 F1
Shirley Rd COVE CV2 .....32 B3
Shorncliffe Rd COVN CV6 .....21 H5
Shortfield Cl
　RCOVN/BALC/EX CV7 .....34 C2
Shortlands RCOVN/BALC/EX CV7 .13 E2
Shortley Rd COVS CV3 .....39 H1
Short St COV CV1 .....3 F5
Shottery Cl COVW CV5 .....29 E3
Showell La RCOVN/BALC/EX CV7 ..19 C5
The Shrubberies TLHL/CAN CV4 ..38 B5
Shuckburgh Crs
　RUGBYS/DCH CV22 .....62 C4
Shulman's Wk COVE CV2 .....24 C4
Shultern La TLHL/CAN CV4 .....38 A3
Shuna Cft COVE CV2 .....25 F4
Shuttle St COVN CV6 .....24 A3
Shuttleworth Rd RRUGBY CV23 ...49 E4
Sibree Rd COVS CV3 .....40 C5
Sibton Cl COVE CV2 .....24 B2
Sidbury Rd COVN CV6 .....22 D5
Siddeley Av COVS CV3 .....31 H5
　KNWTH CV8 .....64 D1
The Sidings RUGBYN/HIL CV21 ...48 A5
Sidmouth Cl COVE CV2 .....24 B4
Sidney Rd RUGBYS/DCH CV22 .....62 C4
Silksby St COVS CV3 .....39 G1
Silver Birch Av BDWTH CV12 .....4 D3
Silverdale Cl COVE CV2 .....14 A4
Silverstone Dr
　RCOVN/BALC/EX CV7 .....13 F3
Silver St COV CV1 .....2 D2
Silverton Rd COVN CV6 .....23 G3
Simon Stone St COVN CV6 .....23 G3
Simpson Gv COVS CV3 .....40 D3

Singer Cl COVN CV6 .....23 H3
Sir Henry Parkes Rd COVW CV5 ...38 A2
　TLHL/CAN CV4 .....37 H2
Sir Thomas White's Rd
　COVW CV5 .....30 A4
Sir William Lyons Rd
　TLHL/CAN CV4 .....37 H3
Sir Winston Churchill Pl
　COVS CV3 .....42 B2
Siskin Cl RRUGBY CV23 .....48 B1
Siskin Dr KNWTH CV8 .....54 D2
Siskin Pkwy East KNWTH CV8 .....54 D3
Siskin Pkwy West KNWTH CV8 .....54 C3
Skipton Gdns COVE CV2 .....24 A5
Skipworth Rd COVS CV3 .....33 F4
Sky Blue Wy COV CV1 .....3 H3
Slade Rd RUGBYN/HIL CV21 .....62 B2
Sleath's Yd BDWTH CV12 .....5 C2
Sledmere Cl COVE CV2 .....14 A5
Sleets Yd BDWTH CV12 .....5 F3
Smarts Rd BDWTH CV12 .....5 E4
Smercote Cl BDWTH CV12 .....4 C4
Smithford Wy COV CV1 .....2 D3
Smiths Orch RUGBYN/HIL CV21 ...62 B1
Smith St BDWTH CV12 .....4 D4
　COVN CV6 .....31 G1
Smiths Yd BDWTH CV12 * 5 C1
Smithy La RRUGBY CV23 .....45 E4
Smorrall La BDWTH CV12 .....4 C4
Snape Rd COVE CV2 .....32 D1
Soden Cl COVS CV3 .....41 E3
Soden's Av KNWTH CV8 .....55 H3
Solent Dr COVE CV2 .....25 F2
Solihull Pkwy
　CHWD/FDBR/MGN B37 .....8 C1
Somerly Cl COVS CV3 .....41 C1
Somerset Rd COV CV1 .....30 D1
Somers Rd RCOVN/BALC/EX CV7 ...12 A2
　RCOVN/BALC/EX CV7 .....17 C2
　RUGBYS/DCH CV22 .....61 E2
Sommerville Rd COVE CV2 .....32 B2
Soredale Cft COVS CV3 .....33 F5
Sorrel Cl TLHL/CAN CV4 .....28 B5
Sorrel Dr RRUGBY CV23 .....48 C1
Southam Cl TLHL/CAN CV4 .....36 D2
Southam Rd RUGBYS/DCH CV22 ...69 G4
South Av COVE CV2 .....31 H4
Southbank Rd COVN CV6 .....29 H1
　KNWTH CV8 .....65 E3
Southbrook Rd
　RUGBYS/DCH CV22 .....61 H3
South Car Park Rd BHAMNEC B40 ..8 D5
Southcott Wy COVE CV2 .....25 E2
Southey Rd RUGBYS/DCH CV22 ...61 F5
Southfield Dr KNWTH CV8 .....65 F1
Southfield Rd RUGBYS/DCH CV22.62 B3
Southleigh Av COVW CV5 .....38 C3
Southport Cl COVS CV3 .....40 C4
South Rdg COVW CV5 .....29 E2
South Rd RRUGBY CV23 .....49 E4
South St COV CV1 .....3 H3
　RUGBYN/HIL CV21 .....48 C5
South View Rd RRUGBY CV23 .....46 A5
South Wy BHAMNEC B40 .....8 D5
Sovereign Rd COVW CV5 .....30 A4
Sovereign Rw COV CV1 .....30 B4
Sparkbrook St COV CV1 .....3 H2
Sparta Cl RUGBYN/HIL CV21.....47 H3
Speedway La KNWTH CV8 .....43 E2
Speedwell Cl RRUGBY CV23 .....48 D2
Speedwell Dr
　RCOVN/BALC/EX CV7 .....34 B3
Spencer Av COVW CV5 .....30 B3
Spencer Rd COVW CV5 .....2 B7
Spencer's La
　RCOVN/BALC/EX CV7 .....26 C4
Sphinx Dr COVS CV3 .....32 A5
Spicer Pl RUGBYS/DCH CV22 .....61 E3
Spindle St COV CV1 .....23 E5
Spinney Cl COVS CV3 .....42 D2
The Spinney RRUGBY CV23 .....46 B4
　TLHL/CAN CV4 .....52 B1
Spon End COVW CV5 .....30 B3
Spon St COV CV1 .....2 B3
Spottiswood Cl
　RUGBYS/DCH CV22 .....60 B4
Spring Cl COV CV1 .....3 H2
Springfield Crs BDWTH CV12 .....5 C3
Springfield Pl COV CV1 .....31 E2
Springfield Rd COV CV1 .....31 E2
Spring La KNWTH CV8 .....65 F2
Spring Rd COVN CV6 .....23 G3
　RCOVN/BALC/EX CV7 .....15 F2
Spring St RUGBYN/HIL CV21.....62 A1
The Square COVE CV2 * 25 F4
　KNWTH CV8 .....65 E3
　RUGBYS/DCH CV22 .....69 H4
Squires Cft COVE CV2 .....25 E2
Squires Wy TLHL/CAN CV4 .....38 A4

Stable Yd *KNWTH* CV8 * 53 H2
Stadium Cl *COVN* CV6 ....23 E1
Stafford Cl *BDWTH* CV12 ....7 F3
Staircase La *COVW* CV5 ....21 F4
Stamford Av *COVS* CV3 ....39 F3
Standard Av *TLHL/CAN* CV4 ....28 D5
Standish Cl *COV* CV2 ....32 D4
Stanier Av *COV* CV1 ....30 B3
Stanley Rd *COVW* CV5 ....38 C1
  RUGBYN/HIL CV21 ....62 D3
Stansfield Gv *KNWTH* CV8 ....66 A3
Stanway Rd *COVW* CV5 ....38 D1
Staples Cl *BDWTH* CV12 ....7 F3
Starcross Cl *COVE* CV2 ....24 B4
Stare Gn *TLHL/CAN* CV4 ....38 A4
Stareton Cl *TLHL/CAN* CV4 ....38 B3
Starley Rd *COV* CV1 ....2 B4
Starley Wy
  CHWD/FDBR/MGN B37 ....8 A2
Startin Rd *RCOVN/BALC/EX* CV7 ...13 G1
Station Av *TLHL/CAN* CV4 ....36 C1
Station Link Rd
  CHWD/FDBR/MGN B37 ....8 B4
Station Rd *HIA/OLT* B92 ....16 B4
  KNWTH CV8 ....65 E3
  RCOVN/BALC/EX CV7 ....34 B3
  RRUGBY CV23 ....49 E4
Station Sq *COV* CV1 ....2 C6
Station St East *COVN* CV6 ....23 F4
Station St West *COVN* CV6 ....23 E3
Station Tower *COV* CV1 * 2 C6
Staveley Wy *RUGBYN/HIL* CV21.....48 C3
Staverton Cl *COV* CV2 ....28 C3
Staverton Leys
  RUGBS/DCH CV22 ....61 H5
Steele St *RUGBYS/DCH* CV22 ....61 E1
Steeping Rd *RRUGBY* CV23 ....46 C4
Steeplefield Rd *COVW* CV6 * 30 B1
Stennels Cl *COVN* CV6 ....22 A3
Stephenson Rd
  RCOVN/BALC/EX CV7 ....14 A1
Stephen St *RUGBYN/HIL* CV21 ....61 G1
Stepney Rd *COVE* CV2 ....31 H2
Stepping Stones Rd *COVW* CV5......30 A2
Stevenson Rd *COVN* CV6 ....22 B3
Stewart Cl *COVW* CV5 ....29 G4
Stirling Cl *COVS* CV3 ....41 G1
Stivichall Cft *COVS* CV3 ....39 E3
Stocks Ct *RUGBYS/DCH* CV22........61 E4
Stocks La *RRUGBY* CV23 ....68 D4
The Stocks *RUGBYS/DCH* CV22 * ...69 G4
Stockton Rd *COV* CV1 ....31 F2
Stoke Gn *COVN* CV6 ....31 H4
Stoke Park Ms *COVE* CV2 * 31 H3
Stoke Rw *COVE* CV2 ....31 H2
Stonebridge Hwy *COVS* CV3 ....39 F5
Stonebrook Wy *COVN* CV6 ....13 G5
Stonebury Av *COVW* CV5 ....28 B2
Stonefield Cl *COVE* CV2 ....25 F3
Stonehall Rd *RUGBYS/DCH* CV22...60 B4
Stonehaven Dr *COVS* CV3 ....53 F1
Stonehills *RUGBYN/HIL* CV21 ....48 B2
Stonehouse La *COVS* CV3 ....40 D5
Stoneleigh Av *KNWTH* CV8 ....65 F1
Stoneleigh Cl *KNWTH* CV8 ....67 E1
Stoneleigh Rd *KNWTH* CV8 ....65 F1
  TLHL/CAN CV4 ....52 A2
Stoneton Crs
  RCOVN/BALC/EX CV7 ....34 B3
Stoney Ct *COVS* CV3 ....41 H2
Stoney Rd *COV* CV1 ....2 D7
Stoney Stanton Rd *COV* CV1 ....31 H1
  COVN CV6 ....23 G4
Stoneywood Rd *COVE* CV2 ....25 E2
Stonleigh Av *COVW* CV5 ....38 C2
Stowe Pl *TLHL/CAN* CV4 ....27 H5
Stratford Rd *COV* CV2 ....31 H2
Strathmore Av *COV* CV1 ....3 G5
Strawberry Flds
  RCOVN/BALC/EX CV7 ....18 A2
Strawberry Wk *COVE* CV2 ....24 C1
Streamside Cl *COVW* CV5 ....20 D3
Stretton Av *COVS* CV3 ....40 D4
Stretton Rd *RRUGBY* CV23 ....57 F4
Stuart Ct *COVN* CV6 ....23 H3
Stubbs Cl *BDWTH* CV12 ....5 E2
Stubbs Gv *COVE* CV2 ....32 A1
Studland Av *RUGBYN/HIL* CV21.....63 E3
Studland Gn *COVE* CV2 ....33 F2
Sturley Cl *KNWTH* CV8 ....65 G1
Sturminster Cl *COVS* CV3 ....33 F2
Styvechale Av *COVW* CV5 ....38 C1
Suffolk Cl *BDWTH* CV12 ....5 E2
  COVW CV5 ....29 E3
Sullivan Rd *COVN* CV6 ....24 A4
Sunbury Rd *COVS* CV3 ....40 D5
Suncliffe Dr *KNWTH* CV8 ....65 F5
Sundew St *COVE* CV2 ....24 C1
Sundorne Cl *COVW* CV5 ....28 D2

Sunningdale Av *COVN* CV6 ....23 E1
  KNWTH CV8 ....65 G3
Sunnybank Av *COVS* CV3 ....40 C4
Sunnyside Cl *COVW* CV5 ....30 A3
  RCOVN/BALC/EX CV7 ....34 D2
Sunnyside La
  RCOVN/BALC/EX CV7 ....34 D3
Sunshine Cl *KNWTH* CV8 ....65 F5
Sun St *RUGBYN/HIL* CV21 ....62 B1
Sunway Gv *COVS* CV3 ....39 E3
Sussex Rd *COVW* CV5 ....30 A2
Sutherland Av *COVW* CV5 ....28 D2
Sutherland Dr *BDWTH* CV12 ....5 F1
Sutton Av *TLHL/CAN* CV4 ....28 A2
Sutton Stop *COVN* CV6 ....14 A3
Swallowdean Rd *COVN* CV6...........21 H3
Swallow Rd *COVN* CV6 ....22 C2
Swanage Gn *COVE* CV2 ....33 F2
Swancroft Rd *COVE* CV2 ....31 H1
Swan La *COV* CV1 ....31 G2
  COVE CV2 ....3 K1
Swanswell St *COV* CV1 ....3 F1
Swift Cl *KNWTH* CV8 ....65 F5
Swift Pk *RUGBYN/HIL* CV21 ....47 H2
Swift's Cnr *COVS* CV3 ....39 H1
Swillington Rd *COVN* CV6 ....30 C1
Swinburne Av *COVE* CV2 ....32 C4
Swindale Cft *COVS* CV3 ....41 G1
Sycamore Gv *RUGBYN/HIL* CV21....47 H5
Sycamore Rd *COVE* CV2 ....24 A1
The Sycamores *BDWTH* CV12 ....4 D3
Sydnall Flds *COVN* CV6 ....13 G4
Sydnall Rd *COVN* CV6 ....13 G3
Sylvan Dr *COVS* CV3 ....38 C3
Synkere Cl *RCOVN/BALC/EX* CV7 ...12 B2
Sywell Leys *RUGBS/DCH* CV22......70 B1

Tachbrook Cl *COVE* CV2 ....24 B1
Tackford Rd *COVN* CV6 ....23 H4
Tainters Hl *KNWTH* CV8 ....65 E1
Talisman Cl *KNWTH* CV8 ....65 H5
Talland Av *COVN* CV6 ....23 H3
Tallants Cl *COVN* CV6 ....23 H3
Tallants Rd *COVN* CV6 ....23 G3
Tamar Cl *RRUGBY* CV23 ....46 C4
Tamar Rd *BDWTH* CV12 ....6 D3
Tamworth Rd
  RCOVN/BALC/EX CV7 ....11 F1
Tanners' La *RCOVN/BALC/EX* CV7 .27 G5
Tanyard *TLHL/CAN* CV4 ....27 H5
Tapcon Wy *COV* CV2 ....33 E1
Tappinger Gv *KNWTH* CV8 ....65 H2
Tarlington Rd *COVN* CV6................21 G5
Tarn Cl *BDWTH* CV12 ....5 F3
Tarquin Cl *COVS* CV3 ....41 E3
Tarragon Cl *COVE* CV2 ....24 C2
Tarrant Wk *COVE* CV2 ....33 F1
Taunton Wy *COVN* CV6 ....22 B1
Tavistock Wk *COVE* CV2 ....24 B4
Taylor Cl *KNWTH* CV8 ....65 G1
Tay Rd *COVN* CV6 ....22 C5
Teachers Cl *COVN* CV6 ....30 B1
The Tea Gdn *RCOVN/BALC/EX* CV7 ..4 D5
Teasel Cl *RRUGBY* CV23 ....48 C1
Ted Pitts La *COVW* CV5 ....21 E1
Telephone Rd *COVS* CV3 ....32 B5
Telfer Rd *COVN* CV6 ....22 C2
Telford Rd *RCOVN/BALC/EX* CV7 ....5 H5
Templar Av *TLHL/CAN* CV4 ....28 D5
Temple Av *RCOVN/BALC/EX* CV7 ...34 A3
Temple St *RUGBYN/HIL* CV21 ....62 B2
Tenby Cl *BDWTH* CV12 ....4 B4
Teneriffe Rd *COVN* CV6 ....23 G2
Tennyson Av *RUGBYS/DCH* CV22....61 F5
Tennyson Cl *KNWTH* CV8 ....65 H5
Tennyson Rd *COVE* CV2 ....32 B3
Terracotta Dr *COVE* CV2 * 31 H2
Terry Rd *COV* CV1 ....3 J6
Tewkesbury Dr *BDWTH* CV12 ....5 H2
Thackeray Cl *RUGBYS/DCH* CV22 ..61 G5
Thackhall St *COVE* CV2 ....3 J1
Thames Cl *BDWTH* CV12 ....6 D2
Thamley Rd *COVN* CV6 ....30 B2
The Thatchings
  RUGBYS/DCH CV22 * 69 H4
Thebes Cl *COVW* CV5 ....19 G3
Theddingworth Cl *COVS* CV3.........41 F1
Thena Gdns *COVN* CV6 ....23 H2
Thickthorn Cl *KNWTH* CV8 ....65 G4
Thimbler Rd *TLHL/CAN* CV4 ....37 H2
Third Exhibition Av *BHAMNEC* B40 ..8 B3

Thirlestane Cl *KNWTH* CV8 ....65 H1
Thirlmere *RUGBYN/HIL* CV21 ....48 B2
Thirlmere Cl *COVW* CV5.................28 B3
Thirlmere Rd *BDWTH* CV12 ....5 F3
Thirsk Rd *COVS* CV3 ....39 F4
Thistle Wy *RRUGBY* CV23 ....48 C1
Thistley Fld East *COVN* CV6 ....22 A5
Thistley Fld North *COVN* CV6.........22 B4
Thistley Fld South *COVN* CV6 ....22 A5
Thistley Fld West *COVN* CV6 ....22 A5
Thomas Landsdail St *COVS* CV3 .....2 E7
Thomas Lane St *COVN* CV6 ....23 H2
Thomas Naul Cft *TLHL/CAN* CV4 ....28 C3
Thomas Sharp St *TLHL/CAN* CV4 ...37 F2
Thomas St *BDWTH* CV12 ....5 F3
  COV CV1 * 2 A4
Thomas Wy *RRUGBY* CV23 ....46 B4
Thompson's Rd
  RCOVN/BALC/EX CV7 ....11 H2
Thomson Cl *RUGBYN/HIL* CV21 .....48 A3
Thornby Av *KNWTH* CV8 ....65 H4
Thorn Cl *RUGBYN/HIL* CV21 ....48 B3
Thorney Rd *COVE* CV2 ....24 A5
Thornhill Ct *COV* CV1 * 31 E1
Thornhill Rd *COV* CV1 ....31 E1
Thornton Cl *COVW* CV5 ....27 H2
Threadneedle St *COV* CV1 ....22 D5
Three Spires Av *COVN* CV6 ....30 B1
Thurlestone Rd *COVN* CV6 ....22 A3
Thurnmill Rd *RUGBYN/HIL* CV21 ....46 C4
Tiber Cl *COVW* CV5 ....28 C2
Tiber Wy *RUGBYN/HIL* CV21 ....47 G2
Tideswell Cl *COVS* CV3..................33 F5
Tidmarsh Cl *RCOVN/BALC/EX* CV7 .34 B3
Tile Hill La *COVW* CV5 ....29 F4
  TLHL/CAN CV4 ....28 B5
Tile Hurst Dr *TLHL/CAN* CV4 ....28 A4
Tilehurst Dr *TLHL/CAN* CV4...........28 A4
Tilewood Av *COVW* CV5 ....28 B2
Timothy Gv *TLHL/CAN* CV4 ....29 F5
Tintagel Gv *KNWTH* CV8 ....65 G3
Tintern Wy *BDWTH* CV12 ....5 H3
Tisdale Ri *KNWTH* CV8 ....65 G2
Tiverton Gv *COVE* CV2 ....32 C1
Tiverton Rd *COVE* CV2 ....32 C1
Tiveycourt Rd *COVN* CV6 ....13 H5
Tocil Cft *TLHL/CAN* CV4 ....38 A5
Tollard Cl *COVE* CV2 ....33 E1
Tom Brown St *RUGBYN/HIL* CV21 ..48 A4
Tom Henderson Cl *COVS* CV3.........41 G2
Tomson Av *COVN* CV6 ....30 B2
Tom Ward Cl *COVS* CV3 ....41 G2
Tonbridge Rd *COVS* CV3 ....40 B3
Topp's Dr *BDWTH* CV12 ....4 D4
Topp's Heath *BDWTH* CV12 ....4 D4
Top Rd *RCOVN/BALC/EX* CV7 ....15 F1
Torbay Rd *COVW* CV5 ....29 F2
Torcastle Cl *COVN* CV6 ....23 G4
Torcross Av *COVE* CV2 ....32 B1
Torpoint Cl *COVE* CV2 ....24 B4
Torrance Rd *RUGBYN/HIL* CV21 .....61 G1
Torrington Av *TLHL/CAN* CV4 ....37 E1
Torwood Cl *TLHL/CAN* CV4 ....37 E3
Totnes Cl *COVE* CV2 ....24 B4
Tove Ct *RRUGBY* CV23 ....46 C4
Tower Rd *BDWTH* CV12 ....5 F3
  RUGBYS/DCH CV22 ....62 B3
Tower St *COV* CV1 ....2 D2
Town Feilds Cl *COVW* CV5 ....21 E4
Townsend Cft *COVS* CV3 ....39 F2
Townsend La *RRUGBY* CV23 ....46 C5
Townsend Rd *RUGBYN/HIL* CV21 ...62 C1
Tredington Rd *COVW* CV5 ....28 C2
Treedale Cl *TLHL/CAN* CV4 ....36 D1
Treforest Cl *COVS* CV3 ....40 D1
Tregorrick Rd
  RCOVN/BALC/EX CV7 ....13 H1
Tregullan Rd *RCOVN/BALC/EX* CV7 .5 G5
Treherne Rd *COVN* CV6 ....22 C3
Trelawney Rd
  RCOVN/BALC/EX CV7 ....13 H1
Trenance Rd
  RCOVN/BALC/EX CV7 ....13 H1
Treneere Rd *RCOVN/BALC/EX* CV7 ..5 F5
Trensale Av *COVN* CV6 ....30 A2
Trentham Gdns *KNWTH* CV8 ....65 H2
Trentham Rd *COV* CV1 ....31 G2
Trent Rd *BDWTH* CV12 ....6 D3
Tresillian Rd *RCOVN/BALC/EX* CV7 ..5 G5
Treviscoe Cl *RCOVN/BALC/EX* CV7 .13 H1
Trevor Cl *TLHL/CAN* CV4 ....36 C1
Trevor White Dr
  RUGBYS/DCH CV22 ....62 A3
Trevose Av *RCOVN/BALC/EX* CV7 ..14 A1
The Triangle *COVW* CV5 ....29 E2
Trident Cl
  LGN/SDN/BHAMAIR B26 ....8 A4
Trinity La *COV* CV1 ....2 D3
Trinity Pk *BHAMNEC* B40 * 8 B5

Trinity St *COV* CV1 ....2 D3
Triumph Cl *COVE* CV2 ....24 A5
Trossachs Rd *COVW* CV5 ....28 A2
Troughton Crs *COVN* CV6 ....23 F4
Troutbeck Rd *COVW* CV5 ....27 H2
Troyes Cl *COVS* CV3 ....39 H2
Truggist La *RCOVN/BALC/EX* CV7 ..27 G5
Trussell Wy *RUGBYS/DCH* CV22.....61 G5
Tudor Av *COVW* CV5 ....28 A2
Tudor Cl *RCOVN/BALC/EX* CV7 ......34 A3
Tulip Tree Av *KNWTH* CV8 ....65 H5
Tulliver Cl *BDWTH* CV12 ....5 E1
Tulliver St *COVN* CV6 ....22 B5
Turchil Rd *RUGBYS/DCH* CV22......61 F1
Turlands Cl *COVE* CV2 ....25 F4
Turner Cl *BDWTH* CV12 ....5 E1
  RUGBYN/HIL CV21 ....61 G1
Turner Rd *COVW* CV5 ....38 C1
Turnpike Cl *RCOVN/BALC/EX* CV7 ..11 G2
Turton Wy *KNWTH* CV8 ....65 H2
Tutbury Av *TLHL/CAN* CV4 ....38 A4
Twickenham Wy *COVS* CV3 ....41 G1
Tybalt Cl *COVS* CV3 ....41 H2
Tylney Cl *COVS* CV3 ....41 H2
Tynemouth Cl *COVE* CV2 ....25 F4
Tynward Cl *COVS* CV3 ....38 C3
Tysoe Cft *COVS* CV3 ....41 H2

Ufton Cft *COVW* CV5 ....29 F4
Ullswater Rd *BDWTH* CV12............5 F3
  COVS CV3 ....39 H2
Ulverscroft Rd *COVS* CV3 ....40 A1
Ulverston *RUGBYN/HIL* CV21 ....48 C3
The Underpass *BHAMNEC* B40 ....8 A5
Unicorn Av *COVW* CV5 ....28 B2
Unicorn La *COVW* CV5 ....28 B2
Union Pl *COVN* CV6 ....23 G4
Union St *RUGBYS/DCH* CV22 ....61 G5
University Rd *TLHL/CAN* CV4 ....52 A1
Uplands *COVE* CV2 ....32 B1
Upper Eastern Green La
  COVW CV5 ....27 F3
Upperfield Wy *COVS* CV3 ....41 G1
Upper Hill St *COV* CV1 ....2 A3
Upper Pk *COVS* CV3 ....41 H2
Upper Prec *COV* CV1 ....2 D4
Upper Ride *COVS* CV3 ....41 H2
Upper Rosemary Hl *KNWTH* CV8....65 E1
Upper Spon St *COV* CV1 ....2 A3
Upper Spring La *KNWTH* CV8 ....65 E1
Upper Well St *COV* CV1 ....2 C3
Upper York St *COV* CV1 ....2 B7
Upton Rd *RUGBYS/DCH* CV22 ....61 F5
Utrillo Cl *COVW* CV5 ....30 A2
Uxbridge Av *COVS* CV3 ....41 H1

Vale Cl *RUGBYN/HIL* CV21 ....48 C3
The Vale *COVS* CV3 ....41 H2
Valley Rd *COVS* CV3 ....40 B2
Van Dyke Cl *COVW* CV5 ....30 A2
Vanguard Av *COVW* CV5 ....27 H3
Vanguard Rd
  LGN/SDN/BHAMAIR B26 ....8 A4
Vardon Dr *COVS* CV3 ....53 F1
Vauxhall Av *COVW* CV5 ....23 G5
Vauxhall Cl *COV* CV1 ....23 G5
Vauxhall St *COV* CV1 ....3 G2
Vecqueray St *COV* CV1 ....3 H4
Ventnor Cl *COVE* CV2 ....32 C1
Vere Rd *RUGBYN/HIL* CV21 ....61 G1
Vernon Av *RUGBYS/DCH* CV22......61 G5
Vernon Cl *COV* CV1 ....3 J4
Vicarage Gdns *KNWTH* CV8 * 65 E1
Vicarage Hl *RUGBYN/HIL* CV21 ......46 C4
Vicarage La *RCOVN/BALC/EX* CV7 ..15 F1
  RUGBYS/DCH CV22 ....57 H3
Vicarage Rd *KNWTH* CV8 ....65 E1
  RUGBYS/DCH CV22 ....61 G5
Victoria Av *RUGBYN/HIL* CV21 ......61 H1
Victoria Ct *COVW* CV5 * 30 A2
Victoria St *COV* CV1 ....3 F1
  RUGBYN/HIL CV21 ....61 H1
Victory Rd *COVN* CV6 ....23 G4
Villa Cl *BDWTH* CV12 ....5 H2
Villa Crs *BDWTH* CV12 ....5 H2

COVN CV6 ....22 C5
St KNWTH CV8 ....65 G2
st COVE CV2 ....3 K2
st COVE CV1 ....2 A4
e Rd COVN CV6 ....13 G4
COV CV1 ....3 F2
l COVE CV2 ....24 B1
GBY CV23 ....48 D1
a Rd COV CV1 ....3 G2
cl COV CV1 ....3 G2

W

Av COVS CV3 ....39 E4
ody Av North COVS CV3 ...38 D4
ody Av South COVS CV3 ...38 C5
eld Cl COVS CV3 ....41 G2
d Pl RUGBYN/HIL CV21 ...63 E4
s Orch KNWTH CV8 ....67 E1
s Wy RCOVN/BALC/EX CV7 ...5 E4
e Rd COVN CV6 ....22 B3
ll Rd RCOVN/BALC/EX CV7 ..10 D4
t St COVE CV2 ....24 A1
Tree Cl KNWTH CV8 ....65 F4
t Wy RUGBYS/DCH CV22 ..60 C3
St TLHL/CAN CV4 ....37 F2
ave Gdns COVE CV2 ....25 F4
ave Rd COVE CV2 ....3 J3
La RCOVN/BALC/EX CV7 ..18 D1
Scott Rd BDWTH CV12 ......5 H4
Cl COVS CV3 ....41 F2
Rd COVS CV3 ....39 G3
ell Cl TLHL/CAN CV4 ....37 F2
nbury Cl COVE CV2 ....24 B1
nbury Rd COVE CV2 ....24 C2
n Rd COVN CV6 ....22 C5
ardens Av COVW CV5 ....21 E5
ardens KNWTH CV8 ....65 H2
am Gn COVE CV2 ....33 F1
Wy RUGBYS/DCH CV22 ...69 H3
ngton Cl COVS CV3 ....41 F1
vell Cl COVE CV2 ....33 E2
Rw COVN CV6 ....23 C4
Fld KNWTH CV8 ....55 H5
Gn TLHL/CAN CV4 ....37 E1
Rd RUGBYS/DCH CV22 ...62 C3
Cl KNWTH CV8 ....65 H1
Av COVW CV5 ....38 D2
ck La COV CV1 ....2 A4
ck Rd COV CV1 ....2 C6
s CV3 ....39 E1
TH CV8 ....57 F1
TH CV8 ....65 E4
ck Rw COV CV1 ....3 H1
ck St COVW CV5 ....38 C1
DCH CV22 ....61 F2
rook La COVW CV5 ....20 D2
rton Cl COVS CV3 ....41 C1
La COVN CV6 ....21 H2
VN/BALC/EX CV7 ....35 F4
Cl COV CV1 ....2 B3
mbe Rd COVE CV2 ....24 D3
call Av COVS CV3 ....39 F4
Fall Cl RCOVN/BALC/EX CV7 ..18 D2
loo St COV CV1 ....3 H1
man Rd COVN CV6 ....31 G1
side COVN CV6 ....14 B2
side Dr RUGBYN/HIL CV21 ..48 B3
smeet Gv COVE CV2 ....24 A5
smeet Rd COVE CV2 ....24 A5
Tower La KNWTH CV8 .....65 F4
fall Cl RCOVN/BALC/EX CV7 ..10 A3
ley Rd KNWTH CV8 ....65 F4
rs Wk COVN CV6 ....24 A3
Dr RRUGBY CV23 ....48 C1
Ellis Rd RUGBYS/DCH CV22 ..61 F2
er Av KNWTH CV8 ....65 G1
er St COVN CV6 ....23 F4
ewood Cl COVE CV2 ....24 D3
Ga RCOVN/BALC/EX CV7 ..34 B4
rd Pl COVN CV6 ....23 E4
rd Rd RUGBYN/HIL CV21 ..48 B5

Welgarth Av COVN CV6 ....21 H5
William Arnold Cl COVE CV2 ....31 H2
Woodside Av North COVS CV3 ......38 C3

Welland Rd RUGBYN/HIL CV21 ..46 C4
William Bree Rd COVW CV5 ....27 H1
Woodside Av South COVS CV3 ......38 C4
Welland Rd COV CV1 ....3 J6
William Bristow Rd COVS CV3 ....39 H2
Woodside Pk RUGBYN/HIL CV21 ..47 H4
Wellesbourne Rd COVW CV5 .....28 D3
William Cree Cl KNWTH CV8 ....57 E1
Woods Piece
Wellfield Cl RCOVN/BALC/EX CV7 ..35 E4
William Groubb Cl COVS CV3 ....41 F2
   RCOVN/BALC/EX CV7 ....12 A2
Wellington Gdns COV CV1 ....2 A4
William McKee Cl COVS CV3 ....41 F2
Woodstock Rd COVS CV3 ....39 G2
Wellington St COV CV1 ....3 C1
William St BDWTH CV12 ....6 A3
Wood St BDWTH CV12 ....5 F1
Wells St RUGBYN/HIL CV21 ......62 A1
   RUGBYN/HIL CV21 ....62 A1
   RUGBYN/HIL CV21 ....47 H4
Well St COV CV1 ....2 D2
Willis Gv BDWTH CV12 ....5 H2
Woodway Cl COVE CV2 ....24 D3
Welsh Rd COV CV2 ....32 A2
Willoughby Av KNWTH CV8 ....64 D4
Woodway La COVE CV2 ....15 E5
Welton Pl RUGBYS/DCH CV22 ..62 C4
Willoughby Cl COVS CV3 ....41 F1
Woodway Wk COVE CV2 ....24 D3
Wendiburgh St TLHL/CAN CV4 ..37 F2
Willoughby Pl
Woolgrove St COVN CV6 ....13 H5
Wendover Ri COVW CV5 ....29 F2
   RUGBYS/DCH CV22 ....62 C4
Wootton St BDWTH CV12 ....5 H2
Wentworth Dr COVN CV6 ....12 C4
Willow Brook Rd KNWTH CV8 .....43 F5
Worcester Cl COVW CV5 ....21 E4
Wentworth Rd
Willow Ctyd COVE CV2 ....24 C3
Worcester Rd KNWTH CV8 ....65 C4
   RUGBYS/DCH CV22 ....61 G3
Willow Gv TLHL/CAN CV4 ....29 F4
Worcester St RUGBYN/HIL CV21 ..47 H5
Wesley Rd RUGBYN/HIL CV21 ..63 F4
Willowherb Cl COVS CV3 ....41 G1
Wordsworth Dr KNWTH CV8 ....65 H3
Wessex Cl BDWTH CV12 ....5 F1
Willow Meer KNWTH CV8 ....65 G2
Wordsworth Rd BDWTH CV12 ......6 A4
West Av BDWTH CV12 ....5 A3
The Willows BDWTH CV12 ....4 D3
   COVE CV2 ....32 B2
   COVE CV2 ....31 H4
Willow Wk RUGBYS/DCH CV22 ..62 B2
   RUGBYS/DCH CV22 ....70 A1
   RCOVN/BALC/EX CV7 ....12 B3
Wilmcote Gn COVW CV5 ....28 D3
Worsdell Cl COVN CV1 ....2 A1
Westbourne Gv
Wilmot Cl RCOVN/BALC/EX CV7 ..34 C1
Worsfold Cl COVW CV5 ....20 D4
   RUGBYS/DCH CV22 ....61 G3
Wilson Cl RUGBYS/DCH CV22 ..60 D2
Wrenbury Dr COVN CV6 ....13 H4
Westbury Ms CV2 * 31 H3
Wilson Gn COVS CV3 ....33 E5
Wren St COVE CV2 ....3 J2
Westbury Rd COVS CV5 ....29 G1
Wilson Gv KNWTH CV8 ....65 H3
Wright St COV CV1 ....31 F1
Westcliffe Dr COVS CV3 ....39 E4
Wilson's La COVN CV6 ....13 G3
Wrigsham St COVS CV3 ....2 E7
Westcotes TLHL/CAN CV4 ....29 E5
Wilton Rd RCOVN/BALC/EX CV7 ..34 C3
Wroxall Dr COVS CV3 ....40 D4
Westfield Rd RUGBYS/DCH CV22 ..61 G2
Wiltshire Cl BDWTH CV12 ....5 F2
Wyatt Ct BDWTH CV12 * 5 G2
Westgate Rd RUGBYN/HIL CV21 ..62 D3
   COVW CV5 ....29 E3
Wych-Elm Cl RUGBYS/DCH CV22 ..60 C3
Westhill Rd COVN CV6 ....22 A5
Wimborne Dr COVE CV2 ....33 E2
Wychwood Av COVS CV3 ....39 F5
Westleigh Av COVW CV5 ....38 C2
Winceby Pl TLHL/CAN CV4 ....28 A5
Wycliffe Gv COVE CV2 ....32 A2
West Leyes RUGBYN/HIL CV21 ..61 G1
Winchat Cl COVS CV3 ....33 E5
Wycliffe Rd West COVE CV2 ....32 A1
Westminster Rd COV CV1 ....2 B6
Winchester St COV CV1 ....3 G2
Wye Cl BDWTH CV12 ....7 E3
Westmorland Rd COVE CV2 ....33 E2
Windermere Av COVS CV3 ....32 D5
Wykeley Rd COVE CV2 ....32 B2
Westonbirt Cl KNWTH CV8 ....65 H1
   COVW CV5 ....28 B2
Wyken Av COVE CV2 ....32 C1
Weston La RUGBYS/DCH CV22 ..69 G3
Windermere Cl
Wyken Cft COVE CV2 ....32 C1
Weston St COV CV1 ....3 F1
   RUGBYN/HIL CV21 ....48 B2
Wyken Grange Rd COVE CV2 ....32 B1
West Rdg COVW CV5 ....28 D1
Winding House La COVN CV6 ......13 E4
Wyken Wy COVE CV2 ....31 H1
West St COV CV1 ....3 H3
Windmill Cl KNWTH CV8 ....65 F1
Wyke Rd COVE CV2 ....32 B2
   RRUGBY CV23 ....46 B1
The Windmill HI COVW CV5 ....20 D4
Wyld Ct COVW CV5 ....29 E1
West View Rd RUGBYS/DCH CV22 ..61 E2
Windmill La RCOVN/BALC/EX CV7 ..10 A2
Wyley Rd COVN CV6 ....30 C1
Westwood Heath Rd
   RCOVN/BALC/EX CV7 ....35 E5
Wyncote Cl KNWTH CV8 ....65 F3
   TLHL/CAN CV4 ....36 B3
   RUGBYS/DCH CV22 ....69 E3
Wynter Rd RUGBYS/DCH CV22 ..61 E1
Westwood Rd COVW CV5 ....30 B5
Windmill Pk
Wythburn Wy RUGBYN/HIL CV21 ..48 C2
   RUGBYS/DCH CV22 ....63 E5
   RCOVN/BALC/EX CV7 * 35 E5
Wyver Crs COVE CV2 ....32 B3
Westwood Wy TLHL/CAN CV4 ..36 D3
Windmill Rd COVN CV6 ....13 H5
Wetherell Wy RUGBYN/HIL CV21 ..48 B2
   RCOVN/BALC/EX CV7 ....13 H1
Wexford Rd COVE CV2 ....24 C2
Windridge Cl COVS CV3 ....40 D3
Whaley's Cft COVN CV6 ....22 B3
Windrush Wy RRUGBY CV23 ......46 C4

Y

Wharf Rd COV CV1 ....31 G1
Windsor St COV CV1 ....2 A4
Yardley St COV CV1 ....3 G1
Whateley's Dr KNWTH CV8 ....65 F3
   RUGBYN/HIL CV21 ....62 B1
Yarmouth Gn TLHL/CAN CV4 ......36 D1
Wheate Cft TLHL/CAN CV4 ....28 C4
Windy Arbour KNWTH CV8 ....65 G4
Yarningale Rd COVS CV3 ....40 D4
Wheatfield Av
Winfield St RUGBYN/HIL CV21 ..62 C1
Yarrow Cl RRUGBY CV23 * 48 C1
   RUGBYS/DCH CV22 ....60 D3
Wingfield Wy COVN CV6 ....22 B1
Yates Av RUGBYN/HIL CV21 ....47 G3
Wheelwright La COVN CV6 ....12 D4
Wingrave Cl COVW CV5 ....20 D5
Yelverton Rd COVN CV6 ....22 D3
Wheler Rd COVS CV3 ....40 B1
Winifred Av COVW CV5 ....30 B5
Yew Cl COVS CV3 ....40 D1
Whernside RUGBYN/HIL CV21 ..48 B2
Winnallthorpe COVS CV3 ....41 F3
Yewdale Crs COVE CV2 ....24 D2
Whetstone Dr RUGBYN/HIL CV21 ..48 D2
Winsford Av COVW CV5 ....29 F2
The Yews BDWTH CV12 ....4 D3
Whichcote Av
Winsford Cl RCOVN/BALC/EX CV7 ..34 B3
York Av BDWTH CV12 ....6 A3
   RCOVN/BALC/EX CV7 ....18 B2
Winsham Wk COVS CV3 ....53 F1
York Cl COVS CV3 ....40 D4
Whiley Cl RRUGBY CV23 ....49 E4
Winster Cl RCOVN/BALC/EX CV7 ..12 B1
York St COV CV1 ....2 A5
Whitaker Rd COVW CV5 ....29 F2
Winston Av COVE CV2 ....24 C2
   RUGBYN/HIL CV21 ....47 H5
Whitburn Rd BDWTH CV12 ....4 B1
Winston Cl COVE CV2 * 24 C3
Yule Rd COVE CV2 ....32 C1
Whitchurch Wy TLHL/CAN CV4 ..37 E2
Winterton Rd BDWTH CV12 ....7 F4
Whitebeam Cl TLHL/CAN CV4 ..28 A5
Winwick Pl RUGBYS/DCH CV22 ..60 D4
Whitefield Cl TLHL/CAN CV4 .....36 C3
Wise Gv RUGBYN/HIL CV21 ....63 E2
White Friars La COV CV1 ....3 E3
Wisley Gv KNWTH CV8 ....65 H2
White Friars St COV CV1 ....3 F4
Withybrook Cl COVE CV2 ....24 C1
Whitehall Rd RUGBYN/HIL CV21 ..62 A1
Withybrook Rd BDWTH CV12 ....7 H3
Whitehead Dr KNWTH CV8 ....65 H1
Witnell Rd COVN CV6 ....22 D5
Whitehead Gv
Wolfe Rd TLHL/CAN CV4 ....37 E2
   RCOVN/BALC/EX CV7 ....34 C2
Wolsey Rd RUGBYS/DCH CV22 ..69 H2
Whitehorse Cl COVN CV6 ....14 A2
Wolston La KNWTH CV8 ....56 B3
Whitelaw Crs COVW CV5 ....21 E5
Wolverton Rd COVW CV5 ....28 D3
Whitemoor Rd KNWTH CV8 ....65 F3
Wolvey Rd BDWTH CV12 ....7 H3
Whiteside Cl COVS CV3 ....41 G1
Woodburn Cl COVW CV5 ....29 E2
Whites Rw KNWTH CV8 ....65 F5
Woodclose Av COVN CV6 ....22 A5
Whitestitch La
Woodcote Av KNWTH CV8 ....64 C1
   RCOVN/BALC/EX CV7 ....18 A1
Woodcraft Cl COVS CV3 ....28 D4
White St COV CV1 ....2 E1
Woodend Cft TLHL/CAN CV4 ....28 B5
Whitley Village COVS CV3 ....40 A2
Woodfield Rd COVW CV5 ....38 B1
Whitmore Park Rd COVN CV6 ..12 D5
Woodford Cl
Whitnash Cl RCOVN/BALC/EX CV7 ..34 B3
   RCOVN/BALC/EX CV7 ....13 E3
Whitnash Gv COVE CV2 ....32 C1
Woodhams Rd KNWTH CV8 ....54 D1
Whittle Cl COVS CV3 ....41 G1
Wood Hill Ri COVN CV6 ....22 D1
   RUGBYS/DCH CV22 ....61 E5
Woodhouse Cl COVS CV3 ....41 F1
Whitworth Av COVS CV3 ....32 A5
Woodland Av COVW CV5 ....38 C2
Whoberley Av COVW CV5 ....29 G5
Woodland Rd KNWTH CV8 ....51 G5
Whoberley Ct COVW CV5 * 29 F3
Woodlands Ct COVW CV5 * 38 D1
Wickham Cl COVN CV6 ....22 A1
Woodlands La BDWTH CV12 ....4 D1
Wickmans Dr TLHL/CAN CV4 ..27 H4
Woodlands Rd BDWTH CV12 ....4 D2
Widdecombe Cl COVE CV2 ....24 C3
   COVS CV3 ....42 C2
Widdrington Rd COV CV1 ....30 D1
Woodleigh Rd TLHL/CAN CV4 ....37 E4
Wigston Rd COVE CV2 ....25 E2
Woodmill Meadow KNWTH CV8 ..65 F1
   RUGBYN/HIL CV21 ....63 F3
Woodridge Av COVW CV5 ....20 C5
Wildcroft Rd COVW CV5 ....29 F4
Woodroffe Wk COVN CV6 ....13 H4
Wildey Rd BDWTH CV12 ....4 C3
Woodshires Rd COVN CV6 ....13 G3
Wildmoor Cl COVE CV2 ....14 A4
Woodsia Cl RRUGBY CV23 ....48 C1

Abbey Clinic
  COVW CV5 ....30 B5
Abbey Fields Swimming Pool
  KNWTH CV8 ....64 D2
Abbey Industrial Estate
  COVE CV2 ....32 D1
Abbots Farm Infant School
  RUGBYN/HIL CV21 ....62 D2
Abbots Farm Junior School
  RUGBYN/HIL CV21 ....63 E2
Abbotsford School
  KNWTH CV8 ....65 E1
Albion Industrial Estate
  COVN CV6 ....23 E4
Alderman Callow School
  TLHL/CAN CV4 ....37 F3
Alderman Green Primary School
  COVE CV2 ....14 B5
Alderman Harris Primary School
  TLHL/CAN CV4 ....37 F3
Aldermans Green
  Industrial Estate
  COVE CV2 ....24 D1
Aldermoor Farm Primary School
  COVS CV5 ....40 C1
Aldermoor Lane Welfare Clinic
  COVS CV5 ....31 H5
Alice Stevens Special School
  COVS CV5 ....40 B4
Allesley Hall Primary School
  COVW CV5 ....29 E2
Allesley Hotel
  COVW CV5 ....21 E5
Allesley Park Medical Centre
  COVW CV5 ....29 F2
Allesley Primary School
  COVW CV5 ....20 D4
All Saints CE Infant School
  BDWTH CV12 ....5 H3
All Saints CE Primary School
  COV CV1 ....3 H6
All Souls RC Primary School
  COVW CV5 ....29 H4
Alpha Business Park
  COVE CV2 ....24 C2
Alvis Retail Park
  COVW CV5 ....30 B2
Annie Osborn Primary School
  COVE CV2 ....24 C4
Arches Business Centre
  RUGBYN/HIL CV21 ....48 B4
Arches Industrial Estate
  COVW CV5 ....30 B3
  RUGBYN/HIL CV21 ....48 B4
Arden Forest Infant School
  BDWTH CV12 ....6 D2
The Arena
  COV CV1 ....2 B4
Arts Centre Cinema
  TLHL/CAN CV4 ....37 G5
Ash Green School
  RCOVN/BALC/EX CV7 ....13 E2
Ashlawn School
  RUGBYS/DCH CV22 ....62 D5
Aston Industrial Estate
  BDWTH CV12 ....6 A3
AT7 Sports Centre
  COVN CV6 ....23 H4
Avon Industrial Estate
  RUGBYN/HIL CV21 ....48 B4
Avon Valley School
  RUGBYN/HIL CV21 ....47 F3
Bablake Junior School
  COV CV1 ....2 B1
Bablake School
  COV CV1 ....2 A1
Baginton Fields Special School
  COVS CV5 ....40 C5
Balsall Common Health Clinic
  RCOVN/BALC/EX CV7 ....34 C2
Balsall Common Primary School
  RCOVN/BALC/EX CV7 ....34 C4
Barkers Butts RFC
  COVW CV5 ....19 H3
Barrs Hill School
  & Community College
  COV CV1 ....30 C2
Bayton Road Industrial Estate
  RCOVN/BALC/EX CV7 ....14 A1
Bede Shopping Arcade
  BDWTH CV12 ....5 G2
Bedworth Health Centre
  BDWTH CV12 ....5 G3
Bedworth Leisure Centre
  BDWTH CV12 ....5 H3
Bedworth RFC
  BDWTH CV12 ....5 E4
Belgrade Theatre
  COV CV1 ....2 C3

Bell Green Health Centre
  COVE CV2 ....24 B2
Berkswell CE Primary School
  RCOVN/BALC/EX CV7 ....26 B3
Berkswell Windmill
  RCOVN/BALC/EX CV7 ....35 E5
Bickenhill Trading Estate
  CHWD/FDBR/MGN B37 ....8 B3
Bilton CE Junior School
  RUGBYS/DCH CV22 ....69 H1
Bilton Grange School
  RUGBYS/DCH CV22 ....70 A3
Bilton High School
  RUGBYS/DCH CV22 ....60 C3
Bilton Industrial Estate
  COVS CV3 ....3 K6
Bilton Infant School
  RUGBYS/DCH CV22 ....60 D4
Binley Business Park
  COVS CV3 ....33 F5
Binley Industrial Estate
  COVS CV3 ....41 H2
Binley Woods Primary School
  KNWTH CV8 ....42 D2
Birmingham International
  Airport
  LGN/SDN/BHAMAIR B26 ....8 A4
Bishopgate Business Park
  COV CV1 ....31 E1
Bishop Ullathorne
  RC Comprehensive School
  COVS CV5 ....38 B5
Bishop Wulstan RC High School
  RUGBYS/DCH CV22 ....61 H1
Blue Coat CE School
  COV CV1 ....3 J7
Bodmin Road Industrial Estate
  COVE CV2 ....32 D1
Bond's Hospital
  & Bablake Old School
  COV CV1 ....2 B3
Boughton Leigh County
  Junior School
  RUGBYN/HIL CV21 ....48 B2
Boughton Leigh Infant School
  RUGBYN/HIL CV21 ....48 C2
Boughton Road
  Industrial Estate
  RUGBYN/HIL CV21 ....48 A3
Bowling Alley
  COVS CV3 ....39 G5
  RCOVN/BALC/EX CV7 ....25 H3
  RUGBYN/HIL CV21 ....48 A3
Brandon Court Leofric
  Business Park
  COVS CV3 ....41 H2
The Brandon Hall Hotel
  KNWTH CV8 ....42 D4
Bridge Works Industrial Estate
  KNWTH CV8 ....65 H1
Broad Heath
  Community Primary School
  COVN CV6 ....23 F5
Broad Heath School
  COVN CV6 ....23 F4
Broad Lane Trading Estate
  COVW CV5 ....27 H2
Broad Street Health Centre
  COVN CV6 ....23 G4
Broad Street Old Boys RFC
  COVS CV3 ....42 A1
Broad Street RFC
  COVE CV2 ....24 B3
Brooke Special School
  RUGBYS/DCH CV22 ....61 G3
Brooke Special School (Sec Site)
  RUGBYS/DCH CV22 ....61 F4
Brooklands Grange Hotel
  COVN CV6 ....29 G1
Broomfield Park Surgery
  COVW CV5 ....30 B4
Brownsover Community School
  RRUGBY CV23 ....48 C1
Brownsover Hall Hotel
  RUGBYN/HIL CV21 ....48 A1
Bulkington CE Junior School
  BDWTH CV12 ....7 F3
Burnsall Road Industrial Estate
  COVN CV6 ....37 H1
Burton Green CE Primary
  KNWTH CV8 ....50 A1
Butlers Leap Industrial Estate
  RUGBYN/HIL CV21 ....48 C5
Caludon Castle School
  COVE CV2 ....32 D2
Campanile Hotel
  COVE CV2 ....25 F3
Canley Gardens Crematorium
  TLHL/CAN CV4 ....38 A3

Cannon Park Primary School
  TLHL/CAN CV4 ....38 A4
Canon Evans CE Infant School
  BDWTH CV12 ....5 F3
Canon Maggs CE Junior School
  BDWTH CV12 ....5 G3
Cardinal Newman RC School
  & Community College
  COVN CV6 ....22 A1
Cardinal Wiseman RC School
  COVE CV2 ....24 D2
Cash's Business Centre
  COV CV1 ....31 E1
Castle Place Industrial Estate
  COV CV1 ....3 G1
Castle Sixth Form Centre
  (Kenilworth School)
  KNWTH CV8 ....65 E5
Cathedral Lanes Shopping Centre
  COV CV1 ....2 D3
Central City Industrial Estate
  COVN CV6 ....31 G1
Central Six Retail Park
  COV CV1 ....2 B6
The Chace Hotel
  COVS CV3 ....40 C4
Chace Primary School
  COVS CV3 ....40 D3
Challenge Business Park
  COV CV1 ....31 E1
Cherry Tree Sports Club
  COVN CV6 ....23 F1
Cheylesmore Welfare Clinic
  COVS CV3 ....39 H3
Christ the King
  Catholic Infant School
  COVN CV6 ....22 A5
Christ the King RC Junior School
  COVN CV6 ....22 A4
Church Lawford Business Centre
  RRUGBY CV23 ....44 D4
Cineworld Cinema
  RUGBYN/HIL CV21 ....48 A3
City Arcade
  COV CV1 ....2 C4
City College Coventry
  TLHL/CAN CV4 ....28 C5
City Farm
  COV CV1 ....3 G1
City of Coventry-Brandon Wood
  Golf Club
  KNWTH CV8 ....42 B4
City Walls & Gate
  COV CV1 ....2 E2
Clarendon House Hotel
  KNWTH CV8 ....65 E1
Clifford Bridge Primary School
  COVS CV3 ....33 F3
Clifton upon Dunsmore
  CE Primary School
  RRUGBY CV23 ....49 E4
Clinton Combined School
  KNWTH CV8 ....64 D4
The Clock Towers Shopping Centre
  RUGBYN/HIL CV21 ....61 H1
Combe Abbey Country Park
  COVS CV3 ....33 G3
Common Lane Industrial Estate
  KNWTH CV8 ....51 H5
Corley Cricket Club
  RCOVN/BALC/EX CV7 ....11 F2
Corley School
  RCOVN/BALC/EX CV7 ....11 E2
Corpus Christi RC Primary School
  COVS CV3 ....41 E2
Coundon Court School
  & Community College
  COVN CV6 ....21 H4
  COVN CV6 ....23 F4
Coundon Primary School
  COVN CV6 ....29 H1
Courthouse Green
  Primary School
  COVN CV6 ....23 H3
Courtyard by Marriott
  KNWTH CV8 ....55 E1
Coventry Airport
  KNWTH CV8 ....54 B3
Coventry & Warwickshire
  Hospital
  COV CV1 ....31 E2
Coventry Athletics Track
  TLHL/CAN CV4 ....37 G3
Coventry Business Park
  COVW CV5 ....29 F4
  COVW CV5 ....30 A5
Coventry Cathedral
  & Visitor Centre
  COV CV1 ....2 E3

Coventry City FC
  (Highfield Road Stadium)
  COVE CV2 ....
Coventry Golf Club
  KNWTH CV8 ....
Coventry Grammar School
  COVW CV5 ....
Coventry Hearsall Golf Club
  COVW CV5 ....
Coventry Muslim School
  COVN CV6 ....
Coventry Preparatory School
  COVW CV5 ....
Coventry RFC
  COVN CV6 ....
Coventry Sports Centre
  COV CV1 ....
Coventry Technical College
  COV CV1 ....
The Coventry Toy Museum
  COV CV1 ....
Coventry Trading Estate
  KNWTH CV8 ....
Coventry University
  COV CV1 ....
Coventry University
  Technocentre
  COV CV1 ....
Coventry Welsh RFC
  COVN CV6 ....
The Crescent School
  RUGBYS/DCH CV22 ....
Criterion Theatre
  COVW CV5 ....
Cross Point Business Park
  RCOVN/BALC/EX CV7 ....
Cross Road Industrial Estate
  COVN CV6 ....
Dalehouse Lane Industrial Estate
  KNWTH CV8 ....
Dartmouth Special School
  COVE CV2 ....
Davenport Lodge School
  COVW CV5 ....
Deedmore Special School
  COVE CV2 ....
De Montfort Hotel
  KNWTH CV8 ....
The Dr Phillips Shopping Centre
  COVE CV2 ....
Dunchurch Boughton
  CE Junior School
  RUGBYS/DCH CV22 ....
Dunchurch Infant School
  RUGBYS/DCH CV22 ....
Dunchurch Trading Estate
  RRUGBY CV23 ....
Durbar Avenue
  Industrial Estate
  COVN CV6 ....
Earl Place Business Park
  TLHL/CAN CV4 ....
Earlsdon Business Centre
  COVW CV5 ....
Earlsdon Primary School
  COVW CV5 ....
Eastern Green Junior School
  COVW CV5 ....
Eastlands County
  Primary School
  RUGBYN/HIL CV21 ....
Eastlands Court Business Centre
  RUGBYN/HIL CV21 ....
Eastwood Business Village
  COVS CV3 ....
Edgewick Community
  Primary School
  COVN CV6 ....
Edgwick Park Industrial Estate
  COVN CV6 ....
Elliott's Field Retail Park
  RUGBYN/HIL CV21 ....
Elmdon Trading Estate
  CHWD/FDBR/MGN B37 ....
English Martyrs
  RC Primary School
  RUGBYN/HIL CV21 ....
Ensign Business Centre
  TLHL/CAN CV4 ....
Ernesford Grange
  Primary School
  COVS CV3 ....
Ernesford Grange School
  & Community School
  COVS CV3 ....
Exhall Business Park
  RCOVN/BALC/EX CV7 ....
Exhall Cedars Infant School
  RCOVN/BALC/EX CV7 ....

Grange Special School
  /N/BALC/EX CV7 ....13 E3
by Holiday Inn
  CV3 ....39 E5
/WTROR B46 ....8 D1
YN/HIL CV21 ....48 A2
Park School
  CV3 ....38 D5
Primary School
  CV3 ....53 E1
mstead Highway
strial Estate
  /CV5 ....38 A1
orth Gate
strial Estate
  /CV5 ....37 H1
il Cemetery
  ....23 H1
il CE Primary School
  ....23 H1
il Leisure Centre
  ....23 E4
ospital
  ....2 C4
Health Centre
  CV2 ....32 C4
ayside Industrial Estate
YN/HIL CV21 ....48 C5
School
mmunity Arts College
  /CV6 ....13 H3
hittle Primary School
  /CV2 ....25 E3
k Bird Primary School
  ....31 G1
er Business Park
/N/BALC/EX CV7 ....13 F4
er Retail Park
  CV6 ....23 C5
anagement College
YS/DCH CV22 ....69 H4
Fentham Junior
ant School
OLT B92 ....16 B5
Farm Industrial Estate
YN/HIL CV21 ....47 G2
Trading Estate
  CV6 ....23 G3
hepherd
imary School
  CV6 ....23 G2
ers End Primary School
/N/BALC/EX CV7 ....4 D5
Industrial Estate
  ....3 H4
Park Primary School
  CV3 ....3 K5
T Golf Club
  CV3 ....32 C3
Farm Primary School
  CV3 ....39 E4
hurst Primary School
  ....14 A4
Central Way
strial Estate
YN/HIL CV21 ....48 C5
ff School
  TH CV12 ....5 G2
nor Hotel
YN/HIL CV21 ....62 A1
ands Industrial Estate
/N/BALC/EX CV7 ....13 H2
Hospital
  CV1 ....3 G5
Road Clinic
  CV1 ....3 G4
Hotel
/N/BALC/EX CV7 ....34 C2
ndustrial Park
  CV6 ....13 F4
d Close Industrial Estate
  CV6 ....23 F5
Lane Industrial Estate
  CV1 ....31 E2
Lane Medical Centre
  CV1 ....31 E2
CE High School
YS/DCH CV22 ....61 G3
sbury Field School
  CV2 ....14 B5
sbury Lock
strial Centre
/N/BALC/EX CV7 ....14 C3
ead Industrial Estate
  CV1 ....3 J5
all Primary School
  CV5 ....30 B4
of England School
/N/BALC/EX CV7 ....34 C3

Heath Business Park
  KNWTH CV8 ....58 A3
Henley College
  ....24 B3
Henley Industrial Park
  COVE CV2 ....24 D4
Henry Bellairs CE
  Junior School
  BDWTH CV12 ....6 A2
Henry Hinde Infant School
  RUGBYS/DCH CV22 ....60 D3
Henry Hinde Junior School
  RUGBYS/DCH CV22 ....60 C2
Henry Parkes Primary School
  TLHL/CAN CV4 ....37 H1
Herald Business Park
  COVS CV3 ....41 G2
Herbert Art Gallery & Museum
  COV CV1 ....2 E4
Hereward College of FE
  TLHL/CAN CV4 ....28 C5
Hill Farm Primary School
  COVN CV6 ....22 C4
Hillfields Health Centre
  COV CV1 ....3 F1
Hillmorton Manor Hotel
  & Restaurant
  RUGBYN/HIL CV21 ....63 F5
Hillmorton Primary School
  RUGBYN/HIL CV21 ....63 G4
Holbrook Park Industrial Estate
  COVN CV6 ....23 E3
Holbrook Primary School
  COVN CV6 ....23 F2
Holiday Inn
  RCOVN/BALC/EX CV7 ....25 G3
Hollyfast Primary School
  COVN CV6 ....21 H4
Holy Family RC J & I School
  COVN CV6 ....12 C5
Homefield School
  RUGBYS/DCH CV22 ....70 A3
Hood Street Industrial Estate
  COV CV1 ....3 G3
Hornchurch Close
  Industrial Estate
  COV CV1 ....2 D7
Hospital of St Cross
  RUGBYS/DCH CV22 ....62 A3
Hotel Ibis
  COV CV1 ....2 E6
Hotel Ibis
  COVS CV3 ....40 A3
Howes Primary School
  COVS CV3 ....39 G4
Hunters Lane Industrial Estate
  RUGBYN/HIL CV21 ....47 H4
Hylands Hotel
  COVS CV3 ....39 F1
Industrial Training Centre
  TLHL/CAN CV4 ....36 D1
Innkeepers Lodge Hotel
  RCOVN/BALC/EX CV7 ....18 B2
Innkeeper's Lodge Hotel
  RUGBYS/DCH CV22 ....69 G4
Jaguar Daimler Heritage Centre
  COVW CV5 ....21 E3
The James Gilbert
  Rugby Football Museum
  RUGBYN/HIL CV21 ....61 H1
John Gulson Primary School
  COV CV1 ....31 E1
John Shelton Primary School
  COVN CV6 ....13 E4
Joseph Cash Primary School
  COVN CV6 ....22 D4
Junction One Retail Park
  RUGBYN/HIL CV21 ....48 A3
Kenilworth Business Centre
  KNWTH CV8 ....65 F4
Kenilworth Castle
  KNWTH CV8 ....64 C2
Kenilworth Golf Club
  KNWTH CV8 ....66 A1
Kenilworth RFC
  KNWTH CV8 ....66 A3
Kenilworth School
  KNWTH CV8 ....65 H2
Kenilworth Wardens Cricket Club
  KNWTH CV8 ....65 H4
Ken Marriott Leisure Centre
  RUGBYS/DCH CV22 ....62 A2
Keresley Grange Primary School
  COVN CV6 ....22 A2
Keresley Health Centre
  RCOVN/BALC/EX CV7 ....12 A2
Keresley Newland
  Primary School
  RCOVN/BALC/EX CV7 ....12 A1

Kingfield Industrial Estate
  COVN CV6 ....22 D5
King Henry VIII School
  COVW CV5 ....2 B7
Knightlow CE (Aided)
  Primary School
  RRUGBY CV23 ....57 H1
Lawford Heath
  Industrial Estate
  RRUGBY CV23 ....59 F5
Lawrence Sheriff School
  RUGBYN/HIL CV21 ....62 A1
Leigh CE Primary School
  TLHL/CAN CV4 ....28 C3
Leyland School
  BDWTH CV12 ....5 G2
Limbrick Wood
  Primary School
  TLHL/CAN CV4 ....28 C3
Little Heath Industrial Estate
  COVN CV6 ....23 H1
Little Heath Primary School
  COVN CV6 ....23 G2
Lodge Farm Campsite
  RRUGBY CV23 ....60 C2
Longford Medical Centre
  COVN CV6 ....13 H3
Longford Park Primary School
  COVN CV6 ....13 H5
Long Lawford Primary School
  RRUGBY CV23 ....46 B4
Lunt Roman Fort
  KNWTH CV8 ....54 A1
Lyng Hall School
  COVE CV2 ....24 B5
Lythalls Lane Industrial Estate
  COVN CV6 ....23 F2
Maguire Industrial Estate
  TLHL/CAN CV4 ....36 D1
Manor Hotel
  RCOVN/BALC/EX CV7 ....18 C2
Manor Park Primary School
  COVS CV3 ....39 F2
Mansfield Medical Centre
  COVS CV3 ....31 H4
Market Hall
  COV CV1 ....2 D5
Martyr's Memorial
  COV CV1 ....2 E6
The Meadows Special School
  TLHL/CAN CV4 ....28 B3
Menzies Leofric Hotel
  COV CV1 ....2 D3
Meriden CE Primary School
  RCOVN/BALC/EX CV7 ....18 B1
Meriden Green Business Park
  COVW CV5 ....19 G3
Middlemarch Business Park
  KNWTH CV8 ....54 C3
  KNWTH CV8 ....54 D1
Midland Air Museum
  KNWTH CV8 ....54 C1
Midland Oak Industrial Estate
  COVN CV6 ....23 F2
Midland Oak Trading Estate
  COVN CV6 ....23 F1
Midlands Sports Centre
  for the Disabled
  RCOVN/BALC/EX CV7 ....36 B2
Midland Trading Estate
  RUGBYN/HIL CV21 ....47 G3
Moat House Primary School
  COVE CV2 ....24 C2
Moseley Primary School
  COVN CV6 ....30 B2
Mount Nod Primary School
  COVW CV5 ....28 D3
Museum of British
  Road Transport
  COV CV1 ....2 D2
Nailcote Hall Hotel
  RCOVN/BALC/EX CV7 ....35 H2
Nation Agricultural Centre
  KNWTH CV8 ....66 D3
National Exhibition Centre
  BHAMNEC B40 ....8 C3
National Motorcycle Museum
  HIA/OLT B92 ....16 B1
Newbold FC
  RUGBYN/HIL CV21 ....47 E3
Newbold Leisure Centre
  RUGBYN/HIL CV21 ....47 E2
Newbold Riverside
  Primary School
  RUGBYN/HIL CV21 ....47 F3
Newdigate Primary School
  BDWTH CV12 ....4 B4
New Inn Industrial Estate
  COVN CV6 ....23 G1

New Oxford Medical Centre
  COV CV1 ....2 C2
Nicholas Chamberlaine School
  BDWTH CV12 ....6 A2
Northbrook Sports Club
  COVW CV5 ....21 F3
Northlands Primary School
  RUGBYN/HIL CV21 ....48 A5
North Warwickshire Golf Club
  RCOVN/BALC/EX CV7 ....17 G3
Novotel
  COVN CV6 ....13 G2
  LGN/SDN/BHAMAIR B26 ....8 A4
Odeon Cinema
  COV CV1 ....2 E4
Old Mill Hotel
  KNWTH CV8 ....53 H1
One Stop Medical Centre
  COV CV1 ....2 C2
Orchard Retail Park
  COVS CV3 ....41 E5
Our Lady of the Assumption
  RC Primary School
  TLHL/CAN CV4 ....28 B5
Paddox Primary School
  RUGBYS/DCH CV22 ....62 C4
Parkgate Primary School
  COVN CV6 ....12 C5
Park Hill Junior School
  KNWTH CV8 ....65 H1
Park Hill Primary School
  COVW CV5 ....28 D2
Parkside Business Park
  COV CV1 ....2 E6
Park Street Industrial Estate
  COVN CV6 ....23 F4
Pattison College
  COVS CV3 ....31 H4
Pearl Hyde Primary School
  COVE CV2 ....33 F1
Pickwick Picture Gallery
  COVN CV6 ....29 H1
Playbox Theatre
  KNWTH CV8 ....65 F3
Pool Meadow Bus Station
  COV CV1 ....2 E3
Potters Green Primary School
  COVE CV2 ....24 D1
The Precinct
  COV CV1 ....2 C3
President Kennedy
  Comprehensive School &
  Community College
  RCOVN/BALC/EX CV7 ....12 B4
Princes Drive Industrial Estate
  KNWTH CV8 ....51 F4
Priors Field CP School
  KNWTH CV8 ....50 C5
Priory Theatre
  KNWTH CV8 ....65 E2
Provost Williams
  CE Primary School
  KNWTH CV8 ....55 H3
Race Leys Primary School
  BDWTH CV12 ....5 G1
Radford Primary School
  COVN CV6 ....30 C1
Ravensdale Primary School
  COVE CV2 ....32 B2
Read Street Industrial Estate
  COV CV1 ....3 H3
Regent Health Centre
  RUGBYN/HIL CV21 ....47 H5
Richard Lee Primary School
  COVE CV2 ....32 C3
Rokeby Infant School
  RUGBYS/DCH CV22 ....61 H4
Rokeby Junior School
  RUGBYS/DCH CV22 ....61 H4
Rowleys Green Industrial Estate
  COVN CV6 ....13 F4
Rugby Athletics Track
  RUGBYS/DCH CV22 ....62 A3
Rugby College
  RUGBYN/HIL CV21 ....62 C2
Rugby FC
  RUGBYS/DCH CV22 ....61 F2
Rugby Golf Club
  RUGBYN/HIL CV21 ....48 D5
Rugby High School for Girls
  RUGBYS/DCH CV22 ....69 H1
Rugby School
  RUGBYS/DCH CV22 ....61 H2
Rugby School Museum
  RUGBYN/HIL CV21 ....61 H1
Rugby School Sports Centre
  RUGBYS/DCH CV22 ....62 A2
Rugby Theatre
  RUGBYN/HIL CV21 ....61 H1

Rugby Welsh RFC
RUGBYN/HIL CV21 ....61 G1
Ryton Gdns
KNWTH CV8 ....56 D3
Sacred Heart RC Primary School
COVE CV2 ....31 H3
**St Andrews Cc Primary
& Middle School**
RUGBYN/HIL CV21 ....48 C5
St Andrews CE Infant School
COVW CV5 ....27 H1
St Andrews RUFC
RUGBYS/DCH CV22 ....62 C5
St Annes RC Primary School
COVS CV3 ....40 C3
St Augustines RC Primary School
COVN CV6 ....22 B4
St Augustines RC Primary School
KNWTH CV8 ....50 D5
**St Bartholomews
CE Primary School**
COVS CV3 ....41 F2
St Christopher Primary School
COVW CV5 ....29 G2
St Elizabeths C Primary School
COVN CV6 ....23 F4
St Francis RC Combined School
BDWTH CV12 ....5 G2
St Giles Junior School
RCOVN/BALC/EX CV7 ....5 E5
St Gregorys RC Primary School
COVE CV2 ....32 D3
St James Medical Centre
COVS CV3 ....40 D4
**St John Fisher
RC Primary School**
COVE CV2 ....24 C5
St Johns CE Primary School
COVW CV5 ....29 F2
St John's Hospital
COV CV1 ....2 D2
St Johns Primary School
KNWTH CV8 ....65 E5
**St John the Divine
CE Primary School**
COVS CV3 ....40 D4
**St John Vianney
RC Primary School**
COVW CV5 ....29 E3
St Josephs School
KNWTH CV8 ....51 G5
St Margarets CE Primary School
COVW CV5 ....43 E5
St Maries Catholic Infant School
RUGBYS/DCH CV22 ....61 H2
St Maries RC Junior School
RUGBYS/DCH CV22 ....61 G2
**St Mary & St Benedict
RC Primary School**
COV CV1 ....3 H1
St Mary's Guildhall
COV CV1 ....2 E4
St Mary's Priory
COV CV1 ....2 D3
St Matthews Bloxam CE School
RUGBYS/DCH CV22 ....61 F2
St Nicholas CE Combined School
KNWTH CV8 ....65 F2
St Osburgs RC Primary School
COV CV1 ....2 A2

St Oswalds CE Primary School
RUGBYS/DCH CV22 ....61 E1
St Patricks RC Primary School
COVE CV2 ....24 C2
St Pauls Cemetery
COVN CV6 ....23 E2
**St Peter & St Paul
RC Primary School**
COVE CV2 ....24 D4
**St Thomas More
RC Primary School**
COVS CV3 ....39 G4
Sandy Lane Business Park
COV CV1 ....30 D1
Seven Stars Industrial Estate
COVS CV3 ....40 B2
**Sherbourne Fields
Special School**
COVN CV6 ....29 C1
Shilton Lane Industrial Estate
BDWTH CV12 ....7 G5
Showcase Cinemas
RCOVN/BALC/EX CV7 ....25 C2
**Sidney Stringer Community
Technology College**
COV CV1 ....3 F2
**Sir Frank Whittle
Business Centre**
RUGBYN/HIL CV21 ....48 C4
Skydome Leisure Complex
COV CV1 ....2 B4
Southfield Primary School
COV CV1 ....3 H3
Sowe Valley Primary School
COVS CV3 ....41 E1
**Sparkbrook Street
Industrial Estate**
COV CV1 ....3 H2
Spon Gate Primary School
COV CV1 ....30 C3
Stag Industrial Estate
COVN CV6 ....23 E3
Stanton Bridge Primary School
COVN CV6 ....23 G5
Star Industrial Park
COVE CV2 ....32 D1
**Station Street West
Business Park**
COVN CV6 ....23 F4
Status Business Centre
COVW CV5 ....30 B5
Stivichall Primary School
COVS CV3 ....38 D3
Stoke Aldermoor Medical Centre
COVS CV3 ....40 C1
Stoke Heath J & I School
COVE CV2 ....23 H5
Stoke Old Boys RFC
COVS CV3 ....32 C5
**Stoke Park School and
Community Technology College**
COVE CV2 ....32 A2
Stoke Primary School
COVE CV2 ....31 H2
Stoke Row Industrial Estate
COVE CV2 ....31 H2
Stonebridge Golf Club
RCOVN/BALC/EX CV7 ....17 G2
Stonebridge Trading Estate
COVS CV3 ....54 C1

Stoneleigh Abbey
KNWTH CV8 ....66 C4
**Stoneleigh Deer Park
Business Village**
KNWTH CV8 ....67 G3
Stoneleigh Deer Park Golf Club
KNWTH CV8 ....67 H2
Stoney Stanton Medical Centre
COVN CV6 ....23 F5
Swanswell Medical Centre
COV CV1 ....2 E1
Swift Valley Industrial Estate
RUGBYN/HIL CV21 ....47 G1
Talisman Theatre & Arts Centre
KNWTH CV8 ....65 E4
**Tanks Glebe Farm
Industrial Estate**
RUGBYN/HIL CV21 ....47 G1
Teachers Centre
COV CV1 ....2 E6
Templar Industrial Park
TLHL/CAN CV4 ....37 F1
Templars Primary School
TLHL/CAN CV4 ....28 D5
Terrace Industrial Estate
RUGBYN/HIL CV21 ....48 A5
Theatre One
COV CV1 ....3 F2
Thorns County Infant School
KNWTH CV8 ....65 F3
**Three Spires
Industrial Estate**
COVN CV6 ....13 H2
**Three Spires
Special School**
COVW CV5 ....21 G5
**Tile Hill Wood
Comprehensive School**
TLHL/CAN CV4 ....28 A4
Tiverton Special School
COVN CV6 ....29 G1
Toffs Country House Hotel
RCOVN/BALC/EX CV7 ....10 D4
Travel Inn
COVS CV3 ....42 A1
RCOVN/BALC/EX CV7 ....34 B1
Travelodge
RRUGBY CV23 ....68 A3
Tribune Trading Estate
RUGBYN/HIL CV21 ....47 H3
Trinity Business Park
HIA/OLT B92 ....8 B5
Tulip Inn Hotel
KNWTH CV8 ....66 D3
University of Warwick
TLHL/CAN CV4 ....37 G5
TLHL/CAN CV4 ....51 H1
**University of Warwick
Sports Centre**
TLHL/CAN CV4 ....37 H4
Wainbody Wood Special School
TLHL/CAN CV4 ....52 A2
Walsgrave CE Primary School
COVE CV2 ....25 F5
Walsgrave General Hospital
COVE CV2 ....33 F1
Walsgrave Health Centre
COVE CV2 ....25 E5
Walsgrave Retail Park
COVE CV2 ....25 G4

**Walsgrave Triangle
Business Park**
RCOVN/BALC/EX CV7 ....
Warwickshire County Council
KNWTH CV8 ....
**Warwickshire Racquet
& Health Centre**
COVS CV3 ....
Webb Ellis Business Park
RUGBYN/HIL CV21 ....
Welfare Clinic
KNWTH CV8 ....
Westfield First School
RUGBYS/DCH CV22 ....
Westfield Lodge College
RUGBYS/DCH CV22 ....
Weston Hall Hotel
BDWTH CV12 ....
West Orchards Shopping Centre
COV CV1 ....
West Side Business Centre
TLHL/CAN CV4 ....
Westwood Business Park
TLHL/CAN CV4 ....
Wheatsheaf Studio Theatre
COVE CV2 ....
**Whitefields Hotel Golf
& Country Club**
RRUGBY CV23 ....
Whitefriars Friary
COV CV1 ....
Whitley Abbey Community School
COVS CV3 ....
Whitley Abbey Primary School
COVS CV3 ....
Whitmore Park J & I School
COVN CV6 ....
Whoberley Clinic
COVW CV5 ....
Whoberley Hall Primary School
COVW CV5 ....
Willenhall Wood Primary School
COVS CV3 ....
Windmill Industrial Estate
COVW CV5 ....
**Windmill Village Golf
& Leisure Club**
COVW CV5 ....
Wolston Business Park
KNWTH CV8 ....
Wood End Health Centre
COVE CV2 ....
Wood End Primary School
COVE CV2 ....
The Woodlands School
TLHL/CAN CV4 ....
Woodside Business Park
RUGBYN/HIL CV21 ....
Woodside Medical Centre
TLHL/CAN CV4 ....
**Woodway Park
Community School**
COVE CV2 ....
Wyken Croft Primary School
COVE CV2 ....
Wyken Medical Centre
COVE CV2 ....

Acknowledgements

The Post Office is a registered trademark of Post Office Ltd. in the UK and other countries.

Schools address data provided by Education Direct.

Petrol station information supplied by Johnsons

One-way street data provided by © Tele Atlas N.V. Tele Atlas

Garden centre information provided by:

Garden Centre Association  Britains best garden centres

Wyevale Garden Centres

Notes

AA **Street by Street** QUESTIONNAIRE

Dear Atlas User
Your comments, opinions and recommendations are very important to us.
So please help us to improve our street atlases by taking a few minutes
to complete this simple questionnaire.

You do NOT need a stamp (unless posted outside the UK). If you do not want to remove this page from your street atlas, then photocopy it or write your answers on a plain sheet of paper.

Send to: The Editor, AA Street by Street, FREEPOST SCE 4598,
Basingstoke RG21 4GY

ABOUT THE ATLAS...

Which city/town/county did you buy?

Are there any features of the atlas or mapping that you find particularly useful?

Is there anything we could have done better?

Why did you choose an AA Street by Street atlas?

Did it meet your expectations?

Exceeded ☐   **Met all** ☐   **Met most** ☐   **Fell below** ☐

Please give your reasons

Where did you buy it?

For what purpose? (please tick all applicable)

To use in your own local area ☐   To use on business or at work ☐

Visiting a strange place ☐   In the car ☐   On foot ☐

Other (please state)

LOCAL KNOWLEDGE...

Local knowledge is invaluable. Whilst every attempt has been made to make the information contained in this atlas as accurate as possible, should you notice any inaccuracies, please detail them below (if necessary, use a blank piece of paper) or e-mail us at *streetbystreet@theAA.com*

ABOUT YOU...

Name (Mr/Mrs/Ms)
Address
                                                                    Postcode
Daytime tel no
E-mail address

Which age group are you in?

Under 25 ☐   25-34 ☐   35-44 ☐   45-54 ☐   55-64 ☐   65+ ☐

Are you an AA member?   YES ☐   NO ☐

Do you have Internet access?   YES ☐   NO ☐

Thank you for taking the time to complete this questionnaire. Please send it to us as soon as possible, and remember, you do not need a stamp (unless posted outside the UK).

ML034z